Gay warriors

Gay Warriors

A Documentary History from the Ancient World to the Present

EDITED BY

B. R. Burg

New York University Press

New York and London

NEW YORK UNIVERSITY PRESS
New York and London

Library of Congress Cataloging-in-Publication Data
Gay Warriors : a documentary history from the ancient world
to the present / Edited by B. R. Burg.
p. cm.
Includes bibliographical references and index.
ISBN 0–8147–9885–3 (cloth : alk. paper) —
ISBN 0–8147–9886–1 (paper : alk. paper)
1. Soldiers—Sexual behavior—History   2. Homosexuality—History.
3. Gay and lesbian studies.   4. United States Armed Forces—Gays.
I. Burg, B. R. (Barry Richard), 1938–
UH630 .G39 2001
355'.0086'642—dc21   2001004522

New York University Press books are printed on acid-free paper,
and their binding materials are chosen for strength and durability.

Manufactured in the United States of America

10 9 8 7 6 5 4 3 2 1

Contents

Editorial Note

Spelling, capitalization, punctuation, and proper names have been standard-ized in most cases to conform with modern usage. Occasional editorial liberties have been taken in the interest of clarity: some abbreviations have been spelled out, sections of manuscript records have been reordered to make them easier to follow, slips of the pen have been silently corrected, the use of upper-case head-ings in military regulations has been eliminated, and trial documents have been arranged to make the threads of testimony more accessible. In no cases have meanings been altered. Many authors of selections included in the book use square brackets liberally. I have, for that reason, chosen throughout to mark ed-itorial insertions with braces, to prevent misunderstanding. Although each se-lection has been edited to eliminate footnotes, extraneous discussions, and the like, I have allowed a small number of duplications to remain in order to pre-serve the continuity of individual selections and chapters, even though the same quotations and information may appear at more than one place. Anyone wishing to consult the annotation of any article or its complete text can locate the original article by using the bibliographical data in the Sources section at the back of the book.

Gay Warriors

Introduction

In the autumn of 1991, presidential candidate Bill Clinton launched an acrimonious national debate over homosexuality. During an appearance at Harvard University, he was asked if he favored rescinding the U.S. military's long-standing ban on service by lesbians and gay men. Clinton responded affirmatively, indicating that he would issue an executive order to that effect, if elected. After his inauguration in January 1993, he discovered a swarm of powerful opponents arrayed against him when he tried to redeem the pledge. In the angry and intemperate exchanges that followed, the arguments over whether or not gays could be allowed to serve openly in the nation's armed forces were pressed indelibly into the public consciousness. Journalists, writers, and scholars of all persuasions went to work examining every conceivable aspect of the relationship between gays and the profession of arms. Newspaper and magazine stories, books, scholarly articles, and investigations by electronic media appeared in staggering numbers. The chronological focus, quite naturally, was on the recent past rather than on earlier ages.

The failure to examine the homoerotic dimension of military service was not a deliberate attempt to submerge an aspect of history that many or even most of the commentators found unpalatable. Problems with retrieving source materials, theoretical uncertainties, and the prodigious difficulties of uncovering the lives of gays-at-arms in earlier centuries created formidable obstacles. Locating the widely distributed references to gay soldiers and Amazons in classical literature, for example, is a lengthy and tedious process. Similarly, medieval knightly orders and mariners who were at sea for years on end are generally thought to have institutionalized homoerotic relationships, but commentaries and source materials on these relationships—scattered as they are throughout the world's archives, manuscript depositories, and libraries—cannot easily be assembled. Gaining access to basic documentation or obtaining useful texts, particularly of regulations and policies dealing with homoerotic relationships in the armed forces of modern nations, can also be difficult and frustrating. The purpose of *Gay Warriors* is to bring together in a convenient format an essential segment of the historical materials that underpin the folklore, legends, truths, and traditions of military homoeroticism through the ages.

The chapters that follow, in most cases, include analytical articles, documents, and historical accounts. Articles were chosen for broad coverage of their subject, insightful scholarship, or usefulness in illuminating the documents. The process for choosing documents was more complex. An assortment of important texts from ancient Greece and Rome deal with the link between soldiers and homoerotic activities. Since none of them is of an inordinate length, chapter 1, on the classical world, contains the major commentaries on the subject and several less well known writings as well. Similarly, almost a score of classical writers dealt with Amazons in their histories, plays, and orations. The passages are brief in most instances, their span often being counted in sentences and paragraphs rather than pages, and almost all are included.

Considerable evidence is available on homoeroticism in armed services from the seventeenth to the mid-twentieth century, but it survives most often only in fragmentary form. Prohibitions against sodomy were, at times, written into army and navy regulations; courts-martial occasionally dealt with such transgressions; a rare diarist wrote of shipboard sexual activity; and oblique references to homoerotic relationships appeared in the work of at least one leading American literary figure.

In the post–World War I era, the United States Navy briefly investigated homosexuality at the Newport Naval Training Station in Rhode Island, but it was not until World War II that sex among armed forces personnel became a matter of abiding interest to the U. S. military. Material from the wartime eras is plentiful and widely dispersed, but several of the more important items are included in chapters 7 and 8.

Throughout the Cold War, when it was assumed in America that unusual behavior of almost any sort by government employees jeopardized national security, the U. S. armed forces regularly rewrote and revised their prohibitions on homosexuality in the ranks and, from time to time, authorized statements, directives, informational reports, and studies of the subject. References to homosexuality in regulations are usually buried in lengthy and convoluted official texts dealing with military personnel, and they are not easy to locate for those without the time to navigate the circuitous paper pathways of the federal bu-reaucracy. The quantity of material dealing with homosexuals in the U. S. armed forces that has been produced since Bill Clinton launched the nation-wide debate on the subject is vast. The selections include only a few source ma-terials that bear on the evolution and application of the "Don't Ask, Don't Tell, Don't Pursue" policy, but each document is representative of the many reports, memoranda, and regulations that set the direction of government agencies throughout the course of the profoundly bitter and divisive struggles over the right of homosexuals to serve openly in the military forces of the United States. The documentary materials in chapter 9 are all extracted from Department of Defense publications or pronouncements. They provide a chronological out-line of policy development through a period of more than five decades.

Over the last fifty years, a host of biographies and biographical sketches have been written about lesbians and gay men who were harassed or ejected from military organizations when their erotic preferences were discovered. Most of these accounts are easily available at any large bookstore, online source, or li-brary, so none have been included in this book.

CHAPTER I

The Classical World

♣

The Greeks of antiquity produced a substantial quantity of literature on both warfare and homosexuality, but junctures where the two subjects intersect are few. The
cities of Ilia and Thebes regularly exploited the homosexual ethos for military purposes, customarily posting pairs of lovers beside each other in battle. Little else is
known of Ilian military practice, but the "Sacred Band of Thebes," organized in
378 B.C., not only was composed entirely of homosexual lovers but formed the hard
core of the formidable Theban army until it was crushed by Philip of Macedon at
Chaeronea in 338 B.C. The Theban commander, Pammenes, advocated pairing
lovers in battle as a principle of military organization, and it was a practice among
his warriors for the elder members of romantically linked pairs to present sets of
armor to the younger members when they came of age.

Plato and numerous other classical authors attested to the military value of
armies made up of lovers. When Epaminondas fell in battle at Mantineia, his
youthful lover died beside him. One of his earlier boy lovers, Kaphisodoros, became the most formidable Theban warrior of his era. Xenophon's reference to the
valor displayed by Episthenes exemplifies the passion of seasoned Thebans of the
370s for impressing young men with their prowess. Among the Spartans, it was
common for lovers to be in battle together, but unlike the Thebans, such pairings
of individuals were not integral to their military organization. Instead, the Spartans practiced a deliberate transference of authority from fathers or families to
groups of older males, who were in turn responsible for younger men, adolescents,
and boys.

References to devoted military couples in classical literature abound in present-day discussions on gays in military service, but the intricacies of these relationships are often treated superficially or entirely ignored. The selection by John Boswell not only explores this relationship but provides a survey of homosexuality in Greek military organizations.

Included after Boswell's article are complete texts in English translation of almost all classical allusions to homosexual or dyadic relationships involving Greek warriors. Although these texts, containing a measure of overlapping material, are frequently cited, and quotations are often extracted from them by scholars and other commentators, they have never before been collected and presented in a single work.

John Boswell

"Battle-Worn: Gays in the Military, 300 B.C."

The most counterintuitive aspect of ancient same-sex eroticism is not its frequency, which is well known, but its long and hallowed relationship to democracy and military valor. Modern military officials tend to find this improbable or even unbelievable. But since sexual orientation was a matter of minor public and ethical concern to most of the city-states of the ancient world, and citizenship was a crucial privilege and obligation of all adult male citizens, many persons who might now be considered "gay" played prominent roles in the military, taking part in the earliest form of democracy through such involvement. A majority of the population of any ancient city-state—women, slaves, noncitizens—could not serve in the army; but they were not voting citizens anyway. Ancient city-states maintained the belief that all those who benefitted from the state had an obligation to defend it.

The association of homosexuals with democracy and the military was intense and widespread, extending from Harmodius and Aristogiton, a pair of lovers who were believed to have founded the Athenian democracy by concerted violence against the last tyrant, who tried to come between them, to the noted generals Pelopidas and Epaminondas, to the great military genius Alexander and his male lover Bagoas.

Of Harmodius and Aristogiton, no less acute a mind than Plato's observed that:

> Our own tyrants learned this lesson through bitter experience, when the love between Aristogiton and Harmodius grew so strong that it shattered their power. Wherever, therefore, it has been established that it is shameful to be involved in sexual relationships with men, this is due to evil on the part of the rulers, and to cowardice in the part of the governed.

In the same *Symposium* Phaedrus argued that no one's behavior is better than that of those who are in love (with other men), because they would rather behave badly in sight of father or comrade than in view of those they love. He even advanced the idea that:

> If we could somewise contrive to have a city or an army composed of lovers and those they loved, they could not be better citizens of their country than by thus refraining from all that is base in a mutual rivalry for honor; and such men as these, when fighting side by side, one might almost consider able to make even a little band victorious over all the world. For a man in love would surely choose to have all the rest of the host rather than the one he loves see him forsaking his station or flinging away his arms; sooner than this, he would prefer to die many deaths: while as for leaving the one he loves in the lurch, or not succoring him in peril, no man is such a craven that the influence of Love cannot inspire him with a courage that makes him equal to the bravest born; and without doubt what Homer calls a "fury inspired" by a god in certain heroes is the effect produced on lovers by Love's peculiar power.
>
> Moreover, only such as are in love will consent to die for others.

Perhaps inspired by this recommendation (although it merely expressed common sense in relation to the social relations of men in antiquity), about twenty years later (378 B.C.) the Theban leader Gorgidas did create such a company of 300 men, composed of pairs of lovers. They were known as the "sacred band" of Thebes, because, as Plutarch later explained, "even Plato calls the lover a friend 'inspired of God.'" Living long after, Plutarch was in a position to know that the troop had played a crucial role in many military engagements, including Tegyrae in 375 and Leuctra in 371, and:

> was never beaten, until the battle of Chaeronea [338 B.C.]; and when, after the battle, Philip—of Macedon, who won the battle—was surveying the dead, and stopped at the place where the 300 were lying, all where they had faced the long spears of his phalanx, with their armor, and mingled one with another, he was amazed, and on learning that this was the band of lovers, burst into tears and said: "Perish miserably they who think that these men did or suffered aught disgraceful."

Much later, in the third century of the Christian era, Athenaeus would echo the idea that young men become exceptionally brave under the influence of love for each other, and added that "this was proved, at any rate, by the Sacred Band organized at Thebes."

The idea that same-sex relationships would compromise the masculinity of military personnel and introduce morale problems is so fixed and unquestionable in the modern U.S. military establishment that this idealization of homosexual relationships in warrior societies may seem preposterous. And some thought it so in ancient times as well. Philip was aware of a contrary prejudice and condemned it vehemently when confronted with the dazzling courage of the Sacred Band. "It is not only the most warlike peoples, Boeotians, Spartans, Cretans, who are the most susceptible to [this kind] of love," noted Plutarch in recording Philip's opinion, "but also the greatest heroes of old: Meleager, Achilles, Aristomenes, Cimon, Epaminondas. Epaminondas, in fact, loved two men, Asopichus and Caphisodorus. The latter died with him at Mantineia and is buried close to him." In his "Life of Pelopidas"—a great military hero even among warlike peoples—Plutarch adds that "Iolaus, who shared the labors of Heracles and fought by his side, was beloved of him. And Aristotle says that even down to his day [fourth century B.C.] the tomb of Iolaus was a place where same-sex lovers plighted mutual faith."

In the *Symposium* Plato also cites the eagerness of the great warrior Achilles to join his military comrade Patroclus in death as an explicit parallel to a wife's being willing to die for her husband. Their bones were burned and mixed together in a golden amphora, as was often done in the case of married heterosexual couples.

Plato also put in the mouth of Aristophanes in the *Symposium* the idea that those males who preferred other males and "delight to lie with them and to be clasped in men's embraces . . . are the finest boys and young men, for they have the most manly nature. . . . Their behavior is due to daring, manliness, and virility, since they are quick to welcome their like."

Romans knew such same-sex hero couples—part of their cultural heritage—and added to them the *Aeneid's* Nisus and Euryalis, a pair of soldiers in the army of Aeneas, who were greatly devoted to each other. In a crucial foot race, Nisus, "remembering the love of Euryalis," essentially threw the race in his favor. The latter, moved by this gesture of love, demanded that Nisus nonetheless receive a prize, which Aeneas granted him. Nisus later begged to be killed in Euryalis's place when the latter was in mortal danger; but instead *both* were slain. Virgil called them both blessed—*fortunati ambo*—and vowed that their devotion would be remembered as long as his poetry.

Hadrian and Antinous—the former one of the most effective commanders of the Roman army and the most outstanding of the so-called "five good emperors"—were among the best known and most romantically idealized couples of antiquity. Statuary of Antinous survives in great abundance, and games and cities were established in his honor after his untimely death. "The loftiest and most typical development of the Hadrianic period was the creation of the character Antinous"—an attachment that no one at the time believed brought Hadrian's masculine or military character into any question.

After the collapse of ancient city-states, however, the ideal of military service for the entire citizenry disappeared. In the Middle Ages, military service in the form of knighthood was possible for (and required of) only the aristocratic followers of great landowners. Most of the males were servile and would not have been welcomed to knighthood. Apart from Joan of Arc, women almost never played any military role. Nonetheless throughout European history an association of military virility and homosexual attachment was common. Richard Lion Heart and Philip II of France, noted warriors of the twelfth century, were lovers and went on crusade together.

Knightly military service as an aspiration for the well-born declined in the later Middle Ages, largely disappeared in the Renaissance and was ultimately replaced by the great mercenary armies of early modern Europe, unrestrained by notions of chivalry or knighthood, who terrorized the entire continent with internecine fighting during Spain's efforts to rule all of Europe or the continent-wide bloodshed following the Protestant Reformation.

Nonetheless, even in the seventeenth century great military figures were often homosexual. Louis XIV was willing to overlook the flagrant homosexuality of the Maréchal de Vendôme—who paid his male servants to have sex with him when he rode about his estate—because the Maréchal was such a fine general. Louis's brother, Philippe, the duke of Orléans, was one of the founding members of a secret society of military men at the court of the Sun King. Its members took an oath to forswear the company of women and to limit their erotic interests to other members of the society. Though Louis was well aware of this, he declined to take action against his brother, whose influence and military genius he feared. Two princes of the royal family joined (the Compte de Vermandois, the admiral of France, and the Prince de la Roche-sur-Yon, who was elected king of Poland); the society was not disbanded until 1682.

The rise of modern nation-states with a new notion of universal conscription linked to general citizenship also included many homosexuals before the middle of the twentieth century, when a general horror of homosexuality as a psychological defect settled on the English-speaking nations of the world. It is not easy to recover records from the eighteenth and nineteenth centuries, when both Europe and the United States had such severe laws against homosexual activity that few people had the courage to leave records that would incriminate them. It was not until the end of the nineteenth century that a European homosexual rights movement appeared, led by sex researchers of the time, but it was brutally exterminated (along with Jews and other nonconformists) by the Nazis.

By the time of World War I, American horror had reached such a pitch that active efforts were made to find, expose and punish homosexuals, of which there turned out to be many in the military. A scandal about homosexual behavior between sailors and local civilians erupted in Newport, Rhode Island, but was ultimately quashed due to the efforts of local clergymen. World War II, a much wider draft, initiated into homosexual relationships many men who would otherwise have lived in rural areas ignorant of the varieties of human sexuality.

As is widely recognized even by opponents of admitting homosexuals openly to the U.S. military, gay and lesbian soldiers have served faithfully and courageously in every conflict since World War II. There is, in other words, an ancient correlation not only of military service and homosexuality, but of democracy in particular with military service on the part of all citizens, which extends from ancient history to the present day. It is perhaps time that one of the leading modern democracies in the world recognized it.

Homer

from *The Iliad,* Books 18, 22-24

"Ah me, son of valiant Peleus; you {Achilles} must hear from me
the ghastly message of a thing I wish never had happened.
Patroclus has fallen, and now they are fighting over his body
which is naked. Hector of the shining helm has taken his armor."
He spoke, and the black cloud of sorrow closed on Achilles.
In both hands he caught up the grimy dust, and poured it
over his head and face, and fouled his handsome countenance,
and the black ashes were scattered over his immortal tunic.
And he himself, mightily in his might, in the dust lay
at length and took and tore at his hair with his hands and defiled it.

There as he sighed heavily the lady his mother stood by him
and cried out shrill and aloud, and took her son's head in her arms, then
sorrowing for him she spoke to him in winged words: "Why then
child, do you lament? What sorrow has come to your heart now?
Speak out, do not hide it. These things are brought to accomplishment
through Zeus: in the way that you lifted your hands and prayed for,
that all the sons of the Achaians be pinned on their grounded vessels by
reason of your loss, and suffer things that are shameful."
Then, sighing heavily, Achilles of the swift feet answered her:
"My mother, all of these things the Olympian brought to
    accomplishment.
But what pleasure is this to me, since my dear companion has perished,
Patroclus, whom I loved beyond all other companions,

as well as my own life. I have lost him, and Hector, who killed him,
has stripped away that gigantic armor, a wonder to look on
and splendid, which the gods gave Peleus, a glorious present,
on that day they drove you to the marriage bed of a mortal.
I wish you had gone on living then with the other goddesses
of the sea, and that Peleus had married some mortal woman.
As it is, there must be on your heart a numberless sorrow
for your son's death, since you can never again receive him
won home again to his country; since the spirit within does not
   drive me
to go on living and be among men, except on condition
that Hector first be beaten down under my spear, lose his life
and pay the price for stripping Patroclus, the son of Menoitios."

"Now I shall go, to overtake that killer of a dear life,
Hector; then I will accept my own death, at whatever
time Zeus wishes to bring it about, and the other immortals.
For not even the strength of Heracles fled away from destruction,
although he was dearest of all to lord Zeus, son of Kronos,
but his fate beat him under, and the wearisome anger of Hera.
So I likewise, if such is the fate which has been wrought for me,
shall lie still, when I am dead. Now I must win excellent glory,
   deep-girdled
Dardanian woman, lifting up to her soft cheeks both hands
to wipe away the close bursts of tears in her lamentation,
and learn that I stayed too long out of the fighting. Do not
hold me back from the fight, though you love me. You will not persuade
   me."

So he {Achilles}, groaning heavily, spoke out to the Myrmidons:
"Ah me. It was an empty word I cast forth on that day
when in his halls I tried to comfort the hero Menoitios.
I told him I would bring back his son in glory to Opous
with Ilion sacked, and bringing his share of war spoils allotted.

But Zeus does not bring to accomplishment all thoughts in men's
  minds.
Thus it is destiny for us both to stain the same soil
here in Troy; since I shall never come home, and my father,
Peleus the aged rider, will not welcome me in his great house,
nor Thetis my mother, but in this place the earth will receive me.
But seeing that it is I, Patroclus, who follow you underground,
I will not bury you till I bring to this place the armor
and the head of Hector, since he was your great-hearted murderer.
Before your burning pyre I shall behead twelve glorious
children of the Trojans, for my anger over your slaying."

Now as the two in their advance were come close together,
first of the two to speak was tall helm-glittering Hector:
"Son of Peleus, I will no longer run from you, as before this
I fled three times around the great city of Priam, and dared not
stand to your onfall. But now my spirit in turn has driven me
to stand and face you. I must take you now, or I must be taken."

So he spoke, and pulling out the sharp sword that was slung
at the hollow of his side, huge and heavy, and gathering
himself together, he made his swoop, like a high-flown eagle
who launches himself out of the murk of the clouds on flat land
to catch away a tender lamb or a shivering hare; so
Hector made his swoop, swinging his sharp sword, and Achilles
charged, the heart within him loaded with savage fury.
In front of his chest the beautiful elaborate great shield
covered him, and with the glittering helm with four horns
he nodded; the lovely golden fringes were shaken about it
which Hephaistos had driven close along the horn of the helmet.
And as a star moves among stars in the night's darkening,
Hesper, who is the fairest star who stands in the sky, such
was the shining from the pointed spear Achilles was shaking
in his right hand with evil intention toward brilliant Hector.

He was eying Hector's splendid body, to see where it might best
give way, but all the rest of the skin was held in the armor,
brazen and splendid, he stripped when he cut down the strength of
  Patroclus;
yet showed where the collar-bones hold the neck from the shoulders,
the throat, where death of the soul comes most swiftly; in this
place brilliant Achilles drove the spear as he came on in fury,
and clean through the soft part of the neck the spearpoint was driven.

Achilles would not allow the Myrmidons to be scattered,
but called out to his companions whose delight was in battle:
"Myrmidons, you of the fast horses, my steadfast companions,
we must not yet slip free of the chariots our single-foot horses,
but with these very horses and chariots we must drive close up
to Patroclus and mourn him since such is the privilege of the perished."

Peleus' son {Achilles} led the thronging chant of their lamentation,
and laid his manslaughtering hands over the chest of his dear friend:
"Good-bye, Patroclus. I hail you even in the house of the death god.
All that I promised you in time past I am accomplishing,
that I would drag Hector here and give him to the dogs to feed on
raw, and before your burning pyre to behead twelve glorious
children of the Trojans for my anger over your slaying."
He spoke, and thought of shameful treatment for glorious Hector.

But the close mourners stayed by the place and piled up the timber,
and built a pyre a hundred feet long this way and that way,
and on the peak of the pyre they laid the body, sorrowful
at heart; and in front of it skinned and set in order numbers
of fat sheep and shambling horn-curved cattle; and from all
great-hearted Achilles took the fat and wrapped the corpse in it,
from head to foot, and piled up the skinned bodies about it.
Then he set beside him two-handled jars of oil and honey
leaning them against the bier, and drove four horses with strong necks
swiftly aloft the pyre with loud lamentation. And there were

nine dogs of the table that had belonged to the lord Patroclus.
Of these he cut the throats of two, and set them on the pyre;
and so also killed twelve noble sons of the great-hearted Trojans
with the stroke of bronze, and evil were the thoughts in his heart against
    them,
and let loose the iron fury of the fire to feed on them.
Then he groaned, and called by name on his beloved companion:
"Good-bye, Patroclus. I hail you even in the house of the death god.
For all that I promised you in time past I am accomplishing.
Here are twelve noble sons of the great-hearted Trojans
whom the fire feeds on, all, as it feeds on you. But I will not
give Hector, Priam's son to the fire, but the dogs, to feast on."

Remembering all these things he {Achilles} let fall the swelling tears, lying
sometimes along his side, sometimes on his back, and now again
prone on his face; then he would stand upright, and pace turning
in distraction along the beach of the sea, nor did dawn rising
escape him as she brightened across the sea and the beaches.
Then, when he had yoked running horses under the chariot
he would fasten Hector behind the chariot, so as to drag him,
and draw him three times around the tomb of Menoitios' fallen
son, then rest again in his shelter, and throw down the dead man
and leave him to lie sprawled on his face in the dust.

So Achilles has destroyed pity, and there is not in him
any shame; which does much harm to men but profits them also.
For a man must some day lose one who was even closer
than this; a brother from the same womb, or a son. And yet
he weeps for him, and sorrows for him, and then it is over,
for the Destinies put in mortal men the heart of endurance.
But this man, now he has torn the heart of life from great Hector,
ties him to his horses and drags him around his beloved companion's
    tomb;
and nothing is gained thereby for his good, or his honor.

Plutarch

from *Moralia*, "Dialogue on Love"

Cleomachus came to help the Chalcidians when the Lelantine War against the Eretrians was at its height. The Chalcidian infantry was thought to have considerable strength, but they found it difficult to resist the enemy cavalry. Accordingly his allies requested Cleomachus, a man of splendid courage, to be the first to charge the horse. His beloved was there and Cleomachus asked him if he was going to witness the battle. The youth said that he was, embraced Cleomachus tenderly, and put on his helmet for him. Filled with ardor, Cleomachus assembled the bravest of the Thessalians about himself, made a fine charge, and fell upon the enemy with such vigor that their cavalry was thrown into confusion and was thoroughly routed. When subsequently their hoplites also fled, the Chalcidians had a decisive victory. It was, however, Cleomachus' bad fortune to be killed in the battle. The Chalcidians point out his tomb in the market-place with the great pillar standing on it to this day. Formerly they had frowned on paederasty, but now they accepted it and honored it more than others did. Now Aristotle says that the circumstances of Cleomachus' death in victorious battle with the Eretrians were different and that the lover embraced by his friend was one of the Chalcidians from Thrace sent as an ally to the Chalcidians of Euboea. And this, he says, is the reason for the Chalcidian popular song:

> Ye lads of grace and sprung from worthy stock,
> Grudge not to brave men converse with your beauty:
> In cities of Chalcis, Love, looser of limbs,
> Thrives side by side with courage.

Anton was the name of the lover and Philistus was his beloved, as the poet Dionysius relates in his *Origins*.

In your city, Thebes, Pemptides, isn't it true that the lover made his beloved a present of a complete suit of armor when the boy was registered as a man? Pammenes, a man versed in love, changed the order of battle-line for the hoplites, censuring Homer as knowing nothing about love, because he arranged the companies of Achaeans by tribes and clans and did not station lover beside beloved in order to bring it about that:

> Shield supported shield and helmet helmet,

for he considered that Love is the only invincible general. It is a fact that men desert their fellow tribesmen and relatives and even (God knows) their parents and children; but lover and beloved, when their god is present, no enemy has ever encountered and forced his way through. In some cases, even when there is no need for it, they are moved to exhibit their love of danger, their disregard for mere life. This was what prompted Theron of Thessaly to place his left hand on the wall, draw his sword, and cut off the thumb, challenging his rival to do the same. When another man had fallen in battle on his face and an enemy was about to kill him, he begged the latter to wait for a moment in order that his beloved might not see him wounded from behind.

It is not only the most warlike peoples, Boeotians, Spartans, Cretans, who are the most susceptible to love, but also the great heroes of old, Meleager, Achilles, Aristomenes, Cimon, Epaminondas. Epaminondas, in fact, loved two young men, Asopichus and Caphisodorus. The latter died with him at Mantineia and is buried close to him; while Asopichus showed himself a most formidable warrior and so redoubtable to his foes that the first man who stood up to him and struck back, Eucnamus of Amphissa, received heroic honors among the Phocians.

As for Heracles, it would be difficult to list all his loves, they are so numerous. For example, believing Iolaus to have been beloved by him, to this very day lovers worship and honor Iolaus, exchanging vows and pledges with their beloved at his tomb. It is also related that Heracles exhibited his talent for healing by rescuing Alcestis from a mortal disease to please Admetus, who was not only in love with his wife, but had also been Heracles' beloved.

Plutarch

from *Lives*, "Pelopidas"

Gorgidas, according to some, first formed the Sacred Band of three hundred chosen men, to whom, as being a guard for the citadel, the State allowed provision, and all things necessary for exercise: and hence they were called the city band, as citadels of old were usually called cities. Others say that it was composed of young men attached to each other by personal affection, and a pleasant saying of Pammenes is current, that Homer's Nestor was not well skilled in ordering an army, when he advised the Greeks to rank tribe and tribe, and family and family together, that:

So tribe might tribe, and kinsmen kinsmen aid,

but that he should have joined lovers and their beloved. For men of the same tribe or family little value one another when dangers press; but a band cemented by friendship grounded upon love, is never to be broken, and invincible; since the lovers, ashamed to be base in sight of their beloved, and the beloved before their lovers, willingly rush into danger for the relief of one another. Nor can that be wondered at; since they have more regard for their absent lovers than for others present; as in the instance of the man, who, when his enemy was going to kill him, earnestly requested him to run him through the breast, that his lover might not blush to see him wounded in the back. It is a tradition likewise, that Iolaus, who assisted Heracles in his labors and fought at his side, was beloved of him; and Aristotle observes that even in his time, lovers plighted their faith at Iolaus's tomb. It is likely, therefore, that this band was called sacred on this account; as Plato calls a lover a divine friend. It is stated that it was never beaten till the battle at Chaeronea: and when Philip, after the fight, took a view of the slain, and came to the place where the three hundred that fought his phalanx lay dead together, he wondered, and understanding that it was the band of lovers, he shed tears and said, "Perish any man who suspects that these men either did or suffered any thing that was base."

It was not the disaster of Laius, as the poets imagine, that first gave rise to this form of attachment amongst the Thebans, but their law-givers, designing to soften, whilst they were young, their natural fierceness, brought, for example, the pipe into great esteem, both in serious and sportive occasions, and gave great encouragement to these friendships in the Palaestra, to temper the manners and characters of the youth. With a view to this they did well again, to make Harmony, the daughter of Mars and Venus, their tutelar deity; since, where force and courage is joined with gracefulness and winning behavior, a harmony ensues that combines all the elements of society in perfect consonance and order.—Gorgidas distributed this Sacred Band all through the front ranks of the infantry and thus made their gallantry less conspicuous; not being united in one body, but mingled with so many others of inferior resolution, they had no fair opportunity of showing what they could do. But Pelopidas, having sufficiently tried their bravery at Tegyrae, where they had fought alone, and around his own person, never afterward divided them, but keeping them entire, and as one man, gave them the first duty in the greatest battles. For as horses run brisker in a chariot than singly, not that their joint force divides the air with greater ease, but because being matched one against the other, emulation kindles and inflames their courage; thus he thought, brave men, provoking one another to noble actions, would prove most serviceable and most resolute, where all were united together.

Virgil

from *The Aeneid,* Book 9

Nisus was guardian of a gate, the son
of Hyrtacus, tenacious warrior,
whom Ida, home of the hunters, sent to serve
Aeneas with his racing javelin and
light arrows. Near him stood Euryalus
his comrade; and no one who served Aeneas
or carried Trojan weapons was more handsome:
a boy whose face, unshaven, showed the first
down of his youth. Their minds and hearts were one;
in war they charged together; and now, too,
they shared a sentry station at one gate.
And Nisus says: "Euryalus, is it
the gods who put this fire in our minds,
or is it that each man's relentless longing
becomes a god to him? Long has my heart
been keen for battle or some mighty act;
it cannot be content with peace or rest.
You see how sure are those Rutulians:
a few lights glitter here and there; they lie
sprawled out and slack with sleep and wine; the night
is still. Hear what I have in mind. The people,

the elders—everyone now urges that
Aeneas be called back, that messengers
be sent to bring him tidings he can trust.
If they agree to give to you instead
the prize that I can claim for such a deed—
since for myself the glory is enough—
then close by that mound there I may have found
a path to reach the walls of Pallenteum."

{Nisus:} "My boy, I cannot take you with me, cannot
bring such a sorrow to your suffering mother—
she is the only one of many matrons
to dare this distant journey and not choose
to wait within Acestes' walls." But he {Euryalus}:
"You weave these pretexts uselessly. My purpose
is set. I have not yielded. Let us hurry."
With that, he wakes new sentrymen. They come
to take their turns; and with the station left
in sure hands, he walks off as Nisus' comrade.

They cross the trenches as they leave and, through
the shadow of the night, make for the camp
that will bring death to them—though before that,
they will be the end of many. Everywhere
they can see bodies sprawling, deep in sleep
and drink, and the tilted chariots on the shore,
men tangled in the harnesses and wheels,
and casks of wine and weapons all about.
And Nisus spoke out first: "Euryalus,
the right hand has to dare; the time invites;
our way is here. You guard and watch from far,
lest any band come at us from behind.
I will act here, to kill and cut a wide
pathway that you can follow." So he speaks,
then checks his voice and drives his sword at once

into the haughty Rhamnes, who by chance
was cushioned on a heap of rugs piled high
while snoring out his sleep from his wide chest.

He cuts down three attendants next to Rhamnes
as they lie sprawled at random around their lances,
and then the charioteer and armor-bearer
of Remus, whom he caught beneath the horses.
He hacks their drooping necks and then lops off
their master's head. He leaves the trunk to gurgle
as it spouts blood; the earth, the rugs are steeped
in warm black gore. Then he kills Lamyrus,
Lamus, and young Serranus, known for beauty.

Euryalus . . . too, is kindled, wild, and falls upon
a vast and nameless rabble, catching Fadus,
Herbesus, Abaris—all three unconscious.

Euryalus is hot for secret slaughter.
He had drawn near the comrades of Messapus,
where he could see the last camp fires flicker
and tethered horses grazing on the grass,
when Nisus, with few words (for he could sense
his comrade was berserk with lust for carnage),
stopped him: "Now let us go; our enemy,
daylight, is near; we have had enough revenge;
we have cut a pathway through these Latin ranks."

But meanwhile horsemen rode up from a force
that hurried out from Latium to carry
an answer to Prince Turnus. While the rest
had halted, readying for battle these
three hundred riders came ahead, and all
were under shield, with Volcens as their captain.
And as they neared the camp, approached the wall,

they saw the pair far off along a path
and heading left; the helmet of the heedless
Euryalus betrayed him, flashing back
moonlight across the shades of gleaming night.
That is enough to stop them. Volcens cries:
"Halt, man! What is this march? Who are you, armed?
Where are you headed?" But the pair do not
attempt to answer, only rushing on
their flight into the forest, trusting the night.

But Nisus now is clear; he had escaped
the enemy and, still unthinking, passed
the place that later is to be called Alban
for Alba Longa—but then King Latinus
kept his tall cattle stalls there—when he halted,
looked back for his lost friend and could not find him.

With this, he tracks and traces back his footsteps
and threads his way through silent thickets until
he hears hoofbeats and trampled brush and signals
of chase and, not long after an outcry;
and sees Euryalus whom now, betrayed
by night and the terrain, bewildered by
the sudden tumult, all the troop are hauling
away as overpowered, he thrashes, hopeless.
But what can Nisus do? What can he use,
what force or arms to dare his comrade's rescue?
Or should he rush to his sure end among
those troops and hurry with his wounds a seemly
death? Quickly then he draws his arm far back;

then, straining all his body, hurled his steel.
Across the shadows of the night it flies,
then strikes the facing back of Sulmo; there
it snaps and, splintered, passes through his midriff.

As Sulmo tumbles over in chill death,
he vomits out a warm stream from his chest;
his long-drawn gasps heave hard against his ribs.
The Latins look around, at every angle.
While they still tremble, Nisus, even fiercer,
now poises a new shaft at his eartip.
The hissing spear drives straight through both the temples
of Tagus; warm, it stuck in his pierced brain.
Though Volcens rages, crazed, he cannot see
whoever was the sender of that shaft
or where he can attack in frenzy. "Yet
until we find him, you shall pay," he cried,
"the penalties of both with your warm blood."
He rushed with drawn sword at Euryalus.
Then, mad with terror, Nisus cries aloud—
he could not hide in darkness anymore
or stand so great a grief: "I did it—I:
your steel, Rutulians, is meant for me;
the crime is mine; he has not dared anything,
nor could he; heaven be my witness and
the knowing stars: he only loved too well
his luckless friend." So was he pleading when
the sword, thrust home with force, pierced through the ribs
and broke the white breast of Euryalus.

But Nisus rushes on among them all;
he is seeking only Volcens, only Volcens
can be the man he wants. The enemy
crowd him; on every side, their ranks would drive
him back, but Nisus presses on unchecked,
whirling his lightning sword until he plunged
it full into the Latin's howling mouth
and, dying took away his foeman's life.
Then pierced, he cast himself upon the lifeless
friend; there, at last he found his rest in death.

Xenophon

from *Anabasis* 8.4

Now there was a certain Olynthian, named Episthenes; he was a great lover of boys, and seeing a handsome lad, just in the bloom of youth and carrying a light shield, about to be slain, he ran up to Xenophon and supplicated him to rescue the fair youth. Xenophon went to Seuthes and begged him not to put the boy to death. He explained to him the disposition of Episthenes; how he had once enrolled a company, the only qualification required being that of personal beauty; and with these handsome young men at his side there was none so brave as he. Seuthes put the question, "Would you like to die in his behalf, Episthenes?" Then the other stretched out his neck, and said, "Strike, if the boy bids you, and will thank his preserver." Seuthes, turning to the boy asked, "Shall I smite him instead of you?" The boy shook his head, imploring him to slay neither the one nor the other, whereupon Episthenes caught the lad in his arms, exclaiming, "It is time you did battle with me, Seuthes, for my boy; never will I yield him up." Seuthes laughed and so consented.

Xenophon

from *The Constitution of the Spartans*

I recall the astonishment with which I first noted the unique position of Sparta among the states of Hellas, the relatively sparse population, and at the same time the extraordinary power and prestige of the community. . . . I ought, as it seems to me, not to omit some remark on the subject of homosexuality, it being a topic in close connection with that of boyhood and the training of boys.

We know that the rest of the Hellenes deal with this relationship in different ways, either after the manner of the Boeotians, where man and boy are intimately united by a bond like that of wedlock, or after the manner of the Eleians, where the enjoyment of beauty is gained by favors; while there are others who would absolutely debar the lover from all conversation and discourse with the beloved.

Lycurgus adopted a system opposed to all of these alike. Given that some one, himself being all that a man ought to be, should in admiration of a boy's soul endeavor to discover in him a true friend without reproach, and to consort with him—this was a relationship which Lycurgus commended, and indeed regarded as the noblest type of bringing up. But if, as was evident, it was not an attachment to the soul, but a yearning merely towards the body, he stamped this thing as foul and horrible; and with this result, to the credit of Lycurgus be it said, that in Lacedaemon the relationship of lover and beloved is like that of parent and child or brother and brother where carnal appetite is in abeyance.

That this, however, which is the fact, should be scarcely credited in some quarters does not surprise me, seeing that in many states the laws do not oppose the desires in question.

Xenophon

from *The Symposium*

Homer makes Achilles get such brilliant revenge for the death of Patroclus not because he was his loved one, but his comrade-in-arms. So with Orestes and Pylades, Theseus and Perithous, and many other demigods: the best of them are celebrated not for sleeping with each other but for being partners in heroic deeds out of admiration for each other.

Are not all noble deeds even today performed for the sake of fame by men willing to endure hardship and danger rather than by men who prefer pleasure to glory? Yet Pausanias, the lover of the poet Agathon, defended people who wallow in debauchery by saying that the most valiant army would consist entirely of lovers and their loved ones. Such men, he thought, would be especially ashamed of deserting each other. This is an astonishing argument: that men addicted to shameless behavior and to ignoring reproach should be ashamed to do something shameful. As evidence he alleged that the Thebans and Eleians follow this practice. At least, he said, they sleep with their loved ones, yet station them next to themselves in battle. But that's a false analogy: with them it's a custom, with us a disgrace. And placing your loved one next to you seems to me to be a sign of distrust, as though you expected him not to act bravely if stationed alone.

The Spartans, on the other hand, believe that if a man so much as lusts after another man's body he'll never attain goodness and beauty. Yet they make their loved ones such models of perfection that even if stationed with foreigners rather than with their lovers they're ashamed to desert their companions. That's because the goddess the Spartans honor is called Shame, not Shamelessness.

CHAPTER 2

Amazons

♣

The Amazons of classical literature have been a puzzling phenomenon from the time of the ancients to the present. Although there was little doubt among at least some writers of two thousand years ago that they once existed, no physical evidence establishes that the Amazons were ever more than mythological beings. Information about them in literary sources is at best fragmentary, hardly more than scattered lines and commentary spread throughout the works of a wide array of Greek and Roman authors. What is clear from their varying descriptions is that writers of antiquity were unable to account for the Amazons, who turned ordinary perceptions of gender upside down. The spectacle of women who lived, worked, and fought in the manner of men defied understanding. Some writers described Amazon groups who married men but even then refused to abandon their masculine pursuits of herding, riding, and warfare in order to adopt the domestic roles considered appropriate to females. Other classical authors wrote of women who lived in entirely female communities, joining with males only to produce the offspring necessary to preserve their numbers. Male children born of these temporary unions were returned to the fathers, mutilated to make them unfit for traditional male roles, or killed.

Neither Greeks nor Romans provided information or speculated on nonprocreative sexuality among the Amazons. In more recent times, the Amazons have been portrayed as lesbian bands or tribes. Whether the classics provide implicit or contextual evidence indicating the practice of homoerotic sexuality among them is unclear. The materials that follow include a large selection of Greek and

Roman works containing the basic sources for pondering the erotic lives of the Amazons.

Sue Blundell
"Amazons," from *Women in Ancient Greece*

A large number of ancient writers tell us about a race of warrior women called Amazons, who lived without men, wore masculine clothing and took part in activities—hunting, farming and above all, fighting—which among Greeks were normally exclusive to males. The Amazons are placed in a variety of geographical locations, but the one mentioned most frequently is the area bordering on the south-eastern shore of the Black Sea (in present-day northern Turkey), around the city of Themiscyra and the river Thermodon. According to one ancient historian, Diodorus Siculus, there was also an earlier race of Amazons who were natives of Libya in North Africa.

The era when the Amazons are supposed to have lived also varies a great deal, but most commonly they are assigned to the period before and during the Trojan War, that is, to a time at least five hundred years before the earliest reference to them, which is in Homer's *Iliad*. For most writers, then, the Amazons are a phenomenon of the distant past, and no author claims ever to have seen them, or even to have met anyone who has seen them. In *Airs, Waters, Places*, a treatise ascribed to the fifth-century physician Hippocrates, some Amazon-type characteristics are attributed to the warrior women of the Sauromatians, a nomadic tribe who in the Classical Age inhabited territory in southern Russia to the east of the River Don. But the author is not describing a race of women living apart from men, and he himself does not refer to them as Amazons. The geographer Strabo in the first century B.C. mentions stories about Amazons which were current in his own time, but is clearly not inclined to believe them himself.

Only one set of narratives places the Amazon story in a specific historical context, that of the late fourth century B.C. Several writers refer to a tale about a meeting between Alexander the Great and a troop of Amazons, under their queen Thalestris, in the far north of the Persian Empire. The historian Arrian gives a slightly different version, referring to a story that Alexander received from the governor of Media a gift of a hundred armed and mounted women, whom the governor called Amazons; the circumspect conqueror at once dismissed them, fearing that his troops would not treat them with much respect, but promised that one day he would visit their queen and make her pregnant. The episode is not given much credence by the majority of the authors mentioning it: Arrian says that it is not included in the most reliable sources for Alexander's life, and that he himself doubts whether Amazons still existed at that time.

Amazonian customs receive a great deal of attention from ancient authors, as well they might. Strabo says that in order to reproduce themselves, the Amazons set aside two months every year for visits to the mountainous area on the border between their own country and that of the Gargarians. The men from the other side of the border made their way to the same region, and sexual intercourse took place in the dark, and at random. At certain fixed times, then, the Amazons' total rejection of men gave way to participation in promiscuous sexual relationships. If the babies which were born as a result were female, they were kept by the Amazons; if they were male, they were handed over to the Gargarians. A number of writers tell us that the right breasts of the girls were either cut off or seared with red-hot bronze instruments when they were infants: this was done to prevent them getting in the way during their later careers as fighters. According to the author of *Airs, Waters, Places*, this was also the custom among Sauromatian women, and had the effect of diverting all the strength and bulk to the right shoulder and arm, which wielded weapons. But the idea that the Amazons lacked one breast must have become popular at quite a late date, since in the numerous visual representations of them produced in the fifth century B.C. they are always shown with the normal two. Clearly one reason why the story caught on was that it offered an explanation (almost certainly a fanciful one) of their name: the Greek word *a-mazon* could be translated as "without a breast."

Needless to say, the absence of men in the Amazon community excites a great deal of comment. The fifth-century tragedian Aeschylus calls them "man-hating" and "manless." As far as Strabo is concerned, it is this feature of their way of life which makes their existence hard to credit, for . . . not only did they manage to survive without men, but they also of course fought against them. They are "a match for men," says Homer, who locates the Amazons in southern Asia Minor and says that the hero Bellerophon and Priam the king of Troy had both encountered them in battle. For Lysias, an Athenian orator of the Classical period, the Amazons . . . pioneered the use of iron and horses in battle, and with these assets they succeeded in enslaving their neighbors and ruling over many lands. The Amazons, then, reject what for a Greek was the ultimate female experience, marriage, and instead engage in the most characteristic of male activities, fighting. The reversal is emphasized by the nature of their religious practices: their favorite deities are said to have been Artemis, the virgin goddess, and the war god Ares.

According to Diodorus, the lifestyle of both the Libyan and the Black Sea Amazons involved an inversion of normal sex-roles rather than complete separatism. In Amazon communities the women were the fighters, rulers and administrators, while the men . . . looked after the home, reared the children and carried out the orders given to them by their wives. While female infants had their right breasts seared to improve their prowess as fighters, the boys were mutilated in their legs and arms so as to make them unfit for war. Both races of Amazons were renowned for their military accomplishments, and succeeded in conquering large parts of Syria and Asia Minor; but eventually both were overwhelmed in battle by the Greek hero Heracles. . . .

For other ancient authors the Amazons, in spite of their separatist habits, were not immune to the lure of sexual desire. The fifth-century historian Herodotus recounts how some Amazons from Themiscyra who had been taken prisoner by a Greek force succeeded in murdering their captors while they were on board ship. They eventually landed on the northern shores of the Black Sea, in the territory of the people known as the Scythians, where they at once stole some horses and took up the profitable pursuit of marauding. When the Scythians at last discovered the sex of these mysterious raiders, they embarked on a deliberate campaign of seduction. A stray Amazon was waylaid by a Scythian, and readily agreed to have sex with him. On the next day they each brought along one of their friends, and before long the entire population of both camps had been brought together by this blind date process. The Amazons were nevertheless reluctant to be drawn into conventional Scythian society, since their customs were incompatible with those of the local women, and it was agreed that the couples should establish a new community to the north-east. This, according to Herodotus, was the origin of the Sauromatian race, whose women in his own day still engaged in hunting and warfare, and wore the same clothes as the men; they also had a law which forbade a woman to marry until she had killed an enemy in battle.

For Herodotus, then, the Amazons' opposition to men could be overcome by the power of sexual attraction. For others it was the force of arms which finally put paid to their unique way of life. The latter was in fact by far the more common explanation of how the Amazons eventually came to grief, and it features in some of the most prominent of their myths. At least as old as the fifth century B.C. is the story that Heracles, for his ninth labor, was given the job of bringing back to Greece the girdle of the Amazon queen Hippolyta. To achieve this, he and his followers fought a battle against the women warriors, in the course of which—according to some accounts—Heracles killed Hippolyta and took the girdle from her dead body.

Some of the versions of the Heracles episode relate how the hero was accompanied on this adventure by his Athenian comrade, Theseus. The latter either captured in battle, or received as a prize, or was amorously pursued by, Hippolyta's sister Antiope—the details vary from story to story, and indeed according to some narratives it was Hippolyta herself rather than Antiope who became the consort of the legendary Athenian king. But one way or another, Theseus came home with an Amazon, thereby precipitating one of the major events in Athens' mythical past. In order to free their queen (or simply, in some versions, in pursuit of their lust for conquest), the Amazons invaded Greece from the north and marched on Athens. From their base on the Areopagus hill they launched a siege of the Acropolis, which was only lifted three months later when the women's army was finally defeated by Theseus' forces.

One final Amazonian exploit features the later queen Penthesileia, who after the death of Hector brought her army to Troy to help defend the city against the Greeks. The hero Achilles faced her on the battlefield, and it was only after his spear had pierced her breast that he came to realize her beauty and to fall in love with her—too late, of course. Here, the two most common causes of the defeat of Amazonian resistance—physical force and love—are combined, and we encounter an analogy frequently made in Greek myth between violent domination and the sexual act. These erotic connotations can be discerned in some of the other Amazonian episodes—Heracles captures the queen's girdle, Theseus carries off an Amazon bride—and were certainly not lost on the sculptors of the Classical Age.

It is impossible to ascertain whether or not the Amazon myth had any substantial basis in reality. No archeological evidence has been uncovered which would remotely suggest the existence, in the Bronze Age or at any later time, of a community consisting entirely of female warriors; nor are there any material remains or contemporary written records which can confirm the notion that the myth preserves a memory of a time when a matriarchal society in Asia Minor was struggling for survival in the face of the growing patriarchal dominance of the incoming Hittite peoples. At present, the most likely candidates for the role of Amazonian prototype seem to be the women of the Sauromatian race, who according to Herodotus and the author of *Airs, Waters, Places* used before their marriages to engage in riding, hunting and fighting. Archeological evidence provides some confirmation of these activities: a few Sauromatian female burials of the sixth to fourth centuries B.C. contain weapons and armor. Travelers' tales about these strange female practices may in themselves have been sufficient to give rise to Amazon myths, especially if the hearer began to speculate, as Herodotus evidently did, about the women's distant ancestors. Genuine warrior women seem often to have excited the male imagination, and it would not be surprising if some such group in the course of time had been mentally transformed into an entire race of female fighters.

Although the origins of the Amazon myth are obscure, there is no doubting its popularity, particularly in Classical Athens: confrontations with Amazons were mentioned frequently by poets, orators and historians, and were a common theme in sculpture, frescoes and vase paintings. Presumably, then, it was a myth that meant something to the population at large; undoubtedly it had gained a place in the official iconography of Athens, since it was chosen for depiction on some very prominent public buildings, including the Parthenon. When we come to consider why this high profile was accorded to the women warriors, the question of whether or not they ever existed becomes irrelevant. No one in fifth-century Athens would have expected ever to encounter an Amazon, or would have believed that this race posed any threat to their city in real life. Nevertheless, the Amazon story seems to have been important to the Athenians.

Whatever the reason for this, we can be sure that it had nothing to do with heartwarming messages about the empowerment of women. The Amazons were outstanding fighters, and they conquered many nations, but in the end they were always beaten by Greeks—by Heracles, by Achilles or, most significantly for the Athenians, by Theseus. . . . Clearly on one level the Amazonian theme in Athenian art can be interpreted as a form of patriotic display. The self-glorification inspired by the myth became very pronounced after the Persian invasions of Greece in 490 and 480 B.C. Like those other legendary foes, the Trojans, the Amazons lived in an area which in the early fifth century was part of the Persian Empire, and their incursion into Greece was seen as foreshadowing the recent Persian onslaughts, which had been directed in particular at the city of Athens.

The identification between Amazons and Persians is confirmed by numerous fifth-century Athenian vase paintings in which the women warriors are provided with Persian dress and weapons—leggings, leather caps, curved bows, axes and hide-covered shields. There can be little doubt that the Amazons were favored by Greek artists partly as an example of the "defeated barbarian" type. In the sculpture which decorated Greek temples, it was customary to refrain from depicting recent historical events, for fear that the gods might be offended by human boastfulness. But myths which provided parallels to those events were quite acceptable; and this would have been one reason why the female invaders were chosen to adorn the Parthenon, the temple which was constructed to replace the one destroyed by the Persians when they sacked Athens in 480 B.C. In these scenes from Athens' heroic past there were intimations of more recent achievements.

However, it is difficult to avoid the conclusion that the Amazons were important to the Greeks, not simply as barbarians, but also as women. Certainly in sculpture their female characteristics are frequently on show, with one breast left exposed, and the buttocks emphasized. These creatures who were so feminine in their physique were nevertheless masculine in their behavior, and this would have presented a paradox which Greek men would have found stimulating but also instructive. In the literary accounts the Amazons can be seen to represent an inversion of everything which a Greek male (in particular, an Athenian male) would have expected of a woman. They were active in the public arena; they were experts in warfare; they were in political control of the state in which they lived; they refused to marry; they were either asexual or sexually promiscuous; and they valued girl babies more highly than males. In later versions of the story, they also, in cutting off a breast, performed a symbolic denial of the characteristic role of women, motherhood. Athenian men may well have found all this female assertiveness very sexy, but they certainly would not have wanted to recommend it to their own womenfolk.

But recommendation was not, of course, what the Amazon myth was offering. This fantasy of a horde of rampant women could be safely enjoyed because of the cautionary nature of its ending: the Amazons were everything that an Athenian woman ought not to be, and ultimately they failed. There can be little doubt that, in a society like that of Classical Athens, one of the myth's functions was the provision of a negative role model. . . . The message of the myth for both males and females alike was that in a civilized society women are passive, chaste and married. The alternative—behaving like an Amazon—was a mark of barbarism, and its consequences were disastrous both for the women themselves and for the state over which they ruled. In this way the personal and political dominance of men was justified and reinforced.

It would be interesting to know whether the Amazon myth was always "correctly" decoded by the Athenian women who encountered it. It is possible that some of them would have found these assertive females inspiring, in spite of their failure. But of course we have no inkling of women's reactions. Presumably the role invented for the Amazons—that of vanquished barbarian invader—would have ensured that the majority of women subscribed to the prevailing view and rejected the warrior women's example.

Aeschylus

from *Prometheus Bound*

On your left hand, is the country of the Chalybes,
    craftsmen in iron.
Beware of them; they are savage, and no stranger can
Approach them safely. After this you reach the river
Hybristes, whose wild torrent justifies its name.
Do not attempt to cross—it is too dangerous—
Until you come to Caucasus itself, the peak

Of all that range, where from the very brows the river
Floods forth its fury. You must cross the topmost ridge
Close to the stars, and take the pathway leading south.
There you will find the warlike race of Amazons,
Haters of men. This race in time to come shall found
The city of Themiscyra, on the Thermodon,
Where the rough jaw of Salmydessus fronts the sea,
An enemy to sailors, stepmother to ships.
The Amazons will most gladly guide you on your way.

Aeschylus

from *The Suppliant Maidens*

King: Women, I find your story incredible. How can
A race like yours be Argive? You resemble rather
Libyans—certainly not women of our country.
The Nile might foster such a plant; and in your faces,
Where the male craftsman molds the female feature, there,
Stamped to the life, is Cyprus; and I hear there are
Women such as you, Nomads, who mount on camels' backs
As we on horses, and ride at ease about the land
That neighbors Ethiopia; if you were armed with bows
I would have guessed you were those famous Amazons,
Who live without men and feed on flesh. But tell me clearly
How you derive from Argos your descent and blood.

Aristides

from *Panathenaic Oration*

But no one, I think, has not heard of their {the Athenians} conduct in behalf
of their own land against whoever attacked them. Yet we must also select and
discuss a small part of these stories. They fought a cavalry engagement against

the Amazons who surpassed their nature by their deeds, and they annihilated them, although no one up to Attica opposed them. Now they had extended their lines equally through both continents, beginning from Thermodon, as it were the center of a circle, and passing through Asia up to Lycia, Caria, and Pamphylia, as if part of their encampment, and through Europe up to their encampment at the city. But now from this point, as if a rope had broken, all snapped back, and the Amazons' march of empire was undone. And here too the city aided the whole race, and now it is doubtful if the Amazons ever existed.

Aristophanes

from *Lysistrata*

Chorus of Old Men: Outrage upon outrage! Things are going from bad to worse. Let us punish the minxes, every one of us that has a man's appendages to boast of. Come, off with our tunics, for a man must savor of manhood; come my friends, let us strip naked from head to foot. Courage, I say, we who in our day garrisoned Lipsydrion; let us be young again, and shake off old. If we give them the least hold over us, 'tis all up! Their audacity will know no bounds! We shall see them building ships, and fighting sea-fights, like Artemisia; nay, if they want to mount and ride as cavalry, we had best cashier the knights, for indeed women excel in riding, and have a fine, firm seat for the gallop. Just think of all those squadrons of Amazons Micon has painted for us engaged in hand-to-hand combat with men. Come, then we must e'en fit collars to all these willing necks.

Arrian

from *Anabasis of Alexander*

Here they say that Atropates, the satrap of Media, gave him {Alexander} 100 women, saying that they were of the race of Amazons. These had been equipped with the arms of male horsemen, except that they carried axes instead of spears, and targets instead of shields. They also say that they had the right breast smaller than the left, and that they exposed it in battle. Alexander dismissed them from the army, that no attempt to violate them might be made by the Macedonians or barbarians; and he ordered them to carry word to their queen that he was coming to her in order to procreate children by her. But this story has been recorded neither by Aristobulus nor Ptolemy, nor any other writer who is a trustworthy authority on such matters. I do not even think that the race of Amazons was surviving at that time, or even before Alexander's time; otherwise they would have been mentioned by Xenophon, who mentions the Phasians, Colchians, and all the other barbaric races which the Greeks came upon, when they started from Trapezus or before they marched down to Trapezus. They would certainly have fallen in with the Amazons there, if they were still in existence. However it does not seem to me credible that this race of women had no existence at all, because it has been celebrated by so many famous poets. For the general account is, that Heracles marched against them and brought the girdle of their queen Hippolyta into Greece: and that the Athenians under Theseus were the first to conquer and repulse these women as they were advancing into Europe. The battle of the Athenians and Amazons has been painted by Micon, no less than that of the Athenians and Persians. Herodotus also has frequently written about these women; and so have the Athenian writers who have honored the men who perished in war with orations. They have mentioned the exploit of the Athenians against the Amazons as one of their special glories. If therefore Atropates showed any equestrian women to Alexander, I think he must have shown him some other foreign women trained in horsemanship, and equipped with the arms which were said to be those of the Amazons.

Demosthenes

The Funeral Speech (7–8)

For the ancestors of this present generation {of Athenians}, both their fathers and those who bore the names of these men in time past, by which they are recognized by those of our race, never at any time wronged any man, whether Greek or barbarian, but it was their pride, in addition to all their other good qualities, to be true gentlemen and supremely just, and in defending themselves they accomplished a long list of noble deeds. They so prevailed over the invading host of the Amazons as to expel them beyond the Phasis, and the host of Eumolpus and of many other foeman they drove not only out of their own land but also from the lands of all the other Greeks—invaders whom all those dwelling on our front to the westward neither withstood nor possessed the power to halt.

Diodorus Siculus

from Book 2

Now in the country along the Thermodon River, as the account goes, the sovereignty was in the hands of a people among whom the women held the supreme power, and its women performed the services of war just as did the men. Of these women one, who possessed the royal authority, was remarkable for her prowess in war and her bodily strength, and gathering together an army of women she drilled it in the use of arms and subdued in war some of the neighboring peoples. And since her valor and fame increased, she made war upon people after people of neighboring lands, and as the tide of her fortune continued favorable, she was so filled with pride that she gave herself the appellation of Daughter of Ares; but to the men she assigned the spinning of wool and such other domestic duties as belong to women. Laws also were established by her, by virtue of which she led forth the women to contests of war, but upon the men she fastened humiliation and slavery. And as for their children, they mutilated both the legs and the arms of the males, incapacitating them in this way for the demands of war, and in the case of the females they seared the right breast that it might not project when their bodies matured and be in the way; and it is for this reason that the nation of the Amazons received the appellation it bears. In general, this queen was remarkable for her intelligence and ability as a general, and she founded a great city named Themiscyra at the mouth of the Thermodon River and built there a famous palace; furthermore, in her campaigns she devoted much attention to military discipline and at the outset subdued all her neighbors as far as the Tanais River. And this queen, they say, accomplished the deeds which have been mentioned, and fighting brilliantly in a certain battle she ended her life heroically.

The daughter of this queen, the account continues, on succeeding to the throne emulated the excellence of her mother, and even surpassed her in some particular deeds. For instance, she exercised in the chase the maidens from their earliest girlhood and drilled them daily in the arts of war, and she also established magnificent festivals both to Ares and to the Artemis who is called Tauropolus. Then she campaigned against the territory lying beyond the Tanais and subdued all the peoples one after another as far as Thrace; and returning to her native land with much booty she built magnificent shrines to the deities mentioned above, and by reason of her kindly rule over her subjects received from them greatest approbation. She also campaigned on the other side and subdued a large part of Asia and extended her power as far as Syria.

After the death of this queen, as their account continues, women of her family, succeeding to the queenship from time to time, ruled with distinction and advanced the nation of the Amazons in both power and fame. And many generations after these events, when the excellence of these women had been noised abroad through the whole inhabited world, they say that Heracles, the son of Alcmena and Zeus, was assigned by Eurystheus the Labor of securing the girdle of Hippolyta the Amazon. Consequently he embarked on this campaign, and coming off victorious in a great battle he not only cut to pieces the army of Amazons but also, after taking captive Hippolyta together with her girdle, completely crushed this nation. Consequently the neighboring barbarians, despising the weakness of this people and remembering against them their past injuries, waged continuous wars against the nation to such a degree that they left in existence not even the name of the race of the Amazons. For a few years after the campaign of Heracles against them, they say, during the time of the Trojan War, Penthesileia, the queen of the surviving Amazons, who was a daughter of Ares and had slain one of her kindred, fled from her native land because of the sacrilege. And fighting as an ally of the Trojans after the death of Hector she slew many of the Greeks, and after gaining distinction in the struggle she ended her life heroically at the hands of Achilles. Now they say that Penthesileia was the last of the Amazons to win distinction for bravery and that for the future the race diminished more and more and then lost all its strength;

consequently in later times, whenever any writers recount their prowess, men consider the ancient stories about the Amazons to be fictitious tales.

Diodorus Siculus

from Book 4

While Heracles was busied with the matters just described, the Amazons, they say, of whom there were some still left in the region of the Thermodon River, gathered in a body and set out to get revenge upon the Greeks for what Heracles had done in his campaign against them. They were especially eager to punish the Athenians because Theseus had made a slave of Antiope, the leader of the Amazons, or, as others write, of Hippolyta. The Scythians had joined forces with the Amazons, and so it came about that a notable army had been assembled, with which the leaders of the Amazons crossed the Cimmerian Bosporus and advanced through Thrace. Finally they traversed a large part of Europe and came to Attica, where they pitched their camp in what is at present called after them "the Amazoneum." When Theseus learned of the oncoming of the Amazons he came to the aid of the forces of his citizens, bringing with him the Amazon Antiope, by whom he already had a son Hippolytus. Theseus joined battle with the Amazons, and since the Athenians surpassed them in bravery, he gained the victory, and of the Amazons who opposed him, some he slew at the time and the rest he drove out of Attica. And it came to pass that Antiope, who was fighting at the side of her husband Theseus, distinguished herself in the battle and died fighting heroically. The Amazons who survived renounced their ancestral soil, and returned with the Scythians into Scythia and made their homes among that people.

Diodorus Siculus

from Book 17

When Alexander returned to Hyrcania, there came to him the queen of the Amazons named Thalestris, who ruled all the country between the rivers Phasis and Thermodon. She was remarkable for beauty and for bodily strength, and was admired by her countrywomen for bravery. She had left the bulk of her army on the frontier of Hyrcania and had arrived with an escort of three hundred Amazons in full armor. The king marveled at the unexpected arrival and the dignity of the women. When he asked Thalestris why she had come, she replied that it was for the purpose of getting a child. He had shown himself the greatest of all men in his achievements, and she was superior to all women in strength and courage, so that presumably the offspring of such outstanding parents would surpass all other mortals in excellence. At this the king was delighted and granted her request and consorted with her for thirteen days, and after which he honored her with fine gifts and sent her home.

Herodotus

The Histories of Herodotus of Helicarnasus 4

It is reported of the Sauromatae, that when the Greeks fought with the Amazons, whom the Scythians call *Oior-pata* or "man-slayers," as it may be rendered, *Oior* being Scythic for "man," and *pata* for "to slay"—it is reported, I say, that the Greeks after gaining the battle of the Thermodon, put to sea, taking with them on board three of their vessels all the Amazons whom they had made prisoners; and that these women upon the voyage rose up against the crews, and massacred them to a man. As however they were quite strange to ships, and did not know how to use either rudder, sails, or oars, they were carried, after the death of the men, where the winds and the waves listed. At last they reached the shores of the Palus Maeotis and came to a place called Cremni or "the Cliffs," which is in the country of the free Scythians. Here they went ashore, and proceeded by land towards the inhabited regions; the first herd of horses which they fell in with they seized, and mounting upon their backs, fell to plundering the Scythian territory.

The Scyths could not tell what to make of the attack upon them—the dress, the language, the nation itself, were alike unknown—whence the enemy had come even, was a marvel. Imagining, however, that they were all men of about the same age, they went out against them, and fought a battle. Some of the bodies of the slain fell into their hands, whereby they discovered the truth. Hereupon they deliberated, and made a resolve to kill no more of them, but to send against them a detachment of their youngest men, as near as they could guess equal to the women in number, with orders to encamp in their neighborhood, and do as they saw them do—when the Amazons advanced against them, they were to retire, and avoid a fight—when they halted, the young men were to approach and pitch their camp near the camp of the enemy. All this they did on account of their strong desire to obtain children from so notable a race.

So the youths departed and obeyed the orders which they had been given. The Amazons soon found out that they had not come to do them any harm, and so they on their part ceased to offer the Scythians any molestation. And now day after day the camps approached nearer to one another; both parties led the same life, neither having anything but their arms and horses, so that they were forced to support themselves by hunting and pillage.

At last an incident brought two of them together—the man easily gained the good graces of the woman, who bade him by signs (for they did not understand each other's language) to bring a friend the next day to the spot where they had met—promising on her part to bring with her another woman. He did so, and the woman kept her word. When the rest of the youths heard what had taken place, they also sought and gained the favor of the other Amazons.

The two camps were then joined in one, the Scythians living with the Amazons as their wives; and the men were unable to learn the tongue of the women, but the women soon caught up the tongue of the men. When they could thus understand one another, the Scyths addressed the Amazons in these words:— "We have parents, and properties, let us therefore give up this mode of life, and return to our nation, and live with them. You shall be our wives there no less than here, and we promise you to have no others." But the Amazons said—"We could not live with your women—our customs are quite different from theirs. To draw the bow, to hurl the javelin, to bestride the horse, these are our arts— of womanly employments we know nothing. Your women, on the contrary, do none of these things; but stay at home in their wagons, engaged in womanish tasks, and never go out to hunt, or to do anything. We should never agree together. But if you truly wish to keep us as your wives, and would conduct yourselves with strict justice towards us, go you home to your parents, bid them give you your inheritance, and then come back to us, and let us and you live together by ourselves."

The youths approved of the advice, and followed it. They went and got the portion of goods which fell to them, returned with it, and rejoined their wives, who then addressed them in these words following:—"We are ashamed, and afraid to live in the country where we now are. Not only have we stolen you from your fathers, but we have done great damage to Scythia by our ravages. As you like us for wives, grant the request we make of you. Let us leave this country together, and go and dwell beyond the Tanais." Again the youths complied.

Crossing the Tanais they journeyed eastward a distance of three days' march from that stream, and again northward a distance of three days' march from the Palus Maeotis. Here they came to the country where they now live, and took up their abode in it. The women of the Sauromatae have continued from that day to the present, to observe their ancient customs, frequently hunting on horseback with their husbands, sometimes even unaccompanied; in war taking the field; and wearing the very same dress as the men.

The Sauromatae speak the language of Scythia, but have never talked it correctly, because the Amazons learnt it imperfectly at first. Their marriage-law lays it down that no girl shall wed till she has killed a man in battle. Sometimes it happens that a woman dies unmarried at an advanced age, having never been able in her whole lifetime to fulfil the condition.

Isocrates

from *Panegyricus*

Now, while the most celebrated of our wars was the one against the Persians, yet certainly our deeds of old offer evidence no less strong for those who dispute over ancestral rights. For while Hellas was still insignificant, our territory was invaded by the Thracians, led by Eumolpus, son of Poseidon, and by the Scythians, led by the Amazons, the daughters of Ares—not at the same time, but during the period when both races were trying to extend their dominion over Europe; for though they hated the whole Hellenic race, they raised complaints against us in particular, thinking that in this way they would wage war against one state only, but would at the same time impose their power on all the states of Hellas. Of a truth they were not successful; nay, in this conflict against our forefathers alone they were as utterly overwhelmed as if they had fought the whole world. How great were the disasters which befell them is evident; for the tradition respecting them would not have persisted for so long a time if what was then done had not been without parallel. At any rate, we are told regarding the Amazons that of all who came not one returned again, while those who had remained at home were expelled from power because of the disaster here; and we are told regarding the Thracians that, whereas at one time they dwelt beside us on our very borders, they withdrew so far from us in consequence of that expedition that in the spaces left between their land and ours many nations, races of every kind, and great cities have been established.

Justin

from *The History of Justin, Taken out of the Four and Forty Books of Trogus Pompeius, 2*

Asia was tributary to the Scythians for the space of one thousand and five hundred years. Ninus, King of the Assyrians did put a period to the tribute. But in this interval of time, two young men of royal blood among the Scythians, Plinos and Scolopythus, being driven from their own country by the faction of the nobility, did draw with them a gallant and numerous train of young men, and sitting down in the coast of Cappadocia, near unto the River of Thermodon, they did inhabit the Themiscyrian Plains which they had conquered to obedience. Being unaccustomed there for the space of many years to plunder their neighbors, they were at last slain through treachery by the conspiracy of the people. Their wives when they observed their punishment to be without children, to be added to their banishment, did put on arms, and first by removing, and afterwards by commencing wars, they did defended their own territories. They also did forbear the desire of marriage with their neighbors, calling it slavery, not matrimony; a singular example to posterity. They did increase their commonwealth without men at the same time when they did defend themselves with the contempt of them. And lest some women should seem more happy than others, they killed those men who did remain alive amongst them, and afterwards prosecuted the revenge of their slaughtered husbands on the destruction of their neighbors. Peace then being obtained by war, lest their nation should fail, they mingled in copulation with their neighbors. If any male children were born, they were killed. They exercised their virgins in the same way of education as they were bred up themselves, not in sloth or the manufactures of wool, but in arms, horses and hunting. The right breasts of every infant virgin being burned off, that afterwards by not drawing of it home, it should not hinder the force of the arrow from the bow. From them they are called Amazons.

They had two queens, Marthesia and Lampedo, who, their forces being divided into two parts, being now renowned for their wealth, did make war by turns, carefully defending their territories. And because authority should not be wanting to their successes, they declared that they were begotten of Mars. The greatest part of Europe being conquered, they seized several cities in Asia, also, and having there built Ephesius and many other towns, they sent home one part of their army laden with a mighty booty. The rest who stayed behind to defend what they had got in Asia were overcome by the concourse of the barbarians and were killed with their queen, Marthesia, in whose place her daughter Oreithyia succeeded in the kingdom, who besides her singular industry in the war, hath been admirable through all ages for the preservation of her virginity. By her prowess so much fame and glory was derived to the Amazons, that the king who imposed the twelve labors upon Heracles did command him as a task impossible to bring him the arms of the queen of the Amazons. Therefore, he sailing there with nine long ships did unexpectedly assault them, the youth of the princes of Greece accompanying him.

Two sisters of the four did then govern the kingdom of the Amazons, Antiope and Oreithyia. Oreithyia was then employed in the wars abroad. When Heracles did steer towards the Amazonian shore, there were but a small and unusual number with Antiope, the queen. Fearing no invasion of an enemy, wherefore it came to pass that a few being awakened by the sudden alarm had recourse to arms, and became an easy victory to their enemies. Many were slain and taken prisoners, amongst whom were the two sisters of Antiope, Menalippe who was taken by Heracles, and Hippolyta by Theseus, who having made his prisoner his reward, did afterwards take her into marriage, by whom he begat Hippolytus.

Heracles after the victory restored Menalippe to her sister, and took for his reward the armor of the queen. And having performed what he was commanded, he returned to the king.

But Oreithyia returning, when she found that a war was made upon her sisters, and that the prince of the Athenians was the chief actor, she persuaded her companions to revenge, alleging that Pontus and Asia were subdued in vain if they still lay open not only to the wars but to the rapines of the Grecians. She desired aid of Sagylus, King of the Scythians, representing that she was of the same generation with him. She made apparent to him the destruction long ago of all the husbands of the Amazons, the necessity that first made the women to take arms, and the causes of the war, and that they had purchased by their virtue that the Scythians should not be found to have women less industrious than were the men.

He, being moved by the temptation of domestic glory, did send his son, Penaxagoras, to her aid with a very great body of horse. But some difference being occasioned before the battle, she being abandoned of her auxiliaries, was overcome by the Athenians. Nevertheless, she had the tents of the Scythians for her receptacle, by whose assistance being untouched by other nations she returned into her kingdom.

After her, Penthesileia enjoyed the Kingdom, who bringing aid against the Greeks, and fighting in the Trojan War amongst the most valiant men, did give many demonstrations of her singular valor, but she being killed at last, and her army consumed, those few that were left being hardly able to defend themselves against their neighbors, did continue until the time of Alexander the Great.

Their queen, Minothea or Thalestris, having obtained of Alexander for thirteen days together to enjoy his company to have issue by him, being returned to her kingdom, not long after was extinguished, and with her the whole name of the Amazons.

Lysias

from the *Funeral Oration*

Well, of old there were Amazons, daughters of Ares, dwelling beside the river Thermodon; they alone of the people round about were armed with iron, and they were first of all to mount horses, with which, owing to the inexperience of their foes, they surprised them and either caught those who fled, or outstripped those who pursued. They were accounted as men for their high courage, rather than as women for their sex; so much more did they seem to excel men in their spirit than to be at a disadvantage in their form. Ruling over many nations, they had in fact achieved the enslavement of those around them; yet, hearing by report concerning this our country how great was its renown, they were moved by increase of glory and high ambition to muster the most warlike of the nations and march with them against this city {Athens}. But having met with valiant men they found their spirit now was like to their sex; the repute that they got was the reverse of the former, and by their perils rather than by their bodies they were deemed to be women. They stood alone in failing to learn from their mistakes, and so to be better advised in their future actions; they would not return home and report their own misfortune and our ancestors' valor: for they perished on the spot, and were punished for their folly, thus making our city's memory imperishable for its valor; while owing to their disaster in this region they rendered their own country nameless. And so those women, by their unjust greed for others' land, justly lost their own.

Pausanias

from *Description of Greece*, Attica, 14

As you go to the portico {in the Athenian acropolis} which they call Painted, because of its pictures, there is a bronze statue of Hermes of the Market-place, and near it a gate. On it is a trophy erected by the Athenians, who in a cavalry action overcame Pleistarchus, to whose command his brother Cassander had entrusted his cavalry and mercenaries. This Portico contains, first, the Athenians arrayed against the Lacedaemonians at Oenoe in the Argive territory. What is depicted is not the crisis of the battle nor when the action had advanced as far as the display of deeds of valor, but the beginning of the fight when the combatants were about to close. On the middle wall are the Athenians and Theseus fighting with the Amazons. So, it seems, only the women did not lose through their defeats their reckless courage in the face of danger; Themiscyra was taken by Heracles, and afterwards the army which they dispatched to Athens was destroyed, but nevertheless they came to Troy to fight all the Greeks as well as the Athenians themselves.

Quintus Curtius
from *History of Alexander* 6

There was, as was said before, neighboring on Hyrcania, a race of Amazons, inhabiting the plains of Themiscyra, about the river Thermodon. They had a queen, Thalestris, who ruled all who dwelt between the Caucasus mountains and the river Phasis. She, fired with desire to visit the king {Alexander}, came forth from the boundaries of her kingdom, and when she was not far away sent messengers to give notice that a queen had come who was eager to meet him and to become acquainted with him. She was at once given permission to come. Having ordered the rest of her escort to halt, she came forward attended by three hundred women, and as soon as the king was in sight, she herself leaped down from her horse, carrying two lances in her right hand. The clothing of the Amazons does not wholly cover the body; for the left side is nude as far as the breast, then the other parts of the body are veiled. However, the fold of the robe, which they gather in a knot, does not reach below the knee. One nipple is left untouched, and with it they nourish their female children; the right is seared, in order that they may more easily stretch their bows and hurl their spears.

With fearless expression Thalestris gazed at the king, carefully surveying his person, which did not by any means correspond to the fame of his exploits; for all the barbarians feel veneration for a majestic presence, and believe that only those are capable of great deeds whom nature has deigned to adorn with extraordinary physical attractiveness. However, on being asked whether she wished to make any request, she did not hesitate to confess that she had come to share children with the king, being worthy that he should beget from her heirs to his kingdom; that she would retain any female offspring but would return a male to his father. Alexander asked her whether she wished to serve in war with him; but she, giving as an excuse that she had left her realm without a guard, persisted in asking that he should not suffer her to go away disappointed in her hope. The passion of the woman, being, as she was, more keen for love than the king, compelled him to remain there for a few days. Thirteen days were spent in satisfying her desire. Then she went to her kingdom, and the king to Parthiene.

Quintus Smyrnaeus

from *The Arrival, Deeds, and Death of Penthesileia the Amazon Queen*

When godlike Hector had been killed by Achilles . . . and the fire consumed him, and the earth hid his bones, at that time the Trojans were staying in Priam's town, frightened of the great might of brave Achilles. Just as cattle refuse to approach a fierce lion in the woods, but the whole herd draws back and runs frightened up through the thick scrub; so the Trojans in their fortress city shrank in terror from the mighty man. They remembered all those whom he had earlier robbed of their lives, as he raged by the streams of Idaean Scamander, all those he killed in flight under the great wall, how he had killed Hector and dragged him around the city, and how he had slaughtered others, when he first brought destruction for the Trojans through the restless sea. These were the things they remembered as they stayed within their fortress city. A dismal sorrow, too, hovered over them, as though Troy were already ablaze with cruel fire.

And then from the streams of the broad river Thermodon there came Penthesileia, wearing the beauty of the gods. She was at once eager for cruel war and bent on avoiding loathsome and ugly talk. She was afraid that someone among her own people would attack her with reproaches about her sister Hippolyta, for whom she felt a growing sorrow. (She had killed her with a heavy spear, quite involuntarily, while aiming at a stag.) This was why she had come to the famous land of Troy. Besides, she had this thought in her warlike heart: she might cleanse herself of the hideous defilement of murder and appease with sacrifices the dreadful Furies. These invisible creatures, angry over her sister, had set about following her at once. For they always dog the feet of wrongdoers, and no one who does wrong can escape the goddesses.

With Penthesileia came twelve other Amazons, all splendid and all longing for war and ugly battle. Distinguished though they were, these were her hand-maids, and Penthesileia far surpassed them all. Just as when in broad heaven the glorious moon shines out conspicuous among all the stars, when the clear upper air breaks through from the thunderclouds, and the great might of the blustering winds is asleep; so was she conspicuous among all the hurrying Amazons.

These were their names: Clonie, Polemousa, Derinoe, Evandre, Antandre, glorious Bremousa, Hippothoe, dark-eyed Harmothoe, Alcibie, Antibrote, Derimacheia, and Thermodosa, moving proudly with her spear. So many were the Amazons who accompanied and surrounded Penthesileia. Just as the Dawn, her heart exulting in her flashing horses, comes down from indestructible Olympus with the fair-tressed Hours, and her splendid beauty shines out among them all, though they are faultless; so Penthesileia came to the Trojan city, pre-eminent among all the Amazons.

The Trojans hurried round from every side, marveling greatly when they saw tireless Ares' daughter in her tall greaves. She looked like the blessed gods, for about her face there was a beauty at once terrible and splendid. Her smile was charming, and under her brows her lovely eyes sparkled like sunbeams. Modesty brought a blush to her cheeks, and a divine grace clothed her strength. The Trojan people, sad though they had been before, were filled with joy. Just as when country folk, longing for the gods to send rain, see from a hill Iris, the rainbow, rising up out of the broad sea, at the time when their farms, yearning for the rain of Zeus, are now parched, and at last the great sky grows dark, and they see the good sign that wind and rain are close and are glad—though before they had been groaning over their fields—so the sons of Troy naturally rejoiced when they saw within their city terrible Penthesileia, eager for war. For when hope of good comes into a man's mind, it softens painful distress.

For this reason, too, the heart of Priam, who had so many causes for groaning and great sorrow, was cheered a little in his breast. Just as when a man who has suffered much with blinded eyes and longs to see the holy light or to die, either through the work of some fine doctor or because a god has taken the darkness from his eyes, at last sees the light of Dawn, he is not so cheerful as he once was, but nevertheless he is cheered a little after a great evil, though he still suffers from a dreadful pain left in his eyes; so Priam the son of Laomedon looked upon terrible Penthesileia: while he rejoiced a little, for the most part he still sorrowed for his sons who had been killed.

But he took the queen into his palace and was zealous in showing her every honor, just as though she were a daughter come home from far away after twenty years. He had a dinner prepared for her with every sort of food, such as glorious kings eat when they have destroyed nations and feast at great banquets to celebrate their victory. He gave her presents, too, beautiful and precious, and promised many more if she would help the Trojans, who were being cut to pieces. She undertook the task and agreed to do what no mortal had ever hoped: she would kill Achilles, destroy the great army of the Greeks, and throw fire on their ships. Foolish girl, she did not know at all Achilles of the good ashen spear, nor how pre-eminent he was in deadly battle.

When Andromache, Eëtion's noble child, heard Penthesileia, she spoke earnestly like this within her own heart: "Poor girl, why do you speak such proud words and have such proud thoughts? You do not have the strength to fight with fearless Peleus' son, but he will quickly send death and ruin upon you. Poor wretch, why are your thoughts so mad? Surely, the end of death has taken its stand close to you, and the fate of doom. Hector was far better with the spear than you are, but for all his might he was defeated and brought great grief to the Trojans, who all looked upon him as a god in the city. He was a great glory to me and to his godlike parents, when he was alive. How I wish the earth had covered me over in the grave before the spear went through his throat and took his life! As it was, I looked in anguish upon a pain beyond telling when the swift horses of Achilles cruelly dragged him about the city. He took from me the husband of my youth and made me a widow; this is my terrible sorrow for all my days."

So in her heart Eëtion's daughter of the fair ankles spoke, remembering her husband. For, truly, great grief increases with good women, when their husbands are dead.

The sun, whirling through its swift course, sank into Ocean's deep stream, and the day was done. When the banqueters had finished their wine and the lovely feast, then the maids prepared a comfortable bed in Priam's palace for brave Penthesileia. She went and lay down, and sweet sleep fell upon her, covering her eyes. Then from the depths of the upper air there came, at the will of Athena, the force of a guileful dream, so that as she looked upon it she might become an evil for the Trojans and for herself, through her longing for the confusion of war. This was what the wise Athena Tritogeneia had in mind. And the grim dream stood over Penthesileia, looking like her father, and urged her to fight boldly face to face with swift-footed Achilles. She, when she heard this, was utterly delighted in her heart, because she thought that on that very day she would accomplish a great deed in the dreadful combat. Foolish girl, who put her faith in a miserable dream of the night, which beguiles in their beds the races of toiling men, filling them with cheating words, and which completely deceived her in urging her to the work of war.

But when the early-born one, the rosy-ankled Dawn, came swiftly up, then it was that Penthesileia, her heart full of courage, leapt from her bed and put about her shoulders the decorated armor that the god Ares had given her. First about her silvery legs she put greaves of gold, which fitted her perfectly. Then she put on her dazzling breastplate, and she proudly placed about her shoulders her great sword, all enclosed in a scabbard beautifully fashioned of silver and ivory. She took up her splendid shield, in outline like the moon when over the deep-flowing Ocean stream it rises half full with curving horns; so marvelously it gleamed. On her head she put her helmet, its top covered with golden plumes. So she put about her body the elaborate armor. She looked like a bolt of lightning that the power of tireless Zeus sends to earth from Olympus, showing to men the strength of noisy rain or the steady blast of whistling winds.

Moving quickly to leave the great hall, she took two javelins to hold beneath her shield and in her right hand a double battle-ax. Eris, terrible goddess of strife, had given her this as a great protection in deadly war. Laughing with pleasure at this weapon, she hurried outside the towers and urged the Trojans into battle where men win glory. The princes gathered there were quick to be persuaded, though they had not previously wanted to stand against Achilles, because he utterly defeated everyone.

She, of course, could not restrain her exultation. The stallion she sat upon was beautiful and very fast. Boreas' wife Oreithyia had given him to her as a present some time ago, when she had gone to Thrace. He stood out even among Harpies, who are swift as hurricanes. Seated on this horse, Penthesileia then left the high houses of the city. Dismal Fates were urging her on to go into a conflict at once her first and her last. Round about, many Trojans on unreturning feet followed the brave girl into ruthless battle, in crowds, like sheep after a ram which runs on ahead, as they all, under the shepherd's skill, go along together; so the sturdy Trojans and the high-spirited Amazons, greatly eager in their might, followed after her. She was like Athena when she went to meet the Giants, or like Eris when she darts through an army raising tumult; such was swift Penthesileia among the Trojans.

Then it was that Priam, noble son of rich Laomedon, raised his long-suffering hands to Zeus the son of Kronos and prayed, turning toward the high temple of Idaean Zeus, whose eyes ever look upon Ilios:

"Hear me, O father, and grant that on this day the Greek host fall beneath the hands of Ares' queenly daughter. And then bring her back safely to my house, having respect for your own vast and mighty son Ares and for Penthesileia herself, because she is terribly like the immortal goddesses and in her descent is from your own stock. Show regard also for my heart, since I have suffered many evils in the deaths of my sons whom the Fates snatched especially from me at the Greeks' hands along the battlefront. Keep your regard for us, while a few of us are still left from the glorious blood of Dardanus, while the city is still unravaged, so that we, too, may have respite from dreadful slaughter and from war."

So he spoke in his earnest prayer. And an eagle, with shrill cries and holding in its talons a dove already dying, darted swiftly on his left. Priam's mind within him took fright, and he thought he would never see Penthesileia alive again and returning from war. The Fates were indeed going to bring this about that day, and Priam's broken heart was full of pain.

The Greeks marveled from afar when they saw the onrushing Trojans and Ares' daughter Penthesileia. The Trojans looked like wild beasts that in the mountains bring groans and death to flocks of sheep. She was like a rush of fire that rages in the dry scrub under a strong wind. This is the sort of thing the Greeks were saying as they gathered together:

"Why, who has roused the Trojans, now that Hector is dead? We said they would never again meet us with any eagerness, but now they suddenly rush on full of desire for battle. Someone in their midst is urging them on to the work of war. You might think him a god, so great is the deed he has in mind. We must put into our hearts an insatiate boldness and remember our trained strength. The gods will help us, too, in our fight with the Trojans this day."

So they spoke. Then, putting their shining armor about them, they poured out from the ships, their shoulders clad in might. The armies came together in the bloody conflict like ravenous wild beasts. They held their fine arms close together, spears, breastplates, sturdy shields, and stout helmets, and recklessly struck one another's flesh with the bronze. The Trojan plain grew red.

Then Penthesileia killed Molion and Persinous, Elissus and Antitheus and manly Lernus, Hippalmus, Haemonides, and strong Elasippus. Derinoe killed Laogonus, and Clonie killed Menippus, who earlier had followed Protesilaus from Phylace to fight the powerful Trojans. His death stirred the spirit of Podarces Iphiclesson, because he loved him especially among his comrades. He immediately threw his spear at godlike Clonie, and the strong shaft went down through her belly. Her black blood quickly flowed out around the spear, and all her entrails followed with it. Penthesileia was naturally greatly angered at this, and she struck Podarces on the thick muscle of his right arm and cut through the blood-filled veins. His black blood gushed from the wound he had received, and he darted to the rear, groaning from the severe pain afflicting his spirit. The people of Phylace felt the greatest longing for him as he hurried away. When he had withdrawn a little from the fighting, he died in the arms of his comrades.

Idomeneus killed Bremousa, hitting her on the right breast with his spear and taking her life instantly. She fell like an ash tree, a towering one that woodcutters cut on the mountains. As it falls it produces a dreadful whistling and a thud; so she uttered a wail as she fell. Doom loosened all her joints, and her soul was mingled with the blowing winds.

Meriones killed Evandre and Thermodosa as they rushed at him in the deadly fighting. He drove his spear into the head of one of them, and the other he struck with his sword under the belly. Their life left them forthwith. The mighty son of Oïleus destroyed Derinoe, running his jagged spear through her collarbone. Tydeusson with his terrible sword cut off the heads of both Alcibie and Derimacheia, necks and all right down to their shoulders. They both fell just like heifers that a man quickly deprives of life by hitting their neck tendons with a strong ax; so they, laid low by the hands of Tydeusson, fell on the Trojan plain, and their bodies were far away from their heads.

Because Penthesileia's strength did not flag at all, but as some lioness in the high mountains darts through a glen deep in the cliffs and leaps upon cattle in her longing for blood, and this greatly cheers her spirit; so then did the warrior girl leap among the Greeks. Their spirits were filled with surprise, and they drew back.

She followed them, just as a wave of the deep-thundering sea follows speeding ships, when a strong wind swells out their white sails, and the headlands roar on every side, as the sea bellows against the long beach; so she kept following and slaughtering the ranks of the Greeks, and, with a heart full of exultation, she threatened them:

"You dogs, how you will pay today for the evil outrage you did Priam. None of you will escape my strength and be a joy to dear parents, sons, and wives, but you will die and lie here a food for birds and beasts; you will find no tomb in the earth. Where is mighty Tydeusson now? Where Achilles? And where Aias? Talk has it that they are your best. But they will not dare to contend with me, for fear I may take their souls from their limbs and dispatch them to the dead."

She spoke and, with proud thoughts, rushed upon the Greeks. Her strength was like the strength of Death, and great was the host she subdued. Sometimes she cut deep with her ax, and sometimes she brandished a sharp javelin. Her nimble horse carried her quiver and pitiless bow, if ever she might need in the bloody turmoil grim missiles and bow. Swift men followed her, brothers and friends of Hector, who had fought his foes hand to hand. Their breasts were full of the breath of mighty war, and with their spears of polished ash they were killing Greeks, who kept falling one after another like swiftly falling leaves or drops of rain. The broad land groaned aloud, wet with blood and packed with corpses. Horses too, pierced with arrows or ashen spears, were neighing for the last time, as they breathed out their strength, while others were biting the dust and writhing. And Trojan horses charging upon them from the rear were trampling them like heaps of grain on a threshing floor where they had fallen with their dead riders.

Many a Trojan was filled with wonder and delight when he saw Penthesileia rushing up through the army like a dark storm which rages on the sea when the sun's might comes together with Capricorn. And in his empty hopes one of them said:

"Friends, how obvious it is that today some one of the immortals has come down from heaven to fight against the Greeks and show kindness to us because of Zeus's bold plan. Zeus is doubtless remembering powerful Priam, who is proud to claim that he is from immortal blood. For I think this is no woman I see before me so brave and wearing such glorious arms, but Athena, or mighty Enyo, or Eris, or Leto's famous daughter Artemis. Today I think she will bring the groans of slaughter upon the Greeks and burn with destructive fire their ships in which they once came to Troy, planning many evils for us; bringing woes from war beyond all checking, they came. But never will they return again to Greece and gladden their native land, because a god is helping us."

So a Trojan spoke, his heart running over with joy. Fool, he did not, of course, know that utter ruin was rushing upon himself and the other Trojans, and upon Penthesileia herself. For great-souled Aias and Achilles the city-sacker had not yet heard at all of the noisy turmoil, but both had thrown themselves down at the grave of Patroclus, filled with thoughts of their friend, and one groaned on this side, one on that. Some one of the blessed gods was keeping them from the turmoil, so that many men might meet with a grim death, destroyed by Trojans and by brave Penthesileia.

She was contriving evil for one man after another, and her strength and her courage alike kept growing ever greater. Never did her spear plunge in vain, but it kept tearing the backs of men running away or the chests of those who charged upon her. She was quite drenched in hot blood, but her limbs were light as she rushed on; no weariness overcame her fearless spirit, but might unconquerable possessed her. For grim Fate, not yet rousing Achilles to dreadful battle, was still glorifying her and, standing far from the fighting, felt a deadly exultation because in a little while she was going to destroy the girl at the hands of Achilles. She was hidden in darkness, but, ever unseen, she urged Penthesileia on and led her to evil destruction, glorifying her for the last time. And Penthesileia kept killing, one here, another there.

Just as when in spring a heifer, longing for sweet grass, leaps inside a dewy garden and, since there is no man there, rushes everywhere, ravaging all the plants just now so flourishing, eating some and destroying others with her feet; so, rushing down through the throng the warrior girl killed some of the Greek youths and drove others to flight.

They had no way of escaping wretched death, but were being killed like bleating goats under the savage jaws of a leopard. It was no longer a desire for battle that possessed the men, but a desire for flight. They were rushing in various directions, some of them with their armor, others throwing their armor from their shoulders to the ground. And horses went running without their drivers. Joy of battle belonged to the attackers; from the dying came many a groan. They had no strength in their afflictions, but short-lived were they all whom she came upon, along the chill edge of battle. Just as when a howling gale presses hard upon tall trees all abloom with flowers and pulls some up by the roots and throws them to the ground and breaks others from their base, and the shattered trees are thrown one upon another; so the great army of Greeks was laid in the dust by the will of the Fates and the spear of Penthesileia.

But when the very ships were going to be set afire by the hands of the Trojans, then it was, doubtless, that steadfast Aias heard the wailing and said to Achilles:

"Achilles, a vast shouting assails my ears, as though a great battle were in progress. Let's go, for fear the Trojans may destroy the Greeks beside their ships and burn up the ships before we get there; that would be a sad disgrace to us both. Men descended from great Zeus ought not to shame the holy stock of their fathers, who themselves, some time ago, along with valiant Heracles, utterly destroyed with their spears Laomedon's Troy, a splendid city. This is what I think will be done now by our hands, since the strength grows great in us both."

The bold might of Achilles was persuaded by what he said, because his ears heard the melancholy clamor. They both rushed for their bright arms, put them on, and took their stand to meet the crowd. Their beautiful weapons clanged loudly, and their spirits were raging like Ares'; so great was the might that shielded Athena Atrytone gave to them both as they pressed on.

The Greeks were glad when they saw the pair of mighty men. They looked like the two sons of great Aloeus who once upon a time thought to put upon broad Olympus high mountains, steep Ossa and lofty Pelion, so that in their eagerness they might actually reach heaven. Such were the two descendants of Aeacus, Aias and Achilles, as they stood to face the ruinous battle, a great joy to the Greeks in their longing, as they both pressed forward to destroy the army of the enemy. Many were the men whom they subdued with their invincible spears. Just as when a pair of destructive lions find fat sheep in the scrub far from their fond shepherds and rush to kill them and then drink all the black blood and fill their great bellies with the inner flesh; so did these two destroy a vast army of men.

When Penthesileia, the skillful warrior, noticed them rushing like wild beasts through the dreadful battle, she started toward them both. Just as in a thicket a grim leopard with destruction in her heart lashes her tail terribly and rushes out to meet oncoming hunters, and they, equipped with fighting gear, await her charge, confident of their spears; so the warrior men lifted their spears and awaited Penthesileia. Their bronze armor was noisy about them as they moved.

Brave Penthesileia first threw a long spear. It landed on Achilles' shield, but broke and was deflected as though from a rock; such were the immortal gifts of skillful Hephaestus. With her hands, she aimed another swift javelin at Aias, and she threatened them both:

"Although just now the spear leapt from my hands to no purpose, I think with this one I shall soon destroy the strength and spirit of you both, who boast of being the mighty ones among the Greeks. Then the misery of war will be lighter for the Trojan horsemen. But please come closer up through the turmoil, so that you may see how much strength rises in Amazons' hearts. My stock, too, is warlike, and no mortal man sired me, but Ares himself, who can never have his fill of the shouts of battle. This is why my might is far better than men's."

So she spoke, but her proud talk made them laugh. Quickly her spear point drove at Aias' solid silver greave. But it did not penetrate inside, for all its eagerness to reach his handsome flesh. For the cruel point had not been fated to mix with that man's blood in the battles of enemies. Aias disregarded the Amazon and leapt into a crowd of Trojans. He left Penthesileia to Peleus' son alone, since he knew in his heart how easy a task she would be for Achilles, strong though she was. It would be like a dove against a hawk.

She gave a deep groan at having thrown her spear without result, and the son of Peleus spoke to her insultingly:

"Woman, how proud you were of your empty words, when you came against us filled with desire for battle. We are easily the best of the heroes upon the earth, and we are proud of our descent from the stock of loud-thundering Zeus. Even swift Hector was afraid of us, though he caught sight of us only from a distance rushing into cruel battle. My spear point killed him, for all his might. You are completely out of your mind in being so bold and threatening us with destruction today. Your own last day will quickly come. No, not even your father Ares himself will save you from me now, but you will die an evil death, just like a young deer that meets a destructive lion in the mountains. Haven't you heard by now about the number of men who fell under my hands by the streams of Xanthus? Or, though you heard, have the blessed gods taken away your wits and senses, so that cruel Fates may gape wide for you?"

With these words, he swooped upon her, brandishing in his powerful hand the long, murderous spear that Chiron made. Quickly he stabbed brave Penthesileia above the right breast. The dark blood flowed swiftly out, and the strength in her limbs was broken at once. The great battle-ax fell from her hand, night veiled her eyes, and anguish sank into her heart. But even so she revived and looked at her enemy, now about to drag her down from her swift horse. She wondered to herself whether she should draw her great sword in her hand and await the onset of Achilles rushing at her, or speedily leap down from her fast horse and entreat the glorious man, offering him at once abundant bronze and gold, which warm the hearts of mortals within them, no matter how bold a man may be. Somehow with these she might persuade the deadly strength of Achilles, or he might let her return home, out of regard for the youth that they shared—and she longed to escape.

These were the thoughts she had; but the gods arranged it otherwise. For the son of Peleus rushed upon her filled with rage and quickly pierced the body of the girl and the wind-swift horse alike. Just as a man hurrying with his dinner pierces meats on a spit over a hot fire, or as a hunter in the mountains throws a cruel javelin and cuts through the mid-belly of a deer, and the strong point, flying right through, is fixed in the base of a tall oak or pine; so Peleus' son with his raging spear cut quite through Penthesileia and her beautiful horse. Still comely, she fell quickly to the ground and rolled in the dust and destruction. Nothing shameful disgraced her beautiful body, but she was stretched out face down, still quivering about the long spear and resting against her swift horse. Just like a fir tree broken by the force of the cold north wind, one which earth nourishes by a spring, a great adornment for herself, the tallest, perhaps, in the long glens and the forest; so did marvelously beautiful Penthesileia fall from her swift horse, and her strength was shattered.

The Trojans, when they saw her cut down in the fight, at once rushed in terror toward the city, their spirits grieving with a sorrow beyond telling. Just as when on the wide ocean sailors who have lost their ship in a heavy wind escape from death—a few of them—after many sufferings in the dreary sea, and at last land appears close by and even a city, and, although their bodies are completely worn out by their cruel troubles, they rush from the sea full of sorrow for the ship and their comrades whom the wave has driven under the dreadful darkness; so the Trojans escaped from the war to their city, all wailing for the daughter of invincible Ares and the soldiers who had died in the savage fighting.

Peleus' son was laughing over her and loudly boastful: "Lie now in the dust and feed the dogs and birds, you wretched girl. Who tricked you into coming against me? I have no doubt you thought you would go home from battle with splendid gifts from old Priam for the Greeks you had killed. The gods did not carry out this idea of yours, because we are far the best of heroes, a great light to the Greeks, a disaster to the Trojans and to you. Unlucky you were, because dark Fates and your own mind roused you to leave women's work and go to war, which frightens even men."

With these words, Peleus' son pulled his ashen spear from the swift horse and dread Penthesileia; both of them, killed by a single spear, were in their death throes. Then he took from her head the helmet gleaming like the rays of the sun or the radiance of Zeus. Though she had fallen in the dust and blood, her face shone out under her lovely brows beautiful even in death. The Greeks who thronged around marveled when they saw her, for she was like the blessed gods. She lay on the ground in her armor like strong Artemis asleep, Zeus's child, when her limbs grow weary as she hunts swift lions in the mountains. Aphrodite of the fine crown, wife of mighty Ares, personally made Penthesileia attractive even among the dead, so that noble Peleus' son too might feel some pain. Many men prayed that they might return home and sleep by wives like her. Achilles could not stop the pain in his heart because he had killed her and had not brought her as a glorious wife to Phthia, land of good horses, for in size and beauty she was faultless and like the immortal goddesses.

Seneca

from *Hippolytus* or *Phaedra*, Act 1, Scene 2

Phaedra: Alas, love sways this powerful scepter here,
   And I fear no returns, none gone from hence
   To the dark house of death find passage thence.
Nurse: Be not too credulous, say the gates of Hell
   Were shut, and Cerberus the sentinel.
   Theseus hath forced the way hath been forbid.
Phaedra: Yet he perhaps would pardon, if did.
Nurse: Why he was cruel to a wife was chaste.
   Antiope can testify his haste.
   But grant we might appease thy angry spouse,
   Yet who can move the stern Hippolytus?
   He doth abhor the very name of wife,
   And obstinately vows a single life.
   Marriage he shuns, an Amazon thou knows.

Strabo

from *The Geography* II

The Amazons are said to live among the mountains above Albania. Theophanes, who accompanied Pompey in his wars, and was in the country of the Albanians, says that Gelae and Legae, Scythian tribes, live between the Amazons and the Albanians, and that the river Mermadalis takes its course in the country lying in the middle between these people and the Amazons. But other writers, and among these Metrodurus of Scepsis, and Hypsicrates, who were themselves acquainted with these places, say that the Amazons bordered upon the Gargarenses on the north, at the foot of the Caucasian mountains, which are called Ceraunia.

When at home they are occupied in performing with their own hands the work of ploughing, planting, pasturing cattle and particularly in training horses. The strongest among them spend much of their time in hunting on horseback, and practice warlike exercises. All of them from infancy have the right breast seared, in order that they may use the arm with ease for all manner of purposes, and particularly for throwing the javelin. They employ the bow also, and sagaris (a kind of sword), and wear a buckler. They make helmets, and coverings for the body, and girdles, of the skins of wild animals. They pass two months of the spring on a neighboring mountain, which is the boundary between them and the Gargarenses. The latter also ascend the mountain according to some ancient custom for the purpose of performing common sacrifices, and of having intercourse with the women with a view to offspring, in secret and in darkness, the man with the first woman he meets. When the women are pregnant they are sent away. The female children that may be born are retained by the Amazons themselves, but the males are taken to the Gargarenses to be brought up. The children are distributed among the families, in which the master treats them as his own, it being impossible to ascertain the contrary.

The Mermodas, descending like a torrent from the mountains through the country of the Amazons, the Siracene, and the intervening desert, discharges itself into the Maeotis.

It is said that the Gargarenses ascended together with the Amazons from Themiscyra to these places, that they then separated, with the assistance of some Thracians and Euboeans, who had wandered as far as this country, made war against the Amazons, and at length, upon its termination, entered into a compact on the conditions above mentioned, namely, that there should be a companionship only with respect to offspring, and that they should live each independent of the other.

There is a peculiarity in the history of the Amazons. In other histories the fabulous and the historical parts are kept distinct. For what is ancient, false, and marvelous is called fable. But history has truth for its object, whether it be old or new, and it either rejects or rarely admits the marvelous. But, with regard to the Amazons, the same facts are related both by modern and by ancient writers; they are marvelous and exceed belief. For who can believe that an army of women, or a city, or a nation, could ever subsist without men? And not only subsist, but make inroads upon the territory of other people, and obtain possession not only of the places near them, and advance even as far as the present Ionia, but even despatch an expedition across the sea to Attica? This is as much as to say that the men of those days were women, and the women men. But even now the same things are told of the Amazons, and the peculiarity of their history is increased by the credit which is given to ancient, in preference to modern accounts.

They are said to have founded cities, and to have given their names to them, as Ephesus, Smyrna, Cyme, Myrina, besides leaving sepulchers and other memorials. Themiscyra, the plains about the Thermodon, and the mountains lying above, are mentioned by all writers as once belonging to the Amazons, from whence, they say, they were driven out. Where they are at present few writers undertake to point out, nor do they advance proofs or probability for what they state, as in the case of Thalestria, queen of the Amazons, with whom Alexander is said to have had intercourse in Hyrcania with the hope of having offspring. Writers are not agreed on this point, and among many who have paid the greatest regard to truth none mention the circumstance, nor do writers of the highest credit mention anything of the kind, nor do those who record it relate the same facts.

Suetonius

The Twelve Caesars, "Julius Caesar"

Having thus secured the goodwill of his father-in-law Piso and his son-in-law Pompey, Caesar surveyed the many provinces open to him and chose Gaul as being the likeliest to supply him with wealth and triumphs. True, he was at first appointed Governor only of Cisalpine Gaul and Illyria—the proposal came from Vatinius—but afterwards the Senate added Transalpine Gaul to his jurisdiction, fearing that if this were denied him, the commons would insist that he should have it.

His elation was such that he could not refrain from boasting to a packed house some days later, that having now gained his dearest wish, to the annoyance and grief of his opponents, he would proceed to "stamp upon their persons." When someone interjected with a sneer that a *woman* would not find this an easy feat, he answered amicably: "Why not? Semiramis was supreme in Syria, and the Amazons once ruled over a large part of Asia."

CHAPTER 3

The Medieval Templars

❧

In the early fourteenth century, the medieval order of the Knights Templar was accused of a series of crimes that included fostering homosexuality within its ranks. The order was judged guilty of most of the charges and disbanded in 1309, but the accuracy of the accusations of homosexuality has been hotly debated over the succeeding centuries. Some believe that the considerable power of the Templars and their vast wealth were, in and of themselves, sufficient cause for the Catholic Church to destroy them, and that the personal hostility of the French king, Philip IV, was also a principal factor in the destruction of the order. Others have argued that while the power and wealth of the Templars might have posed a threat to established ecclesiastical structures, the Templars were, nonetheless, a band of warriors whose rituals and practices were pervaded by homosexuality. While not denying the possibility of widespread homoerotic practices, Anne Gilmour-Bryson maintains in the following article that there is little evidence to portray the knights as a fraternity of warrior homosexuals, explaining that accusations of sexual irregularity numbered only a few among the many crimes charged against the them. Still, accusations of homoerotic practices were included in the almost-identical indictments lodged against the Templars everywhere across Europe. The order's enemies obviously thought such charges sufficiently believable to include them repeatedly in their bills against the knights.

The documents included after Gilmour-Bryson's article indicate that accusations of sexual irregularity constitute only slightly more than 10 percent of the almost one hundred crimes and acts of heresy or apostasy attributed to the Templars.

Many of the enumerated offenses are far more damning, at least in theological terms. Renouncing God, Christ, and the Virgin Mary can hardly be superceded in seriousness. Neither do the charges of homoerotic behavior receive prominent positions within the body of the accusations. They are listed at two separate locations within the middle third of the indictment, indicating perhaps that the Templars' prosecutors did not consider them to be as serious as some of the more prominently featured items in the roster of offenses.

Anne Gilmour-Bryson
"Sodomy and the Knights Templar"

In this article, I will analyze testimony relevant to the charges of the Inquisition that members of the order of Knights Templar throughout Christendom practiced homosexual acts of various sorts from illicit kisses to sodomy. I intend to examine the testimony of Templars in hearings that took place in France and Italy for the most part, since it was in these areas that confessions of guilt were given. My aim is to illustrate how members of the order reacted to the questions concerning these matters, how they described what occurred, and in what terms.

The Evidence

This evidence is by no means unknown. Once the Vatican Archives were opened to scholars and the texts of the trials began to be published in the late nineteenth century, the depositions were available to scholars who could read Latin. The interpretation of this material is a very different matter. Some historians such as Gershon Legman are convinced of the Templars' guilt on the matter of the practice of homosexual acts, though not on the reasons for the indecent acts carried out at reception ceremonies. Konrad Schottmüller, unlike Hans Prutz, was convinced of their innocence. Joseph Marie Antoine Delaville le Roulx did not seem able to make up his mind. Heinrich Finke wrote about the entire Templar affair in great detail. None of them really explored the texts related to accusations of occurrences of homosexual practices themselves in order to derive the maximum amount of information from them. But in any examination of Inquisition testimony, it is impossible to lay aside the effect that torture must have had on the answers given. Work on the answers of all the Templars in all the trials for which we have extant manuscripts has shown that there is a very close correlation between the use of torture, which appears to have been widely used in France and Italy, and confessions of guilt. In other countries, for example, Cyprus, England, Ireland, and the Iberian peninsula, where torture was not used, Templars in the main failed to confess. In spite of the prior existence of torture, attested to by many Templars before the Pontifical Commission, most answers in that hearing seem to have been given in a manner that describes daily happenings in the order in a realistic manner. After all, under the principles of the Inquisition, once a witness had confessed to any of the most serious allegations—the denial of Christ, for example—he had satisfied the criteria to receive absolution provided he promised not to sin again. From that point onward, he could tell the truth without fear of worsening his situation, and this is just what most of the men seem to have done. Notaries, surprisingly, wrote down minor details elicited from the testimony that would never have been deliberately fabricated because there would have been no reason to do so. As an example, various witnesses commented on their specific duties within the order, travels undertaken, the conduct of perfectly normal or standard religious services, and the frequency of attendance at mass. Information of this sort was unrelated to the questioning or to the eventual outcome for the particular witness testifying.

The Templar Order

The Order of Knights Templar, founded in Jerusalem in 1120, became the Western world's first military order. Its exclusively male brethren were devoted to a dual role as members of a religious order who took the normal three vows of chastity, poverty, and obedience, but who also undertook a fighting role in the Holy Land. Their ideology can be seen both in the Templar Rule itself, and in Bernard of Clairvaux's highly idealized portrait of them written about 1128. Yet neither of these sources enables us to form a clear picture of the actual behavior of these men, who have left virtually no written material behind that might illuminate their own thought and behavior. Surveys of comments made by popes and chroniclers in the period 1128–1291 indicate that while considerable criticism was made of all three major military orders, Templars, Hospitallers, and Teutonic knights, the Templars were not generally criticized more often, or more severely, than the other similar groups. Certain notable chroniclers such as William of Tyre and Matthew Paris were frequently critical of them, but they were also critical of any group posing a threat to episcopal authority. The Order of the Temple was an exempt order, subject only to the papacy, and not normally the object of the usual episcopal monastic visitations. Most criticism leveled at the order revolved around its seeming arrogance and pride, its perceived responsibility for some of the military failures in the Holy Land, and, most of all, its alleged possession of wealth and power. The allegations concerning Templar wealth appear to be basically unfounded, but the Templars' role as international bankers and money lenders persuaded some contemporary critics to believe in the existence of very large amounts of funds in the Templar treasury.

The perception of the Templars as arrogant and prideful may have stemmed from the Templars' much greater knowledge of the Holy Land, and their need to cooperate at times with the Muslims. Outsiders, crusaders on their first visit to the Holy Land, often believed immediate and hasty military activity to be the best course. Members of the military orders regularly counseled otherwise. It would not be unlikely that the Templars at times seemed insufferably know-it-all to those who had just arrived from the West, since they were apparently friendly with some local Arabs and most certainly understood the extreme difficulties in taking and, more difficult indeed, in keeping the Holy Land with an insufficient number of troops.

The Charges against the Order

Between 1307 and 1311, the military order of the Knights Templar was charged with permitting and even advocating a wide variety of seemingly heretical acts, and the members themselves were imprisoned, interrogated by tribunals of the Inquisition, charged with up to 127 articles of heresy, blasphemy, sacrilege, improper religious practices, and other perceived faults in their religious life. In

1310 approximately sixty were executed. Although all these actions were taken in at least the name of the pope, in fact, they seem to have been at the instigation of the French king, Philip IV. The pope complained in writing to the king about Philip's interference in what should have been an ecclesiastical matter: the arrest of all members of a renowned religious order. Many of these accusations were completely unrelated to heresy or any other impropriety. Articles 30–33 of the alleged offenses referred to the exchange of various illicit kisses, specifically on the spine, lower back, buttocks, anus, chest, stomach, or penis, presumably a reference to homosexual tendencies on the part of some members of the order. E. G. Rey had an ingenious rationale for seemingly "shameful practices": Since the Templars spent a long time facedown, one behind the other, during the reception ceremony, strangers peeking at this ritual could have mistaken what was going on, believing that they were watching some sort of homosexual act being committed. The few descriptions of initiation ceremonies extant do not, in fact, suggest that the candidates lay prostrate before the receiver. More seriously, article 40 specifically referred to widespread permission being accorded to new members regarding the commission of homosexual acts within the order: "that brothers said to those they received that they could unite carnally with one another." The next five articles of accusation stated that such acts were "licit," that members "should perform and suffer them," and that, moreover, some or many members did so.

Few Templars confessed to any guilt regarding the commission of homosexual acts, although most agreed that such permission was given to them. Considerably more often, the inquisitors obtained confessions regarding the kiss on the mouth, which was licit and usual, less often regarding the kiss on lower parts of the body. Some definite testimony relating to same-sex acts did occur in England (but only by a nonmember of the order), France, and Italy. No confessions of guilt on these matters were received in the Iberian peninsula or Cyprus, or from English Templars themselves. Confessions regarding serious sin, including sexual sin, were all received in areas where torture was used. Since many statements regarding such torture were received by the inquisitors at the Pontifical Commission hearings, it is entirely plausible that no instance of permission to unite carnally was ever given to anyone.

Before considering sodomy and other homosexual acts carried out by the all-male members of the Templar order, it is necessary to look at the issue of what was understood about homosexual acts, particularly sodomy, in the medieval period and before. Jacques Le Goff stated that "the history of medieval sodomy has not been written—neither regarding the practice of it, nor the theory." In the early Middle Ages it is evident that a confusion existed when the word "sodomy" was used. This confusion is partially related to the very different views expressed by historians and theologians in the last fifty years on the original meaning of the story of Sodom and Gomorrah. Some recent scholars have stated that theologians used the term sodomy for a bewildering variety of illicit sex acts. Michel Foucault called sodomy "that utterly confused category," and the sodomite himself "a temporary aberration" in the preindustrial period. John Boswell, whose book of 1980, *Christianity, Social Tolerance, and Homosexuality,* is still the major work in the field, insists that in the eighth and ninth centuries, "sodomy" referred either to any illicit sex act, even heterosexual liaisons between men of the world and women in religious life, or to all "non-procreative and some potentially reproductive sex acts." Vern Bullough agrees essentially with Boswell, stressing medieval writers' disinclination to define sodomy when mentioning it. Early penitentials of the sixth or seventh century did describe sexual acts explicitly, but such specificity was often omitted by later medieval church writers when it was thought that the descriptions themselves might lead the faithful into sin. Pierre Payer firmly states in *Sex and the Penitentials* that in connection with the use of various terms for sodomy in early penitentials, "This study has suggested that the use of these terms probably refers to male anal intercourse." Romano Canosa agrees with him, pointing out that Peter Damian had described the four possible sexual acts between males clearly and realistically around 1050. In an index of increasing gravity, Damian considered first and not very grave, solitary masturbation; next, mutual masturbation between two males; third, intrafemoral coitus; and, last and worst, complete sodomization. Damian was, of course, referring only to clerics who engaged in same-sex acts, but he concluded that this crime was the "worst of all as it carried with it the death of the body, the destruction of the soul, the corruption of the flesh, the extinction of the . . . mind, and the fleeing of the Holy Spirit from the body." As will be seen below, in the case of the Templar trial in the Auvergne, it was perfectly clear that the witness there was describing male anal intercourse. But a problem arises, nevertheless: Can we be sure that all inquisitors and all witnesses understood the term "sodomy," or, more frequently, when they referred to men being told that they might have sex with one another, what did this phrase entail?

In general, even by the time of Gratian, sexual sins *contra naturam* appear to have been catalogued using the Augustinian definition of a male using a part ("member") of his wife for purposes for which it was not intended. This bewildering definition obviously defines as sodomy various acts that might take place during heterosexual intercourse as well as acts that might occur between men though not between women. By this definition oral sex, intrafemoral sex, or heterosexual anal sex would be sodomy. The third Lateran Council of 1179 was the first ecumenical council to give precise penalties for the commission of this act. Ecclesiastics were to be expelled from their orders or confined in monasteries. Laymen were to be excommunicated and removed from the company of the faithful. And in a sentence directly relevant to the alleged activities of senior members of the Templar order with new recruits, "The worst was sodomy between spiritual fathers and spiritual sons." This was precisely the accusation against the Templars in 1307: that the receiver of new members, an older and usually high-ranking member of the order, enjoined the new and much younger recruits to permit sex between the brethren on demand.

It would seem that at various times the official penalty for proven commission of homosexual acts was extremely severe. What is missing, unfortunately, is any knowledge of how often, if at all, these penalties were carried out. For example, Emperor Valentinian had punished homosexuality with burning at the stake in 390, revived in the Theodosian Code. The penalty for persisting in the act of sodomy was particularly severe in the Kingdom of Jerusalem, where in 1120, at the time of the founding of the Templar order, a council enacted a canon directing the punishment as death by burning. If an adult had been found to be a sodomite, he was to be burned. As so often occurs, nevertheless, we have almost no evidence whatever that allows us to know whether such punishments ever took place.

In dealing with the accusations of homosexuality leveled against the Templars, we should consider not only the early definition of sodomy, that of the period of the penitentials, a definition that most certainly appears not to have been necessarily related exclusively to male anal sex, but rather the prevailing view found in the writings of those who influenced theologians in the early fourteenth century, the period of the Templar trials.

Albertus Magnus was one of the most influential theologians to discuss sodomy and to differentiate it from masturbation, adultery, fornication, and bestiality. We may credit him with the statement that homosexuality defied "grace, reason, and nature." He insisted that sodomy was the worst of these sins. Unfortunately, by this time, Albert the Great seems to have assumed that his readers knew what sodomy was since he failed to define it except as sexual relations between persons of the same gender, and consequently we have the possibility that women in lesbian relationships were considered to be committing sodomy. Boswell suggests that other writings of Albertus Magnus clearly show that he intended sodomy to refer principally to anal intercourse between males.

We would expect Aquinas's views to be known to theologians by the time the Templar trials took place; hence his views on homosexual acts and sodomy are certainly relevant. His opinions are closer to those of the period of the Templar trials, but unfortunately they are no more explicit than most of the other eleventh- to thirteenth-century material. Sex acts *contra naturam* are defined as any type of same-sex activity, male/male, or female/female, hence must not have referred only to anal intercourse. Homosexual intercourse was, by definition, included in this list. Aquinas does, nevertheless, reserve special critical scorn for what he calls "unnatural vice," saying that it "flouts nature by transgressing its basic principles of sexuality, it is in this matter the gravest of sins." But within the list of sexual sins, bestiality, which entails having sex with the wrong species, is worse than sodomy, which uses the right species but the wrong sex.

Boswell sees various contradictions in Aquinas's treatment of homosexuality and sodomy in which he vacillated between the point of view that any nonprocreative sex act was "unnatural," and the possibility that some "unnatural" acts were in and of themselves not sinful. In Aquinas's major statements on homosexuality he opines that "vices against nature constitute a species of lust" of which they are the most serious variety, but these unnatural vices include not only homosexuality but "masturbation, intercourse with animals, homosexual intercourse, and non-procreative heterosexual coitus." Aquinas's writings appear to indicate that he did regard homosexuality as a "natural" condition, making it difficult, though theologically necessary, to argue as the church did that it was necessarily evil.

Scholars agree that by the thirteenth and fourteenth centuries, stricter measures began to be taken against marginal peoples: Cathars, lepers, Jews, and homosexuals. Groups that had been tolerated in Christian society no longer were. The establishment of the Office of the Inquisition in 1231 seems to have led to an increased surveillance on human behavior and a concomitant punishment of anyone who did not seem to fall into the mainstream group.

By the end of the thirteenth century, accusations of homosexual practices, sodomy in particular, became common in Inquisition inquiries into important persons, particularly those in the church, for example, Boniface VIII. It is possible that the common people truly did regard homosexual activity as disgusting and against nature, but there is no proof of this. Guy Ménard suggests that "homosexuality inspired horror" since women were regarded as inferior men. Men taking part in homosexual acts were wasting semen or "future human beings." This view contradicts behavior that seems to have been tolerated for many centuries before this date. There is no question that heresy and sodomy came to be linked, as William Monter points out. Sodomy could in most areas be investigated by both secular and religious tribunals. In Aragon, nevertheless, the Inquisition "claimed jurisdiction over all cases of sodomy whether or not heresy was present." Monter also believes that "continuous male homosexual subcultures existed in large Italian cities . . . since the High Middle Ages," a view attacked by Randolph Trumbach, who argues that Monter had seriously misinterpreted his material. Michel Bernos et al. insist that it was the movement into the towns, which occurred before the repressive thirteenth century, that "gave rise to fornication . . . and finally to pederasty." We are told that while homosexuality was condemned in the country, city-dwellers condemned bestiality. Any solid evidence for such attitudes in the early thirteenth century is woefully inadequate.

In conclusion, theologians in the period from the sixth to the fourteenth century frequently referred to sodomy as either the most serious sexual sin or one of the gravest such sins. There is no doubt, however, that they differed in their definition of the act. It could refer to any illicit sexual coupling between men, women, or a man and a woman. I am convinced that by the fourteenth century, the term "sodomy" was used by theologians and inquisitors almost entirely in reference to male intercourse, anal intercourse in particular. There is certainly no evidence to conclude that a gay subculture existed at this time. The fact that penitential books so frequently refer to homosexual acts must lead us to believe, nevertheless, that these acts were committed fairly frequently.

Homosexual Acts and the Templar Charges

Concerning the Templars and other religious orders, accusations of homosexuality were a relative commonplace. Medieval bishops' visitation records mention instances of homosexual acts confessed to by monks or occasionally nuns in various houses. It would not seem that a few confessions by Templars in this regard would have been seen as particularly serious. However, possibly homosexuality was particularly ill-fitting in regard to a "military" order of fighting men. Richard Rorty states that being sodomized is to be a nonmale, which seems to have been the view of many ancient and medieval writers. Or, more realistically, were the homosexual accusations added to the other charges simply because the authors of the allegations hoped that some of them would fit? We are in the period of the use of sexual accusations, often relating to homosexual practices, as standard features in a list of charges of the Inquisition into matters that were more political than heretical. Philip IV had raised the specter of the awfulness of the Templars' conduct in his order of arrest of September 14, 1307. His veiled references to sexual crime underlie several of his statements of pious outrage: "We shudder with violent horror, and in thinking of the gravity [of the accusations] an immense sadness grows in us even more cruelly because there is no doubt that the enormity of the crime reaches far enough to be an offense to the divine majesty, a shame to all christianity, a pernicious example of evil, and a universal scandal. . . . It [the Templar order] is comparable to beasts of the field deprived of a sense of reason, even more, going farther in their lack of reason through its astonishing bestiality." The document continues with a recital of their alleged crimes: denying the divinity of Christ and spitting on the cross. If proved, these would provide proof of heresy existing in the order. The king continues with the more scandalous accusations: naked, they are kissed by the dignitary who receives them at the base of the lower spine, on the navel, and on the mouth, shameful acts in the king's mind except for the usual kiss on the mouth, a common practice in feudal ceremonies. The king relates next that "they are obliged by the vows they take upon profession, and without fearing to offend human law, to give themselves to one another, without refusing, as soon as they are so required, [with] as an effect, a horrific and frightening coupling." The statement given by Philip IV's lawyer and great propagandist, Pierre Dubois, before the Estates General in Paris in 1308, the supposed "remonstrances of the people of France" included the charge of "bougrerie." This word can be used as a general term of opprobrium applied to heretics in general, or as a specific reference to buggery. In any event, Dubois states that the Templars ought to be condemned not for their buggery but for their denials (of Christ), an act that he seems to have found distinctly more despicable. Pierre Dupuy, writing of the condemnation of the Templars in an immensely popular work that was published in 1654, insisted that "the received person kissed the receiver . . . on the base of the spine at that part of the body which is the most foul. And that . . . they were absolutely forbidden to know women carnally, but if they were inflamed by any feelings of desire, they could without fear and without conscience unite with their brothers. . . . Their superiors abused them. . . . One of them confessed that in Cyprus, the Grand Master abused him three times during one night."

Court Records

Testimony given before the courts may furnish some of the most direct evidence available for the ideas and lives of ordinary persons, non-nobles, peasants, and serfs. Since they were normally illiterate at this period, they form a group almost without contemporary written records of their own. Testimony is, nevertheless, necessarily affected by its nature, mediated as it was through the note-taking habits of scribes. No medieval notary took the testimony down verbatim. It was often given in one of the vernacular languages, taken down in note form, and then written up in Latin in standard formal notarial language some time later. And it is this later form that is to be found today in the Vatican and other archives. As Dominick LaCapra notes, "An inquisition register is, as [Carlo] Ginzburg observes, part of the 'archives of the repression.'" But as LaCapra remarks immediately thereafter, "These documents are themselves historical realities that do not simply represent but also supplement the realities to which they refer. . . . An inquisition register is a part of discursive context that embodies hegemonic relations." Ginzburg himself had stated in the preface of the Italian version of *The Cheese and the Worms* that the mere scarcity of testimony on the behavior of the subaltern classes of the past creates an almost impossible obstacle to our research on them. He believed that in spite of this such testimony could reveal their "beliefs, phantasies, and aspirations." It was, unfortunately, an oral culture, "but historians cannot begin to speak with peasants of the sixteenth century." He insists that in spite of the formal nature of the judges' questions and the answers of the accused we can still recognize that there "flowered a deep layer of popular beliefs."

The manuscripts of the depositions of the Templar trials (or, more properly, hearings) are models of their sort given that the notaries involved are almost all papal notaries, or at least properly constituted imperial public notaries. The inquisitors are usually bishops or occasionally archbishops. The official written statements of the three or four notaries who attest to and affix their seals to all of these manuscripts of Templar trials appear at key places on the manuscript. In these attestations, each notary affirms that the official document written by one or more of them is a true record of the proceedings. They list the official list of allegations at the start of each trial manuscript, give the date of each witness's testimony, rarely state whether or not it was given in Latin, and never imply that it was taken down verbatim. The great length of these manuscripts (the trial that I edited in the Papal States and the Abruzzi heard only seven witnesses and was written on 33.75 meters of parchment) indicates the care with which the notaries wrote down even answers that did not suit their presumed agenda: to record the guilty answers. The written instructions sent out by the French king to bailiffs and provosts with instructions not to open them until October 13, 1307, asked them to "isolate the persons [the Templar prisoners] under good and sure guard, first make an inquiry about them, then call in the commissioners of the inquisitor and examine for the truth with care, by torture if necessary; and if they confess the truth, write down their depositions after having called in witnesses."

There are several reasons that underline the great importance of this particular inquiry or inquisition into one of the great medieval religious orders. First, the number of men questioned, about 935, is considerable, a sufficient number to give some credence to the answers. Second, the geographical spread of the inquiry, which has left us with manuscripts from those questioned in England, Scotland, Ireland, Spain, France, Italy, Germany, and Cyprus, is extensive.

There were undoubtedly other trials for which the evidence no longer remains. There is no other prior set of records in which the same questions were asked of so many persons in so many parts of Latin Christendom. It would also seem that the papal or public notaries who took down the evidence were very careful to do so in the proper format: to record at least the sense of what the witnesses said. Unfortunately, for many trials such as the small, regional French inquiries, we have only very brief summaries of a few lines, which cannot, of course, replicate the prisoners' answers. All the large trials—those in England, Paris, the Pontifical Commission, and Cyprus—and the much smaller ones in Brindisi and the Papal States used a form or subset of the official 127 articles of accusation. This coherence makes it possible to compare directly answers given in various trials with one another.

Templar Testimony

I would like now to turn to the testimony itself. Most of the testimony relevant to sexual matters given by Templars during the interrogations is very general in nature, hearsay only, and without mention of who was allegedly committing what illicit act with whom. It is difficult to assess the evidence without considering whether it is "direct evidence" or "hearsay evidence." Although Inquisition records of this sort appear somewhat more reliable than the Renaissance records described by Alan Bray, one would have to agree that, as he said, "they appear to be a sober and objective record of the incidents." Yet I cannot agree that in the case of the Templar depositions, as he found with Renaissance records, "it becomes apparent that these documents are in large part no more than convenient legal fictions." The precise nature of answers that do not conform to the presumed papal wish to obtain confessions of guilt, for example, those of Peter of Bologna before the Pontifical Commission, indicate that in the early fourteenth century such records contained less "fiction" than they seem to have contained later.

In the trial held in the Papal States and the Abruzzi in which seven witnesses were questioned during 1309 and 1310, Andrew Armanni of Mount Oderisio, a serving brother in Chieti, stated that "he had often heard it said by brothers of the order with whom he lived that the grand preceptor who received him [Peter

Peraverde Ultramontanus] and other preceptors [heads of Templar houses] and important brothers in the order used to have boys with whom they committed carnal [acts]." In most instances where it is alleged that specific individuals were involved in homosexual acts with members of the order, or others, the witness implicates someone else, not himself. Although in this case, and in others, the person implicated did, in fact, exist. This man was mentioned often in this trial but was conveniently described as having already died.

This particular response may have implied that whatever homosexual acts took place were not with members of the order, since the Templar order did not accept boys, but with youths who were perhaps employed by the order as servants or agricultural workers. It may, nevertheless, have referred to sex acts committed with young Templars of fifteen or sixteen. It is significant that in this case, and most others, the witness makes the statement that homosexual acts took place without any note of horror, disapproval, or commentary. On the other hand, after describing other acts, notably, the denial of Christ or spitting on the cross, witnesses in various trials expressed regret, or shame, often going off to confess to a priest or higher prelate, in some cases fleeing from the order altogether.

The inquisitors did not dwell on the accusations with sexual significance as they did on the presumed instances of heretical behavior. When interrogating William, a priest interrogated in the same trial, the questioning regarding the denial of Christ or spitting on the crucifix was extremely thorough: "Asked about whether the receivers and those they received had hope [of salvation by Jesus Christ] . . . he said and testified that he used to have and still has hope of receiving salvation through Jesus. He said moreover that the said brothers William and Dominic who forced him to deny Christ, and other brothers of the said order who made others deny Christ, and who denied Christ with their heart, had no hope of receiving salvation through Jesus." Arriving at the questions on permission to have sex with other brothers, William merely answered that "William and Dominic told him that brothers . . . could legitimately have sex with one another. . . . He said and testified that he never did it, nor did he suffer it, that which was contained in the allegation; he did not know about what other brothers did."

Gerard of Piacenza added the first specific information on the subject given in this trial. As well as stating that he had been told that homosexual acts were not a sin, he insisted that he was told by brother Albert of Castro Alquatro that "brother James of Bologna, vicar of brother James of Monte Cuccho," the grand preceptor sought but never found in this trial, "had carnal relations with brother Manfred of Balneoregio." The witness did not express any horror or disgust over the actions of James of Bologna. As mentioned above, expressions of indignation are a feature of many witnesses' testimony in connection with other acts, denying the possibility of salvation through Christ, for example; it is significant that this witness did not demonstrate such an attitude when he gave this testimony.

The last witness in this trial, Walter of Naples, added a new bit of information: "brother Albert after making him deny Christ and spit on the cross, although he spat beside it, told him that he might kiss him on the nude stomach," prior to granting him permission to commit homosexual acts. Nevertheless, Walter never suffered or committed these acts himself and knew nothing about the whole matter. The ritual admission that witnesses were told that they might have sex with other members of the order, but did not do so, is by far the most frequent response to questions on this matter. The intriguing question here, unanswerable from direct evidence, is, first, was such permission to have sex with other brothers routinely given at reception ceremonies, or was it invented by witnesses to satisfy the inquisitors? Since the witness almost always insisted that he himself had never participated in same-sex acts, such an admission would place guilt on others, not on the witness himself. I must stress that no such testimony was given in areas in which torture was not used, such as England or Cyprus.

References to the area of homosexuality were more explicit in the Tuscan trial of 1310–11 in which four of the six witnesses confessed in some way to these charges. The first prisoner insisted that generally the four allegations were correct. Brothers were instructed that male sexual relations were not sinful. Had such an instruction ever been given to new members, the suggestion that it was not a sin would, of course, have removed the important question of deliberate commission of sin from anyone who followed these instructions. But is it credible that Templars could have, or would have, believed such an absurd directive? Regarding specific testimony on this subject, he alleged that it was well known in the order that such behavior took place. In fact, he had seen two men so doing. This evidence was confirmed in substance by the following witness, who insisted that it was public knowledge in the order that such behavior was not a sin.

The third witness in the Florence-Lucca trial confirmed the evidence of his two predecessors and added the names of five Templars, several of them preceptors, who were *maxime subdomite,* very great sodomites. He denied such acts himself. Only one more witness, the sixth, adduced any direct evidence in this matter; he had no proof but offered the information that he had seen and heard that brother James of Bologna and brother Manfred his servant behaved in this manner. Once again, no surprise is expressed at such acts occurring.

The trial in Brindisi in 1310 heard only two witnesses, one of whom confessed to knowledge of homosexual behavior. He spoke of sodomy in particular rather than in the general terms used elsewhere. The word "sodomy" itself in its Latin variants does occur occasionally, but much more often we find the much more vague expression "to unite with one another." He stated that he had heard that brother Hippolyte ordered brother Dennis of Barolo to allow him to commit sodomy. Brother Dennis, Hippolyte's servant, also committed sodomy with Hippolyte and was imprisoned for committing this crime. The Templar Rule explains in no uncertain terms that the penalty for sodomy was expulsion from the order, or in some cases perpetual imprisonment. Sodomy was considered to be one of the most serious crimes any Templar could commit. There were nine sins for which Templars could be "expelled from the house for ever." "The fourth is if a brother is tainted with the filthy, stinking sin of sodomy, which is so filthy and so stinking and so repugnant that it should not be named." Yet, in one of the examples found in the later information on penances composed between 1257 and 1267, it seems evident that same-sex practices seem to have occurred that did not of necessity include anal sex: "At Château Pèlerin there were brothers who practiced wicked sin and caressed each other in their chambers at night; so that those who knew of the deed and others who had suffered greatly by it, told this thing to the Master."

One of the most important early hearings took place in Poitiers in 1308 and heard seventy-two witnesses. It was held particularly in order to convince Pope Clement V of the accuracy of Philip IV's allegations. Since the pope appears to have been convinced of the guilt of the order by this testimony, in spite of the relative lack of importance of the witnesses, its testimony needs close consideration. There is no doubt whatever that torture had been used. The deposition of a knight contained the following statement: "Asked whether he had confessed while being tortured, or even afterwards, he said no. But he said that after the aforesaid tortures, he was placed for three weeks or so in a turret on bread and water, and afterwards he was brought to Poitiers . . . and there he confessed as above spontaneously, of his own will without any coercion." Twenty-two of these men gave specific evidence relating to homosexual acts. A serving brother from Limoges, Peter of Claustro, the second witness, began by stating that "according to a statute of the Templar order one could commit sexual acts with the brothers without sin; he however never did so."

Brother Clement of Pomar insisted not only that he received permission to have carnal relations with other brothers, but that he in fact did so whenever he wished. He expressed no remorse over this act, and since the inquisitors' comments are never included with the transcript, we cannot know what the inquisitors' reactions to his confession were.

The sixth witness, John of Cranaco, in describing his reception into the order, said that when the presiding officer, the receptor, told him that he should have sexual relations with other brothers if he was inflamed with lust, he had removed the habit of the order, in disgust one assumes. The Templar officer ordered him to resume the habit, saying that this was one of the "points of the order." Templars, like most others in religious life, were not permitted to leave the order without permission of the grand master, as he came to be called, or the pope. In fact, even taking the habit off for any reason, and throwing it down, was a serious fault. Robert of Gay continued with an affirmation of homosexual activity as licit by saying that he was told that "if any brother of the order wished to lie with him, he should permit him" to do so; "he also could lie with them" since that was one of the directives of the order.

Raymond of Narbonne spoke if anything more clearly on the subject of homosexual activity. He insisted that he had been told that "it was a greater sin to lie with women [than with men]." Nevertheless, he insisted that he had not sought out men in this way nor had others beseeched him. It seems illogical that if, in reality, this directive was a normal feature of reception ceremonies, so few men were ever approached by others who wanted to have sex with them.

John of Cugy or Cuisi, when asked about homosexual activity, confirmed Raymond's testimony. When asked about the vice of sodomy, he replied that he had been told he might have sex with his brothers but he never did so.

Another witness to testify on this matter in Poitiers said exactly the same thing. Several other witnesses testified in a like manner without adding to our knowledge of the alleged illicit acts. The eighth witness described illicit kisses and the fact that he was told Templars must observe chastity as far as women were concerned. When asked whether he had been told he had permission to have sex with the brethren, he rather surprisingly responded that he could not remember. This response would seem to indicate that it was not a matter of any importance, hence not uncommon. The eighteenth witness, when asked about sodomy, said that he had been told to abstain from women but to have sex with the brothers if he felt the need to do so. Witness Deodatus Jefet, after having given evidence similar to those who testified earlier, added that a Templar knight, William Dersis, had asked him to have sex with him but that he had refused. He did not state that anything happened to him because he refused. No further details were given. If one believes that brothers were ordered to have sex on demand if others asked them to do so, it would not be possible to refuse with impunity, since it would be a fault against the mandatory vow of obedience.

The next witness, another of the few knights to testify in Poitiers, added nothing to the usual recital of permission to commit carnal acts but the denial that such acts ever took place. The last witness of this group offered a similar deposition. In fact, no serious allegations that would confirm the reality that homosexual acts took place in the order occurred in this trial.

The depositions of witnesses at Poitiers appearing in Finke's work are more discursive and fuller than those published by Schottmüller. John of Villiers stated that his receiver and other brothers kissed him "on the mouth, on the navel, and at the base of the dorsal spine." James of Castillon went further, insisting that some of the brothers asked him to have sex with them, but he did not wish to. Hugo of Guamaches only kissed the brethren on the mouth but stated that he was told not to consort with women, "but with the brothers if he became aroused." Several of these men were specifically asked about "the vice of sodomy" but knew nothing about it. A serving brother named Stephen testified at considerable length, saying that brother Paul wished to "corrupt and pollute him with that abhorrent sin, . . . sodomy . . . but he abhorred that sin to such a degree that he hit Paul in the chin breaking three of his teeth and fracturing his jaw." Stephen was taken to task by one of the officials for refusing Paul's request. Although this evidence from Poitiers may seem damning, all scholars today see this particular hearing as notoriously unreliable. The witnesses appearing seem to have been handpicked, perhaps trained in their answers, in order to convince the pope of the Templars' guilt.

By far the most important early trial of the series of interrogations between 1307 and 1311 was that held in Paris in 1307 and took testimony from 138 witnesses. It was twice as large as the Poitiers hearing, and much more important, with evidence heard from a wider variety of Templar witnesses, including knights and priests. All but thirty-one of these men stated that homosexual activity was either permitted or licit, only two that it actually took place.

The first witness in this hearing, Ranier of Larchent, had been received by John of Tours, treasurer of the order some twenty-six years earlier. Ranier offered uncommon evidence on the subject. He related that the psalm "Ecce quam bonum et quam iocundum habitare fratres in unum" was a coded message implying that the brothers might have sex with one another. He gave no testimony whatever on the reality or existence of homosexual acts in the order. It stretches credibility to the utmost to see in one of the psalms an incitement to homosexual acts.

This sort of testimony, which was heard from the group in Paris in 1307, has little substance. It consists of an endless recitation of incitement to commit homosexual activities without any definite evidence of when or where, or indeed whether, such acts were committed. I intend to concentrate here only on those persons who offered different and specific testimony and omit those who merely stated that such behavior was tolerated without the addition of any definite, firsthand information.

A second witness offered direct evidence on this matter. One John of Tortavilla insisted that after receiving the standard advice on homosexuality from a dignitary of the order, Gerard of Villiers, "visitor" (a high official) of France, he had had carnal relations twice with a certain William whose whereabouts were presently unknown to him. He added that he understood from what he had been told that having sex with a member of the order was not a sin, but that had he had sex with a non-Templar it would have been sinful. After all, if some men believed precisely what they were allegedly told, that is exactly what they would have thought. Yet, given the general reputation of the Templar order and its members, it is not credible that all new members were told that homosexual activity was licit.

Another bit of evidence was elicited from brother Peter of Safet, a serving brother, originally from Acre, who insisted that while he was told homosexual activity was licit, he had not participated in such behavior. However, during the night, a Spanish brother was seen coming out of the room of the Master of the Templars, and he sexually abused the witness, who did not dare to deny him because of the master's instructions to him. Peter had been received in Nicosia by James of Molay himself about five years earlier. This testimony would appear to confirm that, in one case at least, sex was forced on low-ranking members of the order by others. In spite of the element of force, Peter did not express any feelings of shame.

When the principal defender of the Templars before the papal commissioners, the priest Peter of Bologna, appeared at the Paris trial, his testimony was completely different from his later appearance, at which time he insisted with great eloquence that the order was completely innocent. In this first appearance, echoing the others, he stated that "the presiding officer told him that he could *se commiscere* [unite] with the brothers and they with him without sin. He however did not believe it, and does not believe it, as he said, because it is a horrible sin, and he said that he never committed that sin." This man was an educated man of the law, eloquent, and used to pleading before the papal curia. His opinion may be one widely held by many important members of the order, but not one necessarily shared by the much more numerous serving brothers or sergeants.

A slight variant on the usual testimony was offered by Fulk of Trecis, who when asked about carnal relations said, "cohabitation with women was prohibited to him, but he was told that the brothers' beds were [common between them] *communes inter ipsos.*" The Templar rule of the order clearly stated that each member was to sleep clothed in his own bed. Poverty and occasional overcrowding might certainly have made it necessary overseas for the Templars to share beds, a perfectly common medieval practice unrelated to sexual behavior. In fact, this directive to share beds with visitors or other Templars when necessary may have influenced serving brothers in particular to think that sexual acts with the brethren were licit.

Hence, although the Paris trial heard ninety-four Templars state that they had been told homosexual relations were licit, even obligatory in many cases, only two persons gave any direct evidence of its existence. The others merely confirmed that they had been told they might or should commit carnal acts with other Templars but were never asked to do so and did not take the initiative themselves.

The hearings of the Pontifical Commission held between 1309 and 1311 heard from 229 men, many of whom had already testified in the earlier Paris trial. This hearing is often accorded the highest status because of its relatively impartial nature. The influence of Philip IV and his councillors was much less than it had been at earlier hearings. The sessions were held before Gilles Aicelin, archbishop of Narbonne, a great expert in the law, and royal councillor. Three other bishops, those of Bayeux, Mende, and Limoges, assisted Aicelin. Although Favier classifies these men as not being royal stooges, none of them is known to have been opposed to the king. They might be described as belonging to the royal camp.

The first two witnesses made no reference to homosexual acts. The third, a serving brother who had only been a Templar for about three years prior to his capture (presumably in 1307) stated that he had never heard anything about the matter until after he was arrested. The next witness, received in Poitiers but at the time of the hearing of the London diocese, insisted that he had never heard that homosexual relations were licit; in fact he considered that "it was a grave sin to do it or to suffer it." He offered hearsay evidence referring to stories that overseas Templars committed that sin ten years earlier, but he did not believe that they did so with any kind of official permission or statute. The knowledge that homosexual acts were considered a sin by the church should have been common to all men entering a religious order. In fact, a witness in the hearing on Cyprus said on the subject that "what was alleged in the article was not true. On the other hand, it is a great sin, and so the brothers, and he himself, said and observed. And he said that any place or land where such a sin [having homosexual relations] was committed ought to be inundated by a flood ['submerged' in the Latin text]." Another Cypriot Templar, preceptor of one of the houses, said that "the accusation was not true. On the contrary, anyone found guilty of the said vice had his habit removed from him and he was condemned to perpetual imprisonment."

In contrast, a sixty-year-old knight, member of the order for twenty-four years, mentioned in several persons' testimonies as a "preceptor" or receiver of new members, stated that he had been told to have sex with brothers of the order rather than with women. He was not told, nevertheless, that homosexual relations were not a sin against chastity. Later in his testimony he stated that he knew of no members actually committing this offense. That the commission of same-sex acts was deemed to be related to age appears in his testimony, in which he said that he had not told an old man received into the order that uniting with his brethren was licit because of his age, while he had so informed a young man at his reception.

A certain serving brother, Theobald of Taverniaco of the diocese of Paris, gave an unusual answer to the queries relating to homosexual acts. When asked regarding allegations 41–45, he replied "that he did not believe the contents of those articles to be true because they could have beautiful and wealthy women, and frequently they did so, because they were rich and powerful, and because of this he and other brothers of the order were frequently banished from their [Templar] houses." While denying the existence of homosexual practices, one of the witnesses explained why earlier men had referred to Templars sleeping two to a bed by saying that it was "for lack of beds that sometimes they slept two together," while specifying that no untoward activities took place since they slept clothed and girdled. Hildegard of Bingen, in her explanation of the Benedictine Rule, rubric 28, on underclothing, added that while in the period before the late eleventh century, particularly the time of Benedict himself, the wearing of underclothing was unusual: "now in our times, because the customs of men indicate it, it is not displeasing to God if monks, because of the blasphemy of sacrilege which they might experience in naked flesh, wear underclothes so that they will not be naked and touch flesh with flesh, and thus be reminded of fleshly sins." Hildegard also explained that at the time of Benedict monks wore a cincture over the tunic since they did not wear underclothes.

One witness, a priest, gave evidence relating to that above concerning the sleeping arrangements, which tends to explain why some postulants, when hearing this advice at their reception ceremonies, might have confused the injunction to share their beds when needed because of overcrowding with an official incitement to perform or permit homosexual acts.

One of the longest, most complete, and most bewildering depositions of this hearing was given by the knight Gerald of Caux, of the diocese of Rodez. He had already received absolution and been reconciled by the lord bishop of Paris. Twelve or thirteen years earlier he had been received as a Templar at Cahors. His reception ceremony had been extremely rigorous. He had been required to answer a series of questions about his belief in "the Catholic faith according to the Roman Church." The vows he was required to take were completely in keeping with the rule and the spirit of the order according to the declaration of Peter of Bologna mentioned above: "Understand well what we say to you; you have sworn and promised by God and the blessed [virgin] Mary that you will always be obedient to the Master of the Temple and any of the brothers of the order . . . that you will observe chastity, the good uses and practices of the order, and live without [personal] possessions unless they have been given to you by your superior." Once he had received the Templar robe, the priest recited the psalm referred to by another Templar earlier, *Ecce quam bonum,* as an incitement to homosexuality. Only, in this instance, it was a normal part of a monastic induction ceremony and not related to sin. As part of a lengthy recital of misdeeds that would cause a member to be cast out of the order, the presiding officer mentioned the following serious offenses: "If they joined with one another, or knew a woman, or were in a suspicious place with her." But after the totally licit ceremony, the presiding official allegedly left the premises leaving the new members with four or five serving brothers. It was almost always in separate ceremonies, after a licit initial ritual, that untoward acts allegedly occurred.

In the recently published edition of the trial of the Templars in the Auvergne, particularly explicit evidence on homosexual acts was given. William of Born, a knight of the diocese of Limoges, related that when he was asked to have carnal relations with other brothers, according to the statute of the order, he had sex with four of them. While the other man lay on the ground holding himself with his feet and his hands, William climbed upon him and introduced his penis into the anus of the prostrate individual. He testified that these acts took place on more than fifty occasions and he had confessed these deeds. Under normal circumstances, the Templar chaplain would have imposed extremely severe penances for such confessions. Had this behavior come to the master's attention, as mentioned above, he would have been expelled from the order. No other Templar of the almost one thousand who testified stated that he had committed homosexual acts so frequently.

Only one other witness at this trial confessed to having had homosexual relations, Robert Courteix, a sergeant from Clermont-Ferrand, who stated that he had sex with three brothers during his forty years in the order. The other twenty-nine Templars denied having committed any such acts.

Conclusion

In conclusion, it seems quite clear that both the inquisitors and the Templars they questioned understood the meaning of the accusations made to them. Whatever confusion may have existed earlier on the nature of sodomy, the accusations against the Templars specified in detail what the alleged illicit acts were: the giving and/or exchanging of kisses not just on the mouth, as usual, but on the navel or bare stomach, the buttocks, the base of the spine (probably meaning the anus), or the penis. Furthermore, brothers were allegedly told at their reception that they could and should have sex with one another, that having carnal relations with other brothers was not sinful, and that many of them, in fact, did so. It is not really credible that any witness misunderstood these questions. Admittedly, the word "sodomy" was not referred to in the official accusations. Perhaps the inquisitors, or the lawyers of Philip IV who framed these accusations, thought the term might not have been understood by all the brethren, many of whom were unlettered. The act of sodomy was referred to in various testimonies, and in the case in the Auvergne, the description is certainly the same as a dictionary definition of the act.

We must surely agree that although a large number of Templars alleged having been told they might commit homosexual acts, and that it was licit to do so, very few of them offered any substantive testimony in that regard. It is impossible to discern whether the alleged permission to engage in homosexual relations was actually given at reception to all, or most, of the brethren. In trials where almost all Templars confessed their guilt (France and most of Italy), those few who described licit or normal receptions do not mention any such permission being given. Those from areas such as Cyprus or England where large trials produced little or no evidence of guilt strongly deny that any permission to have sex with other brethren was ever received. Some hearsay evidence regarding homosexual acts committed by other persons came forth, most of it completely unsubstantiated. A very, very few witnesses, fewer than might have been expected, described having had homosexual relations, even fewer the act of sodomy itself. But was this information merely left out by most witnesses because of shame or fear of punishment? I am very doubtful that witnesses omitted such details for those reasons. These men almost uniformly admitted spitting on the cross, reviling Jesus Christ, and denying that his death redeemed mankind from sin. Surely the mention of homosexual sex acts of some sort after having received permission to engage in them would have seemed infinitely less grave. In the cases where such acts were mentioned, usually as having been engaged in by others, it was unusual for the witness to exhibit any particular disgust, shame, or horror. Those who testified in trials where confessions of guilt did not occur occasionally gave the expected comment that they knew sex acts between men, or sodomy in particular, to constitute an abhorrent sin.

While we can never know the truth about the sexual behavior of the Templars, one must acknowledge that in the order homosexual relations were always regarded as a serious sin to be severely punished. Its frequency was probably on a par with that of any other religious order, possibly even less. Scholars who assert confidently that the Templar order was pervaded by practicing homosexuals have no real evidence on which to base such claims.

After having spent more than twenty years studying this material, I remain convinced that some homosexual acts were practiced in the Templar order, as they were in all other institutes of religion, that the frequency of such behavior was not particularly high, and that most Templars did not regard the practice of homosexual acts with any great horror or loathing, although a few did. The accusation leveled against the order of widespread homosexual behavior does not rest on any firm foundation. My belief has been reinforced, through this study of thousands of pages of trial testimony, that considerable personal and social information is hidden between routine, totally incredible answers, forced by threats or by torture.

Sir William Dugdale

"The Proceedings against the Knights Templars in the Kingdom of England, Anno Domini 1309," from *Monasticon Anglicanum*, 1718

Robert, by divine permission, Archbishop of Canterbury, Primate of all England, to his venerable brethren, R. by the grace of God, of London, H. of Winchester, S. of Salisbury, J. of Lincoln, J. of Chichester, R. of Hereford, W. of Worcester, W. of Coventry and Litchfield, J. of Landaff, W. of Exeter, R. of Ely, J. of Norwich, T. of Rochester, D. of St. Davids, L. of St. Asaph, bishops; and to the venerable lords, J. of Bath and Wells, and A. of Bangor, elects confirmed our church of Canterbury's, and our suffragans, health and brotherly charity in the Lord. Your brotherhood is to understand, that we have received apostolical letters, not canceled, nor abolished nor any way depraved, as appeared at first, the true leaden seal hanging to them, the contents whereof are as follows [Bull, *Faciens misericordiam*]:

Clement, bishop, servant to the servants of God, to the venerable brothers, the Archbishop of Canterbury and his suffragans, health and apostolical blessing. The son of God, the Lord Jesus Christ, using mercy with his servant, would have us taken up into the eminent mirror of the apostleship, to this end, that being, tho' unworthy, his substitute upon Earth, we may, as far as human frailty will permit, in all our actions and proceedings, follow his footsteps. In truth, long since, about the time of our first promotion to the dignity of the pontificate, before we came to Lyons, where we received the honors of our coronation; and also after that, as well there as elsewhere, a secret information had intimated to us, that the master, preceptors and other brothers of the Order of Knighthood of the Temple of Jerusalem, as also the order itself, who had been deputed in the parts beyond the seas for the defense of the patrimony of our same Lord Jesus Christ, were fallen against that Lord himself into the not to be mentioned crime of apostasy, the detestable vice of idolatry, the execrable practice of sodomy, and sundry heresies. But because it was not likely, nor did seem credible, that such religious men, who particularly often shed their blood for the name of Christ, and were thought frequently to expose their persons to danger of death, and who often showed many and great signs of devotion as well in the divine offices, as in fasting and other observances, should be so unmindful of their salvation, as to perpetrate such things, we would not give ear to such insinuations and impeachment of them, being taught so to do by the example of the same Lord of ours, and the writings of canonical doctrine.

But afterwards our most dear son in Christ, Philip, the illustrious King of the French, to whom the same crimes had been made known, not upon a view of avarice, since he does not design to apply or appropriate to himself any thing of the estates of the Templars; nay, has wholly washed his hands of them, leaving the same to be disposed of in his kingdom by persons generally deputed by us and by the prelates of the kingdom of France, but inflamed with zeal for the orthodox faith, following the renowned footsteps of his ancestors, getting what information he properly could of what is aforesaid, he sent us many and great informations for instructing and acquainting of us, by his messengers and letters. The infamy of the Templars daily increasing, in relation to the aforesaid crimes; as also in regard, that a certain knight of that order, who was of great birth, and in no small esteem in that order, sworn before us in private, did depose, that at the reception of the brothers of the said order, this custom, or rather corruption, is observed, that he who is received at the suggestion of the receiver, or of the persons by him deputed, renounces Christ, and spits upon a cross shown him, in contempt of the person crucified; and both the receiver and the person received perform some other things which are not lawful, nor becoming human modesty, as he then confessed, before us; we cannot avoid, the duty of our office requiring the same of us, giving ear to so many and such great clamors.

But when at length, public fame accusing, and the repeated insinuation of the said king, as also of dukes, earls and barons, and other noblemen, likewise of the clergy and people of the said kingdom of France, resorting to our presence upon this account, both personally and by their representatives and syndics, which we mention with grief, it was come to our hearing, that the master, preceptors and other brothers of the said order, and the order itself, were involved in the aforesaid and many other crimes, and the premises seemed in a manner to be proved by many confessions, attestations and depositions of the aforesaid master and several preceptors and brothers of the aforementioned order, made, had and received before many prelates and the inquisitor into heretical deprivations in the kingdom of France, all of them reduced into public writings, and shown to us and to our brethren; and nevertheless the aforesaid report and clamors were grown so strong, and were also heightened as well against the order itself, as against particular persons of the same, that they could not, without great scandal, be passed by, or be tolerated without much danger; we following the steps of him whom we, tho' unworthy, represent, thought fit, for the aforesaid reason, to proceed to inquire into what has been said, and did interrogate and examine many of the preceptors, priests and brothers of the said order, of no small reputation, brought into our presence, having first giving them their oath, that they would tell us the plain and full truth in relation to the premises, they being to the number of 72; and many of our brethren assisting us, and caused their confessions diligently put into authentic writing, by public hands, to be immediately read in ours and the presence of our said brethren; and afterwards, some days being passed, in the consistory, before themselves, and the same to be expounded to each of them in their own vulgar tongue, who persisting in them, expressly and of their own accord, approved of the same as they had been recited.

Afterwards designing in our own person to inquire of the master and chief preceptors of the aforesaid order concerning the premises, we ordered the master, chief preceptors, and brothers of the country beyond the sea, of Normandy, Aquitaine, and Poitou to be brought before us being then at Poitiers; but because some of them were so sick at that time, they could not ride, nor be any way brought into our presence; we desiring with them to know the truth of all the premises, and whether those things were true that were contained in their confessions and depositions, which they were said to have made before the inquisitor into heretical depravity in the kingdom of France, in the presence of certain public notaries and many other good men, and which were exhibited to us and our brethren by the same inquisitor, under public hands, and shown to our beloved sons Berengareus, Cardinal of St. Nerius and Aquileus, and Stephen, Cardinal of St. Ciriacus in Termis, priests, and Pandulphus, Cardinal Deacon of St. Angelo, of whose providence, experience and fidelity, we have undoubted confidence, we commissioned and commanded them, that they should diligently inquire into the truth of the premises of the aforesaid master and preceptors, as well against those and other persons of the said order in general, as against the order itself, and to report to us whatsoever they found in this particular, and to swear to bring back and present to our apostleship their confessions and depositions, put into writing by public hands; they being authorized to grant the same master and brethren, according to the form of the church, the benefit of absolution from the sentence of excommunication, which they had incurred for the premises, if they were true, provided they humbly and devoutly desired absolution, as they ought. The . . . Cardinals going in person to the master and preceptors, signified the cause of their coming.

And in regard to their persons and those of the other Templars in the Kingdom of France, had been delivered up to us, they, by apostolical authority, enjoined them to declare to the said cardinals the truth concerning the premises, freely, without fear of any person, fully and plainly. The . . . master and preceptors of France, of the land beyond the sea, of Normandy, Aquitaine and Poitou, before the said cardinals, in the presence of 4 public notaries and many other good men, having taken their oath on the Holy Gospels of God by them corporally touched, that they would before them deliver the whole and plain truth concerning the premises, did before them singularly, freely and of their own accord without any compulsion or dread, depose, and confess among other things, the renouncing of Christ, and spitting upon the cross, when they were received into the Order of the Templars; and some of them to have received many brothers under the same form, *viz.* of renouncing Christ and spitting on the cross; some of them also confessed some other horrible and indecent things, which we conceal to spare their shame for the present.

They said besides and confessed that those things were true which are contained in their confessions and depositions before made, before the inquisitor into heretical depravity; the . . . confessions and depositions of the said master and preceptors, were put into public writing by four public notaries in the presence of the said master and preceptors, and some other good men; and some days after were read before the same persons, by order of, and in the presence of the said cardinals, and expounded to each of them in his own vulgar tongue; who persisting in the same, did expressly, of their own accord, approve the same as they had been read. And after these confessions and depositions, they, on their knees, with their hands joined, humbly and devoutly, and shedding many tears, begged of the said cardinals absolution from the excommunication, which they had incurred on account of the premises. And those cardinals, in regard that the church does not exclude from its bosom such as return, the master and preceptors having abjured their heresy, expressly granted them the benefit of absolution by our authority, according to the form of the church; and then returning to our presence presented to us the confessions and depositions of the aforesaid master and preceptors, reduced into public writings, by public hands, as aforesaid, and reported what they had done with the said master and preceptors.

By which confessions and depositions, and relation, we find that the aforesaid master and brothers have been heinously guilty of the premises, tho' some in more and others in fewer points. But in regard that we cannot in person inquire into these things in all parts of the world, through which that order is dispersed, and where the brothers of it live, we, by the advice of our brethren, ordain your brotherships, by apostolical writing, that you and some of you, *viz.* in their city and diocese, together with the venerable the Patriarch of Jerusalem, and Archbishop of York, the Bishops of Lincoln, Chichester and Orleans, and our beloved sons the abbots of the monasteries of Lagni, of the Diocese of Paris, and St. Germain des Prèz near Paris, and Master Sicard de Vaur, Canon of Narbonne, our Chaplain and hearer of causes in our place, and Guido Wych, Rector of the Church of Hese, in the Diocese of London, or 8, 7, 6, 5, 4, 3, 2, or one of them, whom we have thought fit to be joined to you in this particular, because of the greatness of the affair, having summoned by public proclamation, by you and those adjuncts, or some one or more of them, in the places to which they are to be summoned, such persons are to be summoned against the singular persons and brothers of the said order, residing in your cities and dioceses, though they be come from other places, or have accidentally been brought thither, that you make diligent inquisition concerning the truth of the articles, we send you enclosed in our bull, and concerning such others as in your wisdom you shall think fit.

It is also our will, that such inquisition or inquisitions being made, judgment of absolution or condemnation be pronounced, as justice shall require, by the provincial council against those singular persons and brothers in the same province, or for them, in relation to those things about which inquisition has been made against them; yet so that the inquisitor or inquisitors of heretical depravity deputed in the said province by the see apostolic, be admitted at the pronouncing of the said sentence, if they shall require to be there with you. Provided, that you no way presume to concern yourselves with inquiring or giving judgment against the said order and the great preceptor of the said order, in the Kingdom of England, against whom we have directed inquisition to be made by certain persons. Given at Poitiers, the 2d day after the ides of August, in the 3d year of our pontificate.

We therefore produce the afore written apostolical letters to the knowledge of your fraternity, that you having got a copy of the same, pursuant to the apostolical mandate, may fulfil what belongs to your care in this part. But the articles which we received enclosed in the true bull {*sic*}, and which we remit to you enclosed under our seal to be opened by you, you are to deliver again sealed with your seal to the bearer, after you have taken and kept a copy of the same; and you are to be careful so cautiously to take the said copy of the articles and to keep it when taken, that the same articles may not be revealed because upon them you are to inquire after the truth. In token of the receipt of what is aforesaid, you venerable brothers to whom the present letters shall come, shall affix your seals to these presents. Given at Wyngham, the 10th day after the calends of October, Anno Domini 1309, and the 16th of our consecration.

Item, at the place, day, and hour aforesaid, in the presence of the aforesaid lords, and before us the mentioned notaries, the articles enclosed in the apostolic bull were exhibited, and opened before us, the contents whereof as under written.

These are the articles upon which inquisition shall be made, against the brothers of the Military Order of the Temple, as against singular persons much exposed and vehemently suspected in relation to the contents of the said articles, and a mighty scandal lying against them, as to these particulars.

The Articles against Singular Persons

1. That at their reception, and some times after, and as soon as they could have conveniency for the same, they renounced Christ, or Jesus, or the person crucified or sometimes God, and sometimes the Blessed Virgin, and sometimes all the saints of God, being induced or admonished so to do by those who received them.
2. Item, That the brothers did this commonly.
3. Item, That the major part of them did it.
4. Item, That sometimes they did it after their reception.
5. Item, That the receivers said, and taught those that were received, that Christ was not true God, or sometimes Jesus, or sometimes the person crucified.
6. Item, That they told those they received that he was a false brother.
7. Item, That they said, he had not suffered for the redemption of mankind; nor been crucified, but for his own crimes.
8. Item, That neither the receivers, nor the persons received, had any hopes of obtaining salvation through him; and this they said to those they received, or something equivalent, or like to it.

9. Item, That they obliged those they received to spit upon the cross, or upon the sign, or sculpture of the cross, and the image of Christ, though they that were received did sometimes spit aside.

10. Item, That they caused the cross to be trampled under foot.

11. Item, That the brothers themselves did sometimes trample on the same cross.

12. Item, That they sometimes pissed and caused others to piss upon the cross; and this they sometimes did on Good-Friday.

13. Item, That some of them, on the said day, or some other of the Holy Week, used to assemble purposely for the trampling and pissing aforesaid.

14. Item, That they adored a certain cat that appeared to them at that assembly.

15. Item, That they did this in contempt of Christ, and of the orthodox faith.

16. Item, That they did not believe the sacrament of the altar.

17. Item, That some of them did not.

18. Item, That it was the greater part.

19. Item, That they neither believed the other sacraments of the church.

20. Item, That the priests of the order did not utter the words by which the body of Christ is consecrated, in the canon of the Mass.

21. Item, That some of them did so.

22. Item, That it was the major part.

23. Item, That those who received them enjoined this same.

24. Item, That they believed and so it was told them, that the great master of the order could absolve them from their sins.

25. Item, That the visitor could do the same.

26. Item, That the preceptors, of whom many were laymen, could do it.

27. Item, That they actually did so.

28. Item, That some of them did it.

29. Item, That the great master confessed these things of himself, even before he was taken, in the presence of great persons.

*30. Item, That at the reception of brothers of the said order or about that time, the receiver sometimes and the person received, now and then kissed one another's mouths, navels, bare bellies and in the anus, or the backbone.

*31. Item, That sometimes in the navel.

*32. Item, That sometimes in the backbone.

*33. Item, That sometimes on the members, or yard.

34. Item, That at the reception they obliged those they received to swear, that they would not quit the order.

35. Item, That they presently regarded them as professed.

36. Item, That the receptions of their brothers were made clandestinely.

37. Item, That none were present but the brothers of the said order.

38. Item, That for this reason, there has been for a long time a vehement suspicion against the brothers of the said order.

39. Item, That the same were very common.

*40. Item, That they told the brothers they received, that they might have carnal copulation with one another.

*41. Item, That it was lawful for them to do so.

*42. Item, That they were to do this to one another, and to be passive.

*43. Item, That it was no sin among them to do this.

*44. Item, That they, or many of them, did this.

*45. Item, That some of them did it.

46. Item, That the brothers themselves had idols in every province, viz. heads; some of which had three faces, and some one, and some had a man's skull.

47. Item, That they adored that idol, or those idols, and more especially in their great chapters and assemblies.

48. Item, That they honored it.

49. Item, That it was as a god.

50. Item, That as their savior.

51. Item, That some of them did it.

52. Item, That the major part.

53. Item, That they said, that head could save them.

54. Item, That it could enrich them.

55. Item, That it gave them all the wealth of the order.

56. Item, That it made the land produce.

57. Item, That it made the trees blossom.

58. Item, That they bound or touched the head of the said idols with a cord wherewith they girt themselves on their shirts, or next the skin.

59. Item, That at their reception, the aforesaid little cords, or others of their length, were delivered to every brother.

60. Item, That they did this in honor of the idol.

61. Item, That they enjoined them to girt themselves with the said little cords, as is said above, and to wear them continually.

62. Item, That generally the brothers of the aforesaid order were received as aforesaid.

63. Item, That they performed these things devoutly.

64. Item, That they did them everywhere.

65. Item, For the major part.

66. Item, That for those who refused the things abovementioned, at their reception, or to observe them afterwards, were killed or imprisoned.

67. Item, That some of them.

68. Item, That the major part.

69. Item, That they were sworn not to reveal the same.

70. Item, That it was on pain of death or imprisonment.

71. Item, That they should not discover the manner of their reception.

72. Item, That they durst not talk of the aforesaid things among themselves.

73. Item, That if any were found to discover, they were put to death or imprisoned.

74. Item, That it was enjoined them not to confess to any but the brothers of the said order.

75. Item, That the brothers of the said order, knowing those errors, neglected to correct them.

76. Item, That they did not depart from the observation of the said errors, and the communion of the said brothers, tho' they had power to depart, and do as aforesaid.

77. Item, That the brothers swore to seek the advancement of the said order by all means, right or wrong.

78. Item, That they thought this no sin.

79. Item, That all that is aforesaid and each particular, are known and manifest among the brothers of the said order.

80. Item, These things are the common talk, common received opinion and report, as well among the brothers of the said order, as abroad.

81. Item, That the said brothers in the aforesaid great multitude, confessed, as well in court as out of it, and before solemn persons, and in several even public places.

82. Item, That many brothers of the said order, as well knights as priests, and others also, in the presence of our lord the pope, and of the lords cardinals, confessed the aforesaid or the major part of the said errors.

83. Item, That they did it upon oath.

84. Item, That they did it in full consistory.

85. Let inquisition be made of every brother, of their receivers, the places in which were received, the times of their receptions, and who were present at the same, and the manner of their receptions.

86. Item, Whether they know or have heard, when or by whom the said errors began, and from whom they had their original, and for what cause, and concerning the circumstances, and all other things relating to what is aforesaid, that shall be thought expedient.

87. Item, Let it be inquired of every one of the brothers whether they know where the said heads or idols, or any of them are, and how they were carried about and kept, and by whom.

Pursuant to the aforesaid bull, Ralph, Bishop of London, in October, enjoined the Archdeacon of London to cause all Knights Templars to be summoned at the time of high mass, on Sunday, in all the churches throughout the city, enjoining them personally to appear at the bishop's palace in London, on the 14th day of November following, to answer such things as should be laid to their charge; or that they should be proceeded against tho' absent.

The First Examined by Way of Trial, without Being Sworn, with the Two Next

In the name of the Lord, amen, in the year of the incarnation of our Lord 1309, in the presence of the lords inquisitors aforesaid, brother William Raven, of the order of Templars, being asked how long he had been in the order of the

Templars, says that he was received into the order of the Templars five years since, at Coumbe, in the diocese of Bath, by brother William More, on the next Sunday after the Feast of All Saints; and there were then present the brothers John Walpole and William Ering, and about 100 secular persons being present, about the hour of prime, in the chapel of the same place, and with him was received brother Geoffrey Frewe, knight, who is dead. He also said he desired the said brothers of the temple that they would admit him into the said order to serve God and the Blessed Virgin Mary, and to end his days in their service.

He says also, that it was asked him, whether his will was fixed so to do; and he answered, it was. And afterwards it was said by the two brothers, who signified to him the rigor of the order, *viz.* that he should not follow his own will in what he did, but the will of the preceptor; and if he were for doing one thing, he would be commanded to do another; and if he would stay in one place, he would be sent to another. Which things being promised, he took an oath on the holy gospels of God to obey his superior, to have nothing of his own, to keep chastity, not to consent to the unjust disinheritance of any person, and not to lay violent hands on any person, unless in his own defense, or on the Saracens.

He also said that this oath was taken in the aforesaid chapel, none being present but the brothers of the said order, and one priest of the said order, whose name he knows not, as he says; and the rule of the order was read to him, by one of the brothers, how he was to behave himself in all things relating to the order; and so he was instructed for a month by a learned serving brother, whose name was John Walpole aforesaid. Being asked whether he had afterwards made any other profession in public or in private, he answered he had not.

The judges and inquisitors enjoined Edmund Verney and William Herdely, the keepers of the said brothers, by no means to permit this Brother William to be with his other brothers, nor to talk to them or any of them; nor no person to come to inquire what was done or to be done in that particular; and this on pain of the greater excommunication to be incurred as if then pronounced.

Done at London in the chapter of the Monastery of the Holy Trinity, in the presence of the brothers, Ralph of Canterbury, the prior of the House of the Holy Trinity, etc.

Brother Hugh of Tadcaster, of the Order of the Temple, being asked how long he had been in the order, etc., says he was received at Farflete, in the diocese of Yorkshire, by Brother William More, in the oratory of that place, a little after sun-rising, and that no secular person was present when he was received; nor is it the custom for any secular person to be present at the reception of the brothers. Being asked concerning the manner of the reception, he says that he, while a secular, was entrusted with the keys in the temple, and desired the master to receive him as a brother, and having been acquainted with the rigorous parts in the Order of the Temple, and substantial parts of the order, as to obedience, chastity and poverty, he was led into the chapel, none being present but the brothers of the order, the chaplains, the knights and servants, all secular persons excluded; having taken his oath on God's holy gospels to observe the aforesaid three substantial points of the said order, and the good and commendable customs of the Order of the Temple, and to his power to advance the affairs of the Holy Land beyond the sea against the enemies of the Christian faith.

He also says, he swore, he would not unjustly disinherit any person, and then the mantle with the cross was delivered to him and the cap put upon his head.

He says also, that at Dynestre, in the chapter where Philip Mews, knight, was received a brother of the said order, he was received after the same manner as himself, and the brothers of the said order are not otherwise received.

Of the Destruction of the Order of the Templars, and the Goodness of William Grenefeld, Archbishop of York, towards Them

In the 2nd year of the pontificate of this pope (Clement above mentioned) the brothers of the Military Order of the Temple of Jerusalem, throughout all England, were on the same day, by the command of Pope Clement, at the instance as was said, of the King of France, apprehended and committed to close custody in London and York. In the mean time strict examination being made as well at York as at London concerning the articles alleged against them by their enemies, before the venerable Fathers William, Archbishop of York, and Ralph Baldock, Bishop of London, especially deputed for this purpose by the pope, the Templars themselves being present, and answering properly to all things objected against them; tho' many things were laid to their charge, yet nothing was found which of right might seem to overthrow their state. But afterwards, the same pope having assembled a general council at Vienna, in the 7th year of his pontificate and of our Lord 1312, being the 7th of pontificate of the aforesaid Father William, on Monday the 3rd of April, having taken the form of judiciary priests, by the advice of some brethren, and of others sitting there, he by apostolical authority condemned, made void, and forever annulled the most renowned order of the said knights of the temple. He moreover prohibited any person for the future entering into the said order or professing in it, or wearing, or receiving its habit, under pain of the greater excommunication to be *ispo facto* incurred by any who should do the contrary.

The aforesaid order being therefore extinguished, the brothers of the Hospital of St. John got most of their possessions, and afterwards enjoyed them. William, the archbishop, being moved with compassion at the state of the Templars of his diocese, who were destitute of all relief; he put them into several monasteries of his diocese, and ordered them to be continually supplied with necessaries at his expense.

CHAPTER 4

Eighteenth-Century Warriors

♣

There are several sodomy cases in English Admiralty records before 1700, but none of the prosecutions involved naval personnel. It was not until the reign of Queen Anne in the early eighteenth century that concern began to grow over what appeared to be a rapid increase in homosexuality. The main factor leading to the spread of the vice, according to several commentators, was the importation of Italian opera into England. Sodomy was no longer considered a simple crime caused by bad character, as was the case in the days of Queen Elizabeth and the early Stuart kings. It had become a foreign menace, a danger adopted from the corrupt, decadent, and ominously Catholic south. Whether or not it was actually on the increase is uncertain, but homoerotic display was surely becoming more frequent. Male brothels were by this time operating with a fair degree of openness in London, and the city hosted a large, conspicuous, and thriving homosexual subculture. The general concern with what the public perceived to be a decline in morality was in large measure responsible for such measures as the founding of the Society for the Reformation of Manners in the 1720s and the decades of antivice crusading that ensued.

The following cases include several of the earliest sodomy prosecutions conducted by the Royal Navy. A leitmotiv of the selections is pederasty, which appears to be involved in most such incidents that have left documentary records. While the courts-martial reflect the escalating concern over shipboard sexuality by the opening decade of the eighteenth century, the worry was occasionally tempered by mercy. In 1745 a Dutch naval lieutenant was tried for buggery on board a Dutch ship in an English port. He was convicted, and according to one account the usual punishment inflicted by lowlanders in such cases consisted of stuffing the sodomite into a sack containing large weights, then tossing the sack overboard. A number of Englishmen intervened in this instance, and the man's life was spared, although he was severely punished nonetheless. A court-martial record from the Revolutionary army in America that concludes the chapter indicates the rebellious colonists were probably less hostile to sodomites than either the English or the Dutch.

Court Martial of James Ball (ADM 1/5266)

At a Court Martial Held on Board Her Majesty's Ship the *Swallow* in Harwich Harbor on Wednesday the 9 of October 1706.

Present: Sir Edward Whitaker, Knight, Commander in Chief of the squadron of Her Majesty's ships ordered to cruise off Dunkirk, etc., President

Captains: Mighell, Haddock, Rumsey, Bertie, Richard Hughes, Hutchins, Vaughn

All duly sworn pursuant to a late act of Parliament, etc.

James Ball, Quarter Master, belonging to Her Majesty's ship, the *Swallow*, was accused and tried for the unnatural and detestable crime of buggery or sodomy by him committed on board the said ship on the body of Walter Jones, a boy aged about thirteen years, and also belonging to the same ship, on the 17th day of July 1706. The court, having strictly and fully examined into the grounds of this information after it appeared to the court by evidence upon oath, and by many other collateral proofs, that the said James Ball did by threat and violence compel the said Walter Jones to suffer the act of buggery, in this the said James Ball's cabin betwixt the hours of 9 and 10 o'clock of the night which said fact he, the said James Ball did then and there commit upon him. And it is resolved by the court that he is guilty of the charge laid against him, and that he falls under the 32nd article of a statute made in the 13th year of King Charles the 2nd which enacts and declares that any person or persons in, or belonging to the fleet that shall commit the unnatural and detestable sin of buggery or sodomy with man or beast, shall be punished with death without mercy, and accordingly the court does adjudge and pass sentence that he, the said James Ball, shall for so doing be hanged by the neck till he is dead, at such time and place as His Royal Highness, Prince George, Lord High Admiral of England, Ireland, etc., shall direct.

Then Walter Jones, the boy aforesaid on whom the said fact was committed, was called into court and further examined as to this matter, but it having appeared to the court by the course of the evidence that the said James Ball did by threatening and by force oblige the said boy to submit to this his wicked action, the court is of the opinion that the said Walter Jones was not consenting to the said act of buggery committed upon him, and therefore the court does acquit the said Walter Jones from this charge.

Act. in cur. {illegible}

{signature illegible} Deputy {?} Judge Advocate

/ss/ {illegible} Edward Whitaker, James Mighell, {illegible} Haddock, {illegible} Rumsey, {illegible} Bertie, Richard Hughes, {illegible} Hutchins, Fra: Vaughn

Court Martial of John Coise (ADM 1/5267)

At a Court Martial Held onboard Her Majesty's Ship, the *St. George* in the River of Lisbon, this 19th July 1709.

Present: Sir Jonathan Jennings, Admiral of the Blue Squadron of Her Majesty's Fleet, President

Captains: Koffy, Long, Trevanion, Cooper, Hopson, Walton, Fotherby, Chamberlen, Thompson, Harland, Kempthorne, Candler, Walpole, Hagar, Sapsford, Story

All being duly sworn according to the act of Parliament on that behalf.

Enquiry being made by the court into the circumstances of the accusation made by John Davis, a boy of about fifteen years old, that John Coise, boatswain of Her Majesty's Ship the *Looe*, committed the act of sodomy upon the said Davis, being his servant; but it only appearing to the court, by the evidence given by the surgeons of Her Majesty's Ships *Advice, Looe* and *Pool*, summoned to examine and search the said boy, that the said detestable sin of sodomy was never committed {illegible} the said Davis, but that however the said boatswain cannot clear himself of some indecent actions {illegible} the said Davis, tending that way; this court has thereupon resolved, that the said Coise falls under the 33 Article, and have therefore dismissed him from his employment of boatswain of Her Majesty's said ship; and that he is not fit to be any more employed in Her Majesty's service.

J. Jennings, K. Koffey, Thomas Long, W. Trevanion, J. Cooper, E. Hopson, G. Walton, Richard Thompson, Charles Fotherby, Peter Chamberlen, {illegible} Garland, Thomas Kempthorne, B. Candler, G. Walpole, J. Hagar, J. Sapsford, Edward Story.

A Copy
F. Hawes, {illegible} Deputy Judge Advocate

The Court Martial of Henry Bicks (ADM 1/5296)

Minutes of a Court Martial Held on Board His Majesty's Ship *Royal William* in Portsmouth Harbor on Monday the 27 day of June 1757, for the Trial of Henry Bicks, a Seaman Belonging to the said Ship for Sodomitical Practices.

Present: Thomas Broderick, Esq., Rear-Admiral of the White Squadron of His Majesty's Fleet, President

Captains: Richard {illegible}, James Douglas, William Gordon, Jonathan Barker, William Harman, Andrew {illegible}, Michael Scarritt, Edward Hughes, Joshua Rowley, Samuel Hood, Thomas Baillie, Thomas Burnet

Being all duly sworn

Lieutenant Willis—Sworn

Court: Do you know the prisoner?
Answer: Yes.

Court: Relate to the court what you know of this detestable crime he is charged with.

Answer: Sunday the 5th June about 11 o'clock at night Mr. Male, mate of the watch, brought down John Booth, a boy, desiring that I would inquire into a complaint that the boy had to make against the prisoner. I asked the boy what he had to say, and he told me that the prisoner had been very troublesome to him that day and made an excuse to the sentinel to pass from the *Magnanime* into the *Royal William* in order to follow the boy. He got into the gun room with him and there pulled down both his own and the boy's breeches, and that he had (as the boy said), buggered him. I asked the boy to explain himself, and how he came to be acquainted with that word, upon which the boy told me that the prisoner had put his thing into his backside. I asked the boy if it did not hurt him, and why he did not cry out for assistance and whether he did not find himself sore. The boy saying that he was very sore, I sent for Mr. Johnson, the surgeon's mate, and desired that he would examine him, who informed me there was no external sign of hurt. I then asked the boy if the prisoner had ever made such an attempt upon him before. He told me that he had on Saturday, the day before, on board the *Magnanime,* under the half deck. He came to him when he was in his hammock and there buggered him four times. I asked him why he did not then call out for assistance. He said he did cry out, and that Edward Gauble, a boy, lay near him. I then asked the boy why he did not between the two attempts complain to his officers, but he made me no answer to that, but I ordered the prisoner from what the boy had said to be put in irons.

On Monday the 13 June about 10 in the morning Thomas Found made another complaint to me that about 2 o'clock that morning, he being then sentinel over the prisoner, he saw him busy under some clothes that were laid over him, upon which the sentinel called to John Chapman, quarter gunner, who was then sentinel at the gunroom door. As soon as he came to him he threw the covering off the prisoner, and discovered the prisoner had got down the breeches of Stephen Fouhead {?}, who was also in irons on the same bolt and that the prisoner had hold of Fouhead's penis. He likewise called Silvanus Hopping, master at arms, to be a witness also.

Mr. Male, masters' mate, sworn

Court: Do you know the prisoner?

Answer: Yes.

Court: How did you first come to the knowledge of this boy's being buggered as he calls it by the prisoner?

Answer: Upon the 5 of this month, I had the first watch, and about 11 o'clock at night Mick Dowling with some others came upon the quarter deck and informed me that Bicks, the prisoner, was concerned with the boy the night before. I went for the boy and after hearing his complaint I carried him to the officer, but I know nothing farther.

John Booth, about 12 years old

Court: Do you know the prisoner?

Answer: Yes, his name is Henry Bicks.

Court: Tell the court what the prisoner did to you.

Answer: On Saturday night he came into my hammock when I was a sleep, and he unbuttoned his breeches and put his private part into my arse 4 times in my hammock that night and twice in this ship.

Court: What time was it when the prisoner was with you in this ship?

Answer: After it was dark.

Court: Did you call out when the prisoner was doing these things to you?

Answer: Yes—I did squeal out a little.

Court: Did he the prisoner ever offer any thing to you in the day time?

Answer: No.

Court: Then how do you know that it was the prisoner that came into your hammock?

Answer: I know him very well. He was my mess mate.

Court: What did the prisoner say to you?

Answer: He spoke to me a few words and asked me how I should like it. I told him I should not like it. The first time, he let down my breeches and pulled me upon him.

Court: How long did he continue with you in your hammock?

Answer: I cannot say how long, but a pretty while. I got out of my hammock and he followed me, and asked me if he should take my hammock down and if I would go and lay with him, but I told him no, and a little while after, I went into my hammock again, and when I was a sleep he came to me and did it again.

Court: Did he threaten you if you complained?

Answer: No.

Court: Who did you complain to?

Answer: To the sentinel over the small beer. He did it to me onboard the *Magnanime* on Saturday and in this ship on Sunday.

Court: Do you know if there was a sentinel upon the stage?

Answer: Yes, there was.

Edward Gauble sworn

Court: Relate to the court what you know of the prisoner buggering the boy, Booth.

Answer: I saw the prisoner in the boy's hammock with him and I heard the boy cry out and say that the man {illegible} him, but I saw nothing.

Court: Did the boy tell you what the man did to him?

Answer: No, I know not what the prisoner did to him, nor the boy never told me, but I saw this man get into the boy's hammock.

Court: Do you know how long the prisoner was in the boy's hammock?

Answer: No, I did not see him get out of the hammock.

Prisoner to the witness: How long did you lay awake after you say I went into his hammock?

Answer: About an hour. I went to sleep a little before 10.

Prisoner to the witness: Was I in the boy's hammock then?

Answer: Yes.

Prisoner: How do you know it was me?

Answer: I am certain it was you. I saw you by the light of the sentinel's candle.

Denis Strand, a marine, sworn

Court: Relate to the court what you know of the prisoner buggering (as it's called) the boy Booth.

Answer: The boy Booth came to me about 1/2 an hour after seven o'clock on the Sunday evening. I was the sentinel over the beer, and he asked me for a drink. I told him there was but little, and bid him call the cooper. There was a man with him (which the boy afterward told me was the prisoner) who said, where do you think he can find the cooper at this time. After which they both went from me and in about three quarters of an hour the boy came to me again, and said there was a man in the ship that wanted to lay with him all night on board the *Royal William*. I asked him what he meant by that, and if the man wanted to bugger him, and the boy said yes. And then I asked him if the man had ever done it to him. He said yes, that he had done it to him four times on Saturday night on board the *Magnanime* and twice that evening in the *Royal William*. I then asked the boy in what manner he did it to him, and the boy told me that he pulled down his breeches and then putting his hand upon his backside said he put his thing in there. I then asked him whether it was a man or a boy, and he said it was his mess mate and as big a man as myself.

James Clark sworn

Court: Do you know the prisoner?
Answer: Yes.
Court: Relate to the court what you know of him.
Answer: I was sentinel at the cabin door, and between 8 and 9 o'clock on Sunday evening the prisoner came to me and asked if I had seen Jonathan Quin. I told him no. He said I suppose he is got between decks a sleep, and he went down and I saw him no more that evening.
Court: What did you know the prisoner by?
Answer: I had a night or two before asked him for a chew of tobacco and he gave me two.

Mr. Johnson, surgeon's mate, sworn

Court: Do you know the prisoner?
Answer: Yes.
Court: Relate to the court what you know of his buggering the boy, Booth.
Answer: I was sent for one evening by Lieutenant Willis to examine the boy, Booth, who had complained of a soreness in his fundament. I did examine him, but could not perceive either soreness or inflammation or that there was any thing more than natural.

Court: Do you think if he had committed sodomy, then there would have been any outward sign?

Answer: I imagine not, but I cannot tell.

Prisoner's defense

William Bean, boatswain's mate, sworn

Prisoner to the witness: Did you not keep me up a Saturday night till 11 o'clock to work the ventilator?

Answer: Yes, I did.

Prisoner: Did you not then bid me go to my hammock?

Answer: I did.

Court: What time did you place the prisoner at the ventilator.

Answer: At 10 o'clock.

Court: Where was he from 8 o'clock till 10?

Answer: I do not know.

Court: Did the prisoner continue at the ventilator all the hour from 10 to 11 o'clock?

Answer: I cannot tell positively because I was upon deck some part of the time, but I saw him there tho' whither he wrought it or no, I cannot say.

Richard Bilton, a seaman, sworn

Prisoner to the witness: Can you tell what time we parted when we were drinking in our berth?

Answer: I do not remember that I saw you after supper which was about 7 o'clock. I continued in the berth till 8, and then I went to my hammock in the bay, and saw nothing of you after supper.

David Hicks, a seaman, sworn

Prisoner to the witness: Do you know what time we parted on Saturday night?

Answer: We were not together at all on Saturday night.

Thomas Towle, a marine, sworn

Court: Relate to the court what you know of the prisoner's behavior with Stephen Fouhead, when they were in irons together.

Answer: On the 13th of this month I was sentinel over them and about 2 o'clock in the morning I saw him, the prisoner, pull down Stephen Fouhead's breeches. He pulled Stephen to him by the private parts, and then pulled a blanket over them, and threw his leg across of Stephen. I saw the master at arms acoming and beckoned to him, and I called John Chapman also, a quarter gunner and sentinel at the gunroom door, who came and saw the prisoner with his leg across of Stephen Fouhead's, and the master at arms went with me, and uncovered the prisoners, and this man had Stephen by his prick, and the prisoner's breeches was also down as far as he could pull them.

Court: What posture were they laying in?

Answer: The prisoner was laying at the back of Stephen Fouhead with his leg over him, and had hold of his prick, who was then dead a sleep and drunk, and the master of arms and myself held him up and we buttoned up his breeches.

Court: Was the prisoner awake then?

Answer: Yes he was, and talked to the quarter gunner and asked him for some tobacco.

John Chapman, quarter gunner, sworn

Court: Relate to the court what you know of the prisoner's behavior with Stephen Fouhead who was in irons with him.

Answer: When I went sentinel I know that Stephen's breeches was up, and in about two hours after I saw them down. I saw the prisoner have hold of Stephen's shoulder with one hand, and have hold of his private parts with the other, and pulled him to him two or three times, and then the master at arms came and uncovered them, and I saw the prisoner draw his hand away.

Silvanus Hopping, master at arms, sworn

Court: Relate to the court what you know of the prisoner's behavior with Stephen Fouhead, who was in irons with him.

Answer: On the 13 of the month between two and three in the morning I wanted a light. I went to the sentinel who was over the prisoner and Stephen

Fouhead, and I found the sentinel at some distance from them, when he saw me he made a motion for me to go to him so I went and he informed me that he had seen something uncommon between the prisoner and Stephen Fouhead, so I went to them and pulled the blanket off, and saw the prisoner have Stephen Fouhead's yard in his hand. I then shook Fouhead two or three times before I could wake him, and at last by the help of the sentinel I got him upon his legs. His breeches was down to his knees, and I asked him how they came so. He told me that he was certain they were buttoned when he laid down, and how they came unbuttoned he could not tell. I then asked the prisoner, Bicks, how he could be guilty of such an action. Who answered that he did not know that he had been guilty of any thing.

Court: Was this prisoner drunk or sober at the time, or had he his breeches down?

Answer: I do not know whether he had or no, but he seemed sober and the other was quite drunk when he was put in irons.

Stephen Fouhead sworn

Court: Did you remember drinking any thing with the prisoner while you was in irons with him.

Answer: I had a can of flip, and believe I might ask him to drink once.

Court: Do you know how your breeches came unbuttoned?

Answer: No, I was very much in liquor, and do not remember any thing about them.

Then the prisoner having no questions to ask, the court was cleared and the following questions proposed:

Question 1: Has the charge been proved against the prisoner?
Agreed that it has been proved in part.
Question 2: What article of war does the prisoner fall under?
Agreed under a part of the second article
Question 3: What kind of punishment does he deserve?
Agreed: For him to have corporal punishment, and to be turned out of the service with a halter about his neck and a bill pinned upon his breast setting forth

the time after which he was discharged, he having been first punished with 500 lashes.

/s/ Robert Hardy
Appointed by the court to act as Deputy Judge Advocate

The Court Martial of Robert Garbut (ADM 1/5301)

Minutes of the Proceedings at a Court Martial Assembled on board His Majesty's Fireship, the *Strombollo*, at the Nore this 23 of October 1762. At the Trial of Robert Garbut, Boatswain of His Majesty's Sloop, *Spy*, for Attempting Sodomitical Practices with John Pyle, Belonging to the Said Sloop.

Present: William Gordon, Esq., Commander In Chief of His Majesty's Ships and Vessels at the Nore etc., President

Captains: John Falkingham, James Shirley, John Brooks, William Williams

The prisoner was brought into court by the marshal, and all persons who thought proper to be present were admitted.

The order for trying Robert Garbut, boatswain of the *Spy*, dated the 19th of October 1762 was read.

The court was sworn first, then the judge advocate agreeable to {the} act of Parliament.

The charge exhibited against the prisoner in a letter from Captain Hayward of the *Spy* sloop dated the 6th day of October 1762 directed to Commodore Gordon, as also another letter from Captain Hayward dated the {illegible} of the said month, directed to John Cleveland Esq., Secretary of the Admiralty.

The first evidence in support of the charge was Thomas Robertson, gunner of the *Spy*, who being called, deposed as follows:

On the 26th of last month, between the hours of nine and ten at night as I was coming out of the carpenter's cabin, I heard some of {*sic*} people calling one another buggerers. I said it was very bad language to be used on board a king's ship, on which five of the men came up after me, and told me that there was a young lad belonging to the fore top that had been guilty of sodomy with Mr.

Garbut. I asked them the lad's name. They told me John Pyle. I went on the forecastle and asked Pyle if ever he had been guilty with Mr. Garbut. He told me that Mr. Garbut, six or seven different times had attempted to commit sodomy with him. I asked him why he did not make a complaint there of to the commanding officer. He said he was afraid the boatswain would use him ill if he did. I told him that if he did not go immediately and complain, I would myself, on which he went and made a complaint to the officer of the watch. After he made the complaint he went down to the boatswain's cabin, and then the door was shut on them; this I saw myself.

Question: How long have you and the boatswain been brother officers in the *Spy?*

Answer: About two years.

Question: During that time had you ever any reason to suspect the boatswain of these practices?

Answer: He had been confined three or four months before for the same practices, in Captain Philips's time.

Question: Did you yourself ever at any time seem him guilty of any action of this nature, either in appearance or reality?

Answer: At no time.

Prisoner's question: You have been with me many times in my cabin both by night and day; did you ever see me guilty of any thing of this nature?

Answer: No never.

Evidence withdrew.

John Pyle examined:

The first time of the boatswain's attempt on me, he called me into his cabin to give me some marlin spikes. He took hold of my yard. He then ordered me out of his cabin. Next night he called me down again and took hold of my yard, and gave me a dram. He then ordered me out of his cabin as before. He called me down the next night but I did not go. The night after this, he again called me down, and I went down. He gave me a dram and pulled down my breeches, and attempted to bugger me. The next night he called me down and gave me three drams. He then pulled down my breeches, took hold of my yard, and again attempted to commit sodomy with me.

Question: Did he at any of these times commit sodomy with you?

Answer: No, he did not. I would not suffer him, but he attempted it.

Question: What was the manner of his attempt?

Answer: He pulled down my breeches, took hold of my yard, and attempted to get upon me.

Prisoner's question: When you came into my cabin did I pull down your breeches?

Answer: Yes.

Question: Where was I then?

Answer: Sitting on your bedside.

Question: Did I ever ask to bugger you?

Answer: Yes.

Evidence withdrew.

Isaac Cox being called, deposed as follows:

At sea in the boatswain's cabin, I saw him. The boatswain have John Pyle's yard in his hand. On seeing of this I immediately went and made a complaint to the officer of the watch.

Question: Did you ever see any thing further between them than what you have just now mentioned?

Answer: No, nothing.

Question: Are you positive it was the boatswain you saw?

Answer: Yes, I am sure it was him.

Evidence withdrew.

James Butler Broadbill, surgeon's mate, deposed as follows:

On the 26th of September last, I was called off the forecastle between nine and ten o'clock at night, and was told that Mr. Garbut, the boatswain, and John Pyle was committing of sodomy in the said boatswain's cabin, on which I went down to the cabin and looked thro' the keyhole and saw a man's yard in another man's hand as I took it to be, and whilst I was thus looking thro' the keyhole, I happened to strike the door with the sleeve of my coat twice. The yard was then dropped, and a bottle with a funnel was taken up as if they had been to put some liquor in it, on which I turned round and said to the people, that Mr.

Garbut was, I believed, only creating of pleasure to himself with his hand. The people then told me that Pyle was actually in with the boatswain and that they were sure he was concerned with him, and desired I would look again. Accordingly I looked thro' a crevice that was higher up than the keyhole and could see a yard in a man's hand {illegible} and Mr. Garbut's head and shoulder. I could see plainly in motion, but could not see anything of Pyle. I then desired the people to acquaint the officer of the watch immediately.

Question: Why did you not (seeing the boatswain in such a {illegible}) immediately break open his cabin?

Answer: I called on the commanding officer, but was afraid to break open his cabin door for fear of troubles.

Evidence withdrew.

James Sheerer, master, being called, deposed as follows:

On the complaint being made to me as officer of the watch, I immediately went to the door of the boatswain's cabin, where I saw a great many people standing. I looked thro' a crevice and saw the boatswain sitting on a locker in the after part of his cabin with a basin in his hand, as if he was making water. In a little after the door of the cabin was opened and John Pyle came out. I asked him what he had been about in the boatswain's cabin at this time of night. He answered, nothing, but on questioning him a little further, he confessed the boatswain and he had been handling one another's private parts. I then took him down to the lieutenant and acquainted him of what I had seen and heard, who told me that as he had the morning watch he would present it to the captain.

Question: What hour of the night did this happen?

Answer: At half past nine.

Question: How long have the boatswain and you been shipmates together?

Answer: About fourteen months.

Evidence withdrew.

Lieutenant George Insell, deposed as follows:

At half past nine at night on the 26th of September last, the master came down and acquainted me of this affair, on which I told him that as it was my morning watch, I would acquaint the captain which I accordingly did. Captain Hayward after enquiring into the truth of the affair, thought proper to have the boatswain confined, and ordered me to see him put into confinement which I immediately did.

Evidence withdrew.

Robert Garbut being put to his own defense, proceeded thus:

I never asked to commit the crime alleged against me in my life to my knowledge. That I took John Pyle into my cabin to draw off a bottle of brandy, and when he came into my cabin, he drew the door after him. After it was drawn off, he and I drank together two or three drams.

David Melvil, evidence for the prisoner:

Prisoner's question: Whether you ever knew me guilty of the crime laid against me?

Answer: Not to my knowledge.

Evidence Withdrew.

Philip Smith called by the prisoner:

Prisoner's question: Did you ever see or hear of my being guilty in an affair of this nature?

Answer: No. I never saw you guilty of any practice of the kind, but I have heard of it.

The Court was then cleared, and the president put the following question to the court:

Question: Is the charge of an attempt to commit the detestable crime of sodomy proved against the said Robert Garbut?

Answer: Unanimously proved.

Question: What article of war does he fall under?

Answer: Part of the second article.

Question: What punishment must be inflicted in consequence?

Answer: Unanimously, to be dismissed from His Majesty's service as an officer, and to be publicly drummed on shore with the usual marks of ignominy.

The sentence was then drawn up and signed.

Audience admitted.

Robert Garbut, the prisoner, was called into court and the sentence was read by the judge advocate.

The original sentence sent up on the {blank} October 1762.

The above is a copy of the minutes taken in court by James Bruce, Deputy Judge Advocate.

{Enclosed with the court-martial record is the following letter of James Bruce, the presiding judge advocate, to John Cleveland, Esq., Secretary of the Admiralty.}

Sir,

I have the honor to transmit {to} you the minutes of a court martial assembled for the trial of Robert Garbut, boatswain of His Majesty's sloop, *Spy*, as also an order for my officiating as judge advocate at the said trial, and a certificate of the number of days I was employed thereon, for which service I beg you will be pleased to move my Lords Commissioners of the Admiralty for their order that I may be paid. I am with the greatest respect—

Sir, Your most humble and obedient servant

James Bruce

Sheerness 31st October 1762

{To:} John Cleveland Esq.

The Gentleman's Magazine, February 1745

About the same time a court martial was held on board the Dutch admiral's ship at Spithead for the trial of the 1st lieutenant of one of their ships, for committing sodomy on the boatswain's son. He was found guilty, and ordered to be tied up in a sack with a large weight fastened to it, and flung overboard at high water (which is the usual punishment inflicted by the Dutch for crimes of that nature committed at sea), but his life was spared upon intercession of some

English gentlemen, and his sentence changed into a whipping, after which he was stripped of his clothes, and set on shore at Gosport in an old jacket and trousers to shift for himself. The admiral immediately dispatched to Holland an account of his proceedings to the States General, in order for the confiscating of the delinquent's estate and effects, worth £500 per ann. sterling.

George Washington

"General Orders"

At a general court martial whereof Colo. Tupper was president (10th March 1778) Lieut. {Frederick Gotthold} Enslin of Colo. Malcom's regiment tried for attempting to commit *sodomy*, with John Monhort a soldier; secondly, for perjury in swearing to false accounts, found guilty of the charges exhibited against him, being breaches of the 5th article, 18th section of the Articles of War and do sentence him to be dismissed the service with infamy. His Excellency the Commander in Chief {George Washington} approves the sentence and with abhorrence and detestation of such infamous crimes orders Lieut. Enslin to be drummed out of camp tomorrow morning by all the drummers and fifers in the army never to return; the drummers and fifers to attend on the grand parade at guard mounting for that purpose.

CHAPTER 5

Britain and the Wars against Napoleon

♣

Record keeping, particularly judicial record keeping, improved substantially from the late eighteenth century onward. This is nowhere more apparent than in the transcripts of Royal Navy sodomy trials. Accounts of proceedings from the Napoleonic wars onward contain far more information than is found in the documents from earlier cases.

It is not possible to speculate on the extent of sodomy in the navy on the basis of the number of courts martial during the period, but examination of the few dozen trials held at the Public Record Office indicates that punishments meted out to those convicted became progressively more brutal with the passing years. The severity reached its peak during the dark days when England felt most threatened by Napoleon's seemingly invincible armies. During that time, mariners convicted of sodomy could expect to swing from yardarms of His Majesty's ships.

Despite the limited number of cases, some trends are apparent. Almost all the defendants in the courts-martial were adults, while most of their partners in sodomy were boys. Threats or physical compulsion often characterized the sexual contacts between these men and their boys, and most of the accused were officers who had private cabins or similarly isolated berthing accommodations on board ship, where they could engage in sexual activity unobserved by ordinary crewmen. The men were most often brought to trial on the basis of accusations leveled against them by the unwilling boy or boys who were forced to engage with them in an assortment of sex acts. There are few cases involving pairs of consenting adults, and in each of those, the participants' lack of discretion led to their discovery by a third party and a subsequent report to a ship's lieutenant or captain.

Arthur N. Gilbert

"The *Africaine* Courts-Martial: A Study of Buggery and the Royal Navy"

On February 1, 1816, Captain Edward Rodney of the *Africaine* hanged four members of the ship's crew for buggery. At the same time, two others were punished for "uncleanness," a catchall term for all sexually deviant behavior. One, John Parsons, received 200 lashes, while the other, Jack Hubbard, was given 170 out of his sentence of 300, because the surgeon decided he could not take any more punishment without endangering his life. When the executions were completed, the bodies were sent to the hospital, according to custom, and Captain Rodney read the Articles of War to the assembled crew.

The *Africaine* had a reputation as a "man-fucking ship" long before evidence of sodomitic practices came to the attention of Captain Rodney, who was the youngest son of the famous English Admiral George Rodney. There were several reports of "uncleanness" on the ship early in 1815 and, on one occasion, two seamen were punished for "lying on a chest together one night." Until September, however, there was not sufficient evidence to justify a court-martial trial. In that month, while the ship was sailing home from the East Indies, a seaman named James Green was told by a shipmate, Dominico Gadize, who was later implicated himself, that Raphael Seraco and William Dane committed "unnatural acts," and on the basis of this information, Green decided to keep watch on these seamen in the future.

The *Africaine* made its way from the Cape of Good Hope to Saint Helena while Green watched and waited for evidence. Seraco and another seaman, James Cooper, soon suspected Green's intention, and it was not long before harsh words were exchanged. A few days after the ship left Saint Helena, Green went down to the galley and observed Frank Jean "occasionally catching hold of him [Cooper] by the private Parts." He also uttered some "expressions in

Italian" which Green believed to be indecent. Soon afterward, Seraco came into the galley and, in Green's words, "caught Cooper by the arm but Cooper said to him, 'It won't do yet.'"

On the basis of this rather flimsy evidence, Green reported his suspicions to Captain Rodney on October 8. Gadize had already informed the captain of his concern, noting that he and Sergeant Clarke of the marines had tried to find out if the crime had been committed. While they, too, had no hard evidence, they claimed "their suspicions were increased from conversations they had overheard." The captain determined to conduct an investigation of these charges, but, as one might expect, the crew members were reluctant to offer any information that might incriminate themselves or their shipmates. Rodney, however, was resourceful, and he convinced Cooper and Dane "that a discovery would in all probability sooner or later take place." If they were convicted, Rodney informed them, they faced "dreadful consequences," but a voluntary confession might predispose a Court-Martial Board to be merciful. Cooper and Dane then confessed to committing buggery and, in the process, implicated others. After that, accusations and counteraccusations flew thick and fast until 23 of the crew were implicated. Several were put in irons, and the *Africaine* sailed home with a major problem for the Royal Navy.

On the long voyage, Rodney and his lieutenants tried to determine which crew members were telling the truth. William Dane and James Cooper, who made the initial confession, had accused a number of others. Dane, for example, claimed he caught {Raphaelo} Treake and Seraco committing sodomy, while Cooper testified that in June of 1815, he "saw Raphaelo Seraco with his yard actually in the posterior of John Westerman." Cooper confessed to buggery in which he took "both the active and passive part in the intercourse" with Seraco, and to committing the "same crime with John Charles 4 times." Dane, furthermore, accused one of the ship's officers, Midshipman Christopher Beauchamp. In the captain's words, Dane "positively declared to us, that on or about the 12th June 1815, while a party of men were employed cutting wood in the neighborhood of Simons Town, and during the night while they were laying down in a tent, Mr. Beauchamp (who lay next to him) placed his yard between his thighs and in that position effected an emission."

Confessions and accusations were the order of the day. George Parsons said that Frank Jean had attempted sodomy on him while he was sleeping. Dane accused Emanuel Cross of buggering him "on the flag stones of the Galley," while Seraco claimed that in February 1815 he saw Cross with "his yard against the backside of the boy Christopher Jay and Cross's backside in quick motion as if he was committing the unnatural crime." Jay supported Seraco's testimony, claiming that on one occasion Cross had "effected an emission" between his thighs by leaning him against a gun on the main deck, and that three weeks later he committed the "unnatural crime" in his hammock.

In the atmosphere of fear and suspicion on the *Africaine*, any offense remotely related to buggery brought the captain and his lieutenants onto the scene. On October 13, four men were examined because they claimed that William Brown, a boatswain's mate, had said, "God must put it into men's heads to commit the unnatural crime of buggery." Following this line of reasoning, Brown had declared that "if God was to put it into his head to fuck a man he would as soon do it as fuck a woman." Thomas Wayman, a cook, and James Gibson, quartermaster, testified that Brown embellished his theological discourse by telling his shipmates that "he would do it to the skipper, any of the officers or ship's Company, even to Jesus Christ if he was in his coffin."

In spite of the diligence shown by the officers in investigating charges, it was difficult to separate truth from falsehood. Further, the number of implicated sailors and marines was so great it would have been ludicrous to try them all for buggery. Raphael Seraco alone had accused 23 crew members, and the thought of 15 or 20 men hanging from the yardarm of the *Africaine* was too much for even the most ferocious moralist. The navy rarely hanged that many men for mutiny, a crime most officers admitted was more dangerous to the ongoing life of the service than buggery.

When the *Africaine* reached Portsmouth harbor in December, the Admiralty Office became involved in the case almost immediately. Special investigators were sent to Portsmouth to determine which members of the crew should be formally tried before a Court-Martial Board. Once again, most of the crew were questioned, this time by Captain George Jones aboard the *Queen Charlotte*, where the courts-martial would later be held, and supporting evidence was gathered as well. For example, it was customary in buggery trials to call in a ship's surgeon to examine the men for signs of penetration. Needless to say, too much time had passed for rectal examination, but the surgeon's role was still important, as in the case of James Cooper, who had developed an inflamation of the urethra. Surgeon James McDonnell was asked to identify its cause, and while he thought it unlikely that Cooper had any contact with women on the voyage home—making buggery a possible cause—he admitted he could not "speak definitely" to the cause of the complaint. McDonnell was also called to examine Frank Jean, who claimed he was incapable of committing buggery because he was impotent. The surgeon found "Frank Jean's parts of generation perfect."

Even with professional investigators interrogating the crew of the *Africaine*, it was impossible to learn the truth. Several factors affected the decisions on which crew members to try and who would testify against them. It is possible that racial considerations played some role in these decisions. Two of the seamen tried and hanged for sodomy were Italians, and the English had long believed this was a popular pastime in Italy. Buggery was known commonly as *le vice Italien*, and one eighteenth-century English writer referred to Italy as "the mother and nurse of sodomy," while eminent legal authorities such as Edward Coke claimed "the Lombards had brought into the realm the shameful sin of sodomy." The two principal witnesses in the courts-martial trials were Emanuel Cross, described as a black or Spaniard from Santo Domingo, and Frank Jean, a Portuguese sailor from Madeira. The pretrial and trial testimony contains racial slurs against these two men, and their willingness to cooperate fully with the prosecution may have stemmed from racial and ethnic prejudice against their shipmates.

More significant was the fact that in the atmosphere of terror surrounding the December interrogations, those under suspicion would have testified to anything if they felt that cooperation with the prosecution would free them. This is not to say that the prosecutors behaved improperly. Charles Bicknell later claimed, and there is no reason to doubt him, that during the investigation it was made clear to each man that he was "not bound to incriminate himself" and that there was no promise of pardon for cooperation with the prosecutors. During one trial, the prosecutor's assistant, John Purcell, testified that neither Cross nor anyone else was offered a pardon during the pretrial investigation. Still, Cross, the star witness in all the trials, had been accused of buggery by Seraco, Hubbard, and Jay. A reading of the pretrial evidence suggests that as strong a case for conviction and death could have been constructed against Cross as against Seraco or any of those ultimately executed. While Cross was not specifically offered a pardon, it seems clear he believed this would be his reward for cooperation. During one trial, he stated that he was unsure whether he would be tried by court-martial, but "the impression on my mind was that I always had a hope of being liberated because I never did anything with any person."

A number of other crew members—indeed several who had confessed to buggery—also escaped trial. Jay, a 14-year-old boy who claimed that Cross had buggered him three times, was set free, perhaps because his testimony implicated the main witness. Rainbow Archer, another boy, was freed because he agreed to testify against Treake. William Dane and James Cooper, who made the original confessions, were not tried because they testified against Seraco, Westerman, Charles, Treake, and, in Dane's case, Christopher Beauchamp, one of the officers tried for buggery.

On December 27, Seraco and Westerman were tried for buggery and sentenced to death. On January 1, Seraco was again brought to trial, this time with Charles, and both men pleaded not guilty to the charge of buggery. Some of the evidence presented at the trial was strictly of the hearsay variety. For example, Benjamin Horlick was asked if the two prisoners were suspected of unnatural acts. He replied, "Yes they were. There were not many in the ship, but had suspicion of them." More specifically, Emanuel Cross testified that he had seen Westerman and Charles under a tarpaulin on the quarterdeck and saw the tarp move. He also stated that on another occasion he saw both prisoners in the act. Charles, he said, "lifted up his shirt and his backside was bare—Seraco stood behind him with his shirt up. He put his yard into the backside of Charles— they moved the same as between a man and a woman."

James Cooper gave what was, perhaps, the most damning testimony: "Seraco put the question to me whether I would let him fuck me. I told him I did not much mind. He connected with me forward on the Starboard side. He entered my backside—I did the same with him three times. John Charles the prisoner was the first who mentioned the thing to me or I should never have had such a thought in my head." The trial lasted one day, and both men were sentenced to death—Seraco for the second time.

On January 2, Raphaelo Troyac (alias Treake) and Joseph Tall were tried for the same offense. Cross testified he had seen the prisoners committing buggery three times. John Clarke added that he had been propositioned by Treake, who offered him a new jacket if he would commit the "unnatural crime" with him. Clarke stated, "It was known fore and aft the ship by everyone that those in the galley were guilty of it." Thomas Bottomy told the court he had caught Treake and Westerman committing buggery, and that Treake had propositioned him, while William Dane said he had seen Treake and Seraco do it quite openly in the galley. Finally, Rainbow Archer testified that Treake had attempted sodomy, but when he could not effect entry, emitted upon his thighs. On January 3, Treake and Tall (who was granted a royal pardon soon after) were sentenced to death.

The Court-Martial Board and the Admiralty Office were uneasy about the mounting list of death sentences. Further, there was some question whether or not the trials had been conducted according to accepted legal practice, so the first trial Minutes were forwarded to the attorney general and the solicitor general for an opinion. On January 3, three legal officers of the crown, Jervis, Garrow (attorney general), and Shepherd (solicitor general), handed down the opinion that "no doubt can be entertained that the capital offence of which the Prisoners have been found guilty and sentenced to death has in point of law been repeatedly perpetrated by them, if the facts deposed by these several witnesses are true." They further concluded that there was no reason to suspect the witnesses were influenced by "malice or revenge" or other "corrupt and improper motives."

Still, there was one disturbing aspect of the trials of concern to the crown lawyers. Evidence had been introduced at the trials that implicated one or another of the prisoners in unnatural acts with others who were not on trial—a violation of the English law practice of excluding information that did not bear *directly* on the charge. On January 5, the lawyers objected to James Cooper's testimony in the Seraco-Charles trial on the ground that "he was directed to relate everything he knew *relative to the charge* but his evidence had no relation to those charges but to the imputation of unnatural practices with himself." Seraco and Charles were accused of sodomitic practices *with each other*, and evidence of buggery with other members of the crew was not admissible.

On the following day, the attorney general made a fuller statement of his objection to the practice of allowing extraneous evidence in the Treake-Tall case: "I am bound to say that if the conviction of these prisoners had taken place at any Court of Sessions where evidence like that which has been received and admitted and I had been called upon by the Secretary of State to report on it, I should have felt myself bound to advise that the Sentences should not be carried into execution."

Garrow argued that it was possible that the Court-Martial Board members, "who might have hesitated to find Tall (a man of good character) guilty on the single testimony of Cross," convicted him because several witnesses testified that he had committed unnatural acts with others. The other crown lawyers concurred, and on January 9, they recommended that the Treake-Tall sentences not be carried out. Nevertheless, they agreed that it was perfectly proper to try Treake a second time (or a third time, presumably), but not again for committing sodomy with men on the *Africaine* not specifically mentioned in the charge.

On this basis, Treake was tried again for buggery with a 17-year-old boy, George Hubbard. Once again Emanuel Cross was called into court, and he testified that he had observed Treake and Hubbard—who was always the "woman"—three times. On one occasion, he recalled, they "went through the Act and had not shame, and they finished—and they deliberately buttoned their trousers up without being affected by my presence." Again, however, extraneous evidence was allowed. Cross continued, "As far as I can recollect I have seen Treake with four or five besides Hubbard." Another "witness" for the prosecution admitted he had never seen Treake and Hubbard engaged in "unnatural acts" but claimed he heard talk of Treake buggering Westerman, and that "all the scandalous behavior in the *Africaine* has been owing to Treake and Seraco, they are the origin of the whole of it." Treake was sentenced to death once more, and Hubbard to 300 lashes.

The trials continued. John Parsons was put on trial for uncleanliness, but the evidence was not substantial and he was acquitted. Ten days later he was again tried for uncleanliness with another sailor and given 200 lashes.

On January 15, the first of the ship's officers, Midshipmen Christopher Beauchamp and James Bruce, were brought before the Court-Martial Board. The main witness in this case was Frank Jean, who claimed he had seen them commit sodomy but could not testify that he had seen the "yard" of either of them penetrate the anus of the other. While proof of penetration was defined in various ways in the eighteenth century, in this case the court refused to convict. Jean had seen "motion," but not penetration. Emanuel Cross's testimony was even more circumstantial: he had seen Beauchamp and Bruce go into the roundhouse together and observed Bruce "come out buttoning his trousers" a few minutes later.

Unlike many of the seamen tried for buggery, Beauchamp was reasonably well educated and was able to fashion an intelligent and competent defense. With Bruce and Crutchly, he combed the standard legal texts of the day on the long voyage back to England and during early January before he came to trial. He began, for example, by quoting Blackstone's commentary on sodomy: "It is a crime which ought to be strictly and impartially proved but it is an offense of so dark a nature, so easily charged and the negative so difficult to be proved that the accusation should be clearly made out for if false it deserves a punishment inferior only to that of the crime itself." Beauchamp tried to discredit his principal accusers on three closely related grounds: (*a*) they were motivated by revenge; (*b*) they were sodomites themselves; and (*c*) they were testifying against him in order to save their own lives. Cross admitted under examination that "Mr. Beauchamp has often beat me for not coming to work, very often four or five times with a bamboo but as it was his duty, I do not wish to complain." He noted that this had not influenced his testimony, but needless to say, we cannot tell if this were true.

Both Cross and Jean were accused of buggery in the pretrial hearings. Cross admitted that he had been put in irons on one occasion for, in his words, "having pulled down the trousers of the soldiers," but he claimed he had been falsely accused. Beauchamp described Jean as a "sodomite as he is clearly proved before you to have been in the other trials," and accused him and Cross of trying "to screen themselves and elude their own prosecution of their infernal guilt." Because of the suspicion that these two principal witnesses were testifying to save themselves, the court questioned Cross closely on this matter. Cross's answers were ambiguous: "I am not certain, on condition, I told everything I knew a Pardon was held out to me. . . . but then he [Jones] said 'if you will tell all the truth and everything you know you shall be pardoned.'"

It was clear the prosecution did not have enough evidence to convict Beauchamp and Bruce of buggery, but the two men were also on trial for "uncleanliness." The evidence on this charge was not particularly strong either, but the prisoners were at a great disadvantage because they had confessed to the crime. Beauchamp argued that the confessions were meaningless because:

terrified as we were in the idea of being prosecuted for the horrible crime imputed to us, dismayed and alarmed—we submitted to an examination of us separately made, and in the duress of our situation, our minds and feelings every moment distorted by hope and fear without a friend to counsel us . . . and in the hope amidst such a confusion of feelings that an acknowledgment of the minor offense of boyish indecent indisposition would insure us compassion and avert the evil we feared . . . we confessed.

Bruce and Beauchamp were found guilty of the lesser charge and "rendered incapable and unworthy of ever serving His Majesty, His Heirs or Successors, in any capacity again." They were to have their uniforms stripped from them on the *Africaine*, and sentenced to two years of solitary confinement in the Marshalsea prison.

On January 16, a third officer, W. L. Crutchly, was tried for sodomy and uncleanliness with George Parsons. The only witness with direct evidence was Cross, who claimed he had seen "the prisoner Crutchly put his yard into the orifice of the boy Parsons." On the uncleanliness charge, Cross testified he "saw the boy's hand go up and down on his [Crutchly's] yard. Doing what is called frigging, until an emission took place." Crutchly presented his defense along the same lines as Beauchamp's. He argued that Cross understood he would be pardoned for testifying against others, and described him as "an individual whose very looks and manners are hellish not only assimilated to the horrible crime he perpetrates but constantly whilst he was giving his evidence against me . . . even in Court ferocious and malicious." Like Beauchamp, Crutchly was convicted on the uncleanliness charge and given the same sentence. Because of his youth, Parsons received only six months in prison.

Although Crutchly had been dismissed from the service and Treake sentenced to death, each was tried before yet another Court-Martial Board. Crutchly claimed that he was no longer under the jurisdiction of the Court-Martial Board, but his petition was dismissed. In the third Treake trial, the prisoner was accused of sodomy with Thomas Bottomy, John Westerman, and Seraco. No one could testify to penetration during the act with Seraco, but once again Emanuel Cross came forward and told the court: "I am positive of having seen the yard of Treake between the faces or cheeks of the boy's [Bottomy's] backside, but I cannot take upon myself to swear beyond that they moved to-gether for the spate of four or five minutes."

Of greater importance was the testimony of Bottomy, who not only con-fessed that Treake had buggered him but stated he had seen him do it to West-erman as well. Frank Jean also said he had seen Treake and Westerman. Treake was sentenced to death once again—this his third capital sentence of the month.

On January 30, the series of courts-martial finally ended when Crutchly was tried again, this time for "scandalous actions" and uncleanliness with William Lockhart. Henry Ball and John Whitly said they saw the two embrace and kiss each other, and this was sufficient to convict Crutchly of the charge.

The corporal and capital punishments were carried out on February 1, 1816. Admiral Hornsborough reported to the Admiralty Office that "the four men died truly penitent acknowledging the justice of their sentences and admon-ishing their shipmates to take warning from their unhappy fate not to be guilty of such detestable practices."

In the meantime, an inquiry was launched by the Admiralty Office into con-ditions on the *Africaine* to discover why "immorality" was rife on that particu-lar ship. On January 21, William Crocker instructed Hornsborough to conduct an investigation of the "state of the discipline of the *Africaine* and neglect of the performance of Divine Service and the reading of the Articles of War." Crocker wrote that since buggery and "uncleanliness" had been practiced on the *Africaine* for a long time, there was "strong suspicion that the state of discipline was extraordinarily lax." On January 31, Hornsborough replied that three cap-tains had been appointed to board the *Africaine* and investigate the situation thoroughly. The investigating team spent most of its time questioning the ship's lieutenants on whether or not Captain Rodney was a good disciplinarian. All the lieutenants supported Rodney. Lt. William Sturgess said the captain had in-vestigated several reports of uncleanliness, but found no evidence, and that "Captain Rodney had paid as much attention to the discipline of his ship" as other captains he had served under. Lt. McAldon testified that "Captain Rod-ney has always paid the utmost attention to the general discipline of the *Africaine*." The lieutenants did admit, however, that divine services were sel-dom held on the ship, and the Articles of War were read infrequently.

The report of the three captains was forwarded to the Admiralty Office, and on February 5 the office signified "their regret and displeasure at his [Rodney's] neglect in not having caused the Articles of War to be read . . . and that he did not, although there was no chaplain, provide as is usually done in similar cases for the performance of divine service or the observance of the Lord's Day on board the *Africaine*." No further action was taken against Captain Rodney or any member of his crew.

Discussion

The *Africaine* courts-martial are interesting for a number of reasons. They are an excellent example of the problems encountered in courts of law when morals or victimless crimes are at issue. The Court-Martial Boards faced serious difficulties in determining the nature of admissible evidence. In a murder trial, for instance, it was fairly simple to define and rule out all evidence without specific bearing on the crime. In buggery cases, admissible evidence was far more problematic. Was a purported bugger on trial for committing sodomy with a particular individual, or for an inclination toward buggery in general? Conforming to traditional English practice, the attorney general and solicitor general suggested that testimony of buggery or unclean acts other than those cited in the specific charge was extraneous evidence, but in making this decision they opened the door to what could be an endless series of trials of the same man for every illicit sexual act he had performed. By making each relationship and act a separate crime, it was possible to try Parsons, Crutchly, and Treake several times over, with Treake receiving three death sentences in one month—surely some kind of naval record.

Blackstone, Hale, and other English jurists had warned that sodomy, like rape, was difficult to prove and even more difficult to disprove. While it is reasonably certain that buggery was prevalent on the *Africaine*, it is by no means clear that all the men punished for it were actually guilty. Much of the evidence came, as we have seen, from two "eyewitnesses," Frank Jean and Emanuel Cross. It is likely that both men would have been capitally convicted themselves if they had not agreed to cooperate with the prosecution. Further, Cross, in particular, seems to have had an unusual penchant for being "in the right place at the right time." Indeed, it is amazing how often he "witnessed" acts of buggery and uncleanliness, and was close enough to testify to penetration as well.

We also get a vivid picture of the terror that the "abominable and detestable sin" conjured up in the minds of many men in the early nineteenth century. While Beauchamp was probably overstating his own aversion to sodomitic practices to clear his name, it is evident that his fear was quite real when he described sodomy as "a crime which would to God t'were never more seen on earth from those shades of hellish darkness whence to the misery of Man its propensity has been vomited forth." It is possible that Beauchamp and Crutchly really did confess to uncleanliness simply out of fear of the buggery charges.

Finally, it is safe to say that few crimes in the eighteenth and early nineteenth centuries were treated with such severity as buggery. While buggery was difficult to prove, when it was demonstrated to the satisfaction of the Court-Martial Board the resultant sentence was usually death. Conviction for unclean or indecent behavior meant a lashing far in excess of those usually demanded for mutiny, desertion, or robbery. Indeed, the sentences given to Parsons and Hubbard were relatively mild compared to the number of lashes inflicted on other men convicted of deviant behavior during this period.

After the *Africaine* courts-martial, the number of trials for uncleanliness and buggery declined. Attitudes toward crimes of all sorts were changing rapidly, and the harsh penal code that characterized the eighteenth century was giving way to the more enlightened practices of the nineteenth century. In 1829, the Royal Navy held its last court-martial in which a man received the death sentence for buggery, but it was not until 1861 that the crime was formally removed from the capital list in England.

The Court Martial of Bartlet Ambler (ADM 1/5369)

Minutes of Proceedings at a Court Martial Held onboard His Majesty's Ship *Salvador del Mundo* in Harmoaze on Monday the 22nd Day of April 1805.

Present: The Right Honorable William Earl of Northesk, Rear Admiral of the White and Second Officer in the Command of His Majesty's Ships and Vessels at Plymouth, President

John Sutton, Esquire, Rear Admiral of the Blue

Captains: Charles Boyles, Thomas Byam Martin, John Cooke, the Right Honorable Lord Cochrane, William Lechmere, James Nicoll Morris, Richard King, Josias Rowley

Robert Liddel, Deputy Judge Advocate

Being all the admirals and captains of post ships according to seniority

The prisoner was brought into court and the evidence {illegible} audience admitted.

Read the order of the Right Honorable the Lords Commissioners of the Admiralty, dated the 25th of March 1805. The Right Honorable William, Earl of Northesk, Rear Admiral of the White and Second Officer in the Command of His Majesty's Ships and Vessels at Plymouth to Try Mr. Bartlet Ambler, mate of His Majesty's sloop, *Tisiphone,* for having been guilty in several instances of a breach of the 29th Article of War.

Read the warrant appointing a judge advocate.

Then the members of the court and the judge advocate, in open court and before they proceeded to trial respectively took the oaths directed by act of Parliament passed in the 22nd year of the reign of King George the Second.

Read the 29th Article of War.

A letter from Captain William Foote, commander of His Majesty's Sloop, *Tisiphone,* to William Marsden, Esq., etc., was then read as follows:

> His Majesty's sloop, Tisiphone {illegible} etc.
>
> March 19th 1805.
>
> Sir:
>
> Whereas it having been represented to me that Bartlet Ambler, mate of His Majesty's sloop *Tisiphone,* under my command has been guilty in several instances of a breach of the 29th Article of War, I have to request my Lords Commissioners of the Admiralty will be pleased to give directions that a court martial may be held on him for such misconduct. I have the honor to be, Sir, your most obedient, humble servant.
>
> W. Foote
>
> To William Marsden Esq., Admiralty

All the witnesses except the first to be sworn, being then ordered to withdraw and to attend their examinations separately, they all withdrew accordingly and the court proceeded to trial as follows:

Evidence in support of the charge:

John Davy, a volunteer of the third class onboard His Majesty's sloop, *Tisiphone*, aged thirteen years, having been interrogated and instructed into the nature of an oath, was sworn and examined as follows:

Prosecutor: Relate all you know respecting the charge against the prisoner.

Witness: About 3 months ago, one night after the gunroom had done tea, about 7 o'clock, the prisoner called me as he was sitting alone in his cabin and said to me are you in a great hurry? Not knowing what he meant, I said I was in no great hurry. He then put out his light that was in his cabin and drew the curtain of his cabin door. He sat down. I stood before him. He unbuttoned his breeches. He took my hand and put it into his breeches and told me to turn round. He then unbuttoned my breeches. He took me round the middle. I refused it and wanted to go out. He said don't be frightened. I shant hurt you. After I was turned round he took his cock and put it in my arse. He tried to put it in so far as he could. He put it in so hard that {it} made me cry out. I thought they heard it in the gunroom. After he had done that, he found I would not let him put it in my backside, he began putting it between my thighs and the water ran down my thighs. And then he told me to button up my breeches, and I had scarce buttoned up my breeches when he said be sure don't tell no person. I'll be very good to you, but if you tell any person of it I'll get you flogged. I did not make him any answer but went out of the cabin.

About a month after, I was going by the gunroom door about the same time in the evening as when the prisoner first called me into his cabin. The prisoner called me to his cabin door and said he wanted me. I thought he was going to do as he did the first time so I refused to go in. O says he, come along in and he took me by the coat and hauled me in. After I was in I refused to bide in. I said I did not like no such works. He then blew out the light and drew the curtain. He unbuttoned his breeches and took my hand and put it in his breeches and put his cock in my hand and told me to draw it to and fro. Then unbuttoned my breeches. I told him I did not like to bide there. Says he, don't be afraid, I shant hurt you. He told me to turn round. I wanted to go out, but he held me round the middle and I could not. Then he took his cock and put it in my backside again. He made me bend down, then, he put it in so hard that I stood upright as I could, and would not let him put it in my backside. Then he began putting it between my thighs again. The water ran down my thighs. Then I wiped my thighs and buttoned up my breeches and went out. I went into the gunroom and told the gunroom servant, James Ford, of it.

Somewhat less than a month after that, I was in the master's cabin about nine o'clock at night making up my master's bed. The prisoner came to me and asked me for a light. I said, Sir, if you please. When he was taking a light he said come over to my cabin bye and bye. I have some thing to give you. Very well, Sir, says I. So I made up my master's bed and the cabin to right and blew out the light. I was going into the gunroom. The prisoner stopped me. I asked him what he wanted of me. I saw him sit down. I went into the cabin. Then he blew out the light. Then I wanted to go out and he would not let me. I told him I was in a hurry. Says he, I suppose you are not in a hurry for a minute. Then he unbuttoned his breeches and he unbuttoned mine. Then he told me to turn round. I was standing facing him, and while I was so standing he put his cock between my thighs. Then he told me to turn round. I turned round and then he put his cock in my backside. He began putting it in so hard as he could. I told him I did not like no such works. Then he told me to button up my breeches, and he gave me three pence half-penny. There was no person in the gunroom then but the other servant, James Ford, and me, so I told him how the prisoner served me, and I told him that I would make it known and told him what the prisoner had given me.

Prisoner: Are you sure it was me that was in the cabin and treated you as you have related?

Answer: It was him and no person else.

Court: Have you ever consulted with the other boys who are witnesses in this case as to what you should say in evidence against the prisoner?

Answer: No. I never mentioned a word to any of them nor did any person ever say any thing to me about what I should say.

The witness withdrew.

John Wilcott, a volunteer of the third class onboard His Majesty's sloop, *Tisiphone*, aged 12 years, having been interrogated and instructed into the nature of an oath, was sworn and examined as follows:

Prosecutor: Relate all you know respecting the charge against the prisoner.

Witness: About 3 months ago, I was on deck playing along with the boys. The prisoner told me to come down below that he wanted me. I went down and he came down and had me into his cabin. I did not know what he was going to do to me. He unbuttoned my breeches and then he took and laid me down on his bed. Then he pulled my trousers down. Then he put his cock into my arse and kept on shoving and when he had done with me he gave me 3 pence and told me I should not tell any body.

About a fortnight after, the prisoner called me down and said he wanted me to clean his shoes. He called me into his cabin. Then he pulled my breeches off and laid me down. Then I sung out and he stopped my mouth with his hand. He took his cock and shoved it up my arse as hard as ever he could. When he had done with me, he told me that I should not tell any body of it. If I did, that he would get me flogged the next minute.

About a month after the second time, I was down by my master {in} the carpenter's cabin. Then the prisoner called me into his cabin. I did not know what he wanted with me. I went into the cabin. Then he blowed the light out and drawed the curtain. Then he unbuttoned my breeches and laid me on his bed. Then he buggered me, by shoving his cock up my arse. When I went out he said if I did tell any body he would get me flogged.

Court: Have you ever consulted with the other boys who are witnesses in this case as to what you should say in evidence against the prisoner?

Answer: No. I never did.

Court: How many times have you been flogged and for what?

Answer: Nine times. Once for not having my master's kettle boiled. The other times for skylarking, or playing about at marbles, etc.

Court: Did you tell any body of what the prisoner had done to you?

Answer: When the boy Oliver, a supernumerary, went round in the gun brig to Plymouth to be paid with a division of the people, he told what the prisoner had done to other boys, and when they came back to the *Tisiphone*, the boatswain taxed me with it and I confessed it to him.

Court: Was the boatswain or your master on bad terms with the prisoner?

Answer: I do not know that they were.

Court: Before this business happened to you, did you ever hear from any other of the boys that they had been served so by the prisoner?

Answer: No. I never heard it from any of them.

The witness withdrew.

Richard Hopkins, a volunteer of the third class onboard His Majesty's sloop, *Tisiphone,* aged 13 years and 6 months, having been interrogated and instructed into the nature of an oath, was sworn and examined as follows:

Prosecutor: Relate all you know respecting the charge against the prisoner.

Witness: About 4 months ago, since Christmas, I was on deck. The prisoner called me down into his cabin and he got a light. Then he put me on the bed, and put the light out and shut the cabin door. He unbuttoned my breeches. Then he unbuttoned his breeches. Then he put his cock in my bottom. Then I cried out and somebody knocked at the door. Then he put his hand to my mouth to stop my noise. He said if I told he would have me flogged. About an hour after that, the prisoner called me into his cabin again and I would not go. About ten minutes after he called me into the cabin again. I went in. The prisoner unbuttoned my breeches. Then he unbuttoned his breeches. He shut the door and blew the candle out. He then let me out of the cabin without doing any thing to me.

Court: How long is it since you first told of these circumstances?

Answer: About a month ago to the lieutenant onboard the *Tisiphone.*

Court: Did you feel the prisoner's prick within your body?

Answer: I did and I singed out.

Court: How long did the prisoner's prick remain in your body?

Answer: Not above a minute.

Court: What did you feel in consequence of his prick being in your body?

Answer: I could not hold my water at that time.

Court: Did you feel any thing come from the prick of the prisoner while it was in your body?

Answer: No.

Court: Have you ever consulted with the other boys who are witnesses in this case as to what you should say in evidence against the prisoner?

Answer: No.

Court: Before the business happened to you, did you ever hear from any other of the boys that they had been served so by the prisoner?

Answer: Not before. But Wilcott told me that the prisoner had served him so, after I had been so treated.

Court: Did you tell Wilcott first what had happened to you? Or did he first tell you what had happened to him? And what other boys were present at the time?

Answer: He told me first what had happened to him. No other boy was present at the time.

Court: Have you ever been flogged on board the *Tisiphone?*

Answer: Yes, twice, for having broke things of my master's.

Court: What other boys have you spoken to since about this matter?

Answer: To none.

Court: How came it to be known that the prisoner had treated you as you have related?

Answer: One of the boys who came round in the gun brig told it. I do not know how he came to know it.

Court: Did you tell of it to any of the officers?

Answer: No.

Prisoner: You have said that while you was in my cabin some one knocked at the door. Did that person then speak?

Answer: No. No person spoke then.

Prisoner: Did a person at the time you heard the knock at the cabin door speak to me or ask me a question?

Answer: No. I did not hear any person speak.

Prisoner: If I forced you and stopped your mouth as you have stated, why did you not inform some person of it as soon as you got out of the cabin?

Answer: He said if I spoke of it to any body he would have me flogged.

The witness withdrew.

Joseph Gammicliff, a volunteer of the 3rd class onboard His Majesty's sloop, *Tisiphone*, aged 12 years and 11 months, having been interrogated and instructed into the nature of an oath, was sworn and examined as follows:

Prosecutor: Relate all you know respecting the charge against the prisoner.

Witness: One night about 7 or 8 months ago, before Christmas, about 10 o'-clock, the prisoner asked me to come into his cabin. He asked me where my father and mother lived. I told him. Afterward he put out the light and threw me upon the bed. He unbuttoned my trousers and then unbuttoned his own. He then put his cock in my arse. Every time I made an attempt to cry out he stopped my mouth. And he told me if I told any person of it he would get me flogged. Then he told me to go along. A good while after, the prisoner asked me to step into his cabin. I told him I could not come in. I went away. The prisoner asked me to go in another time but I would not go in.

Court: Have you ever consulted with the other boys who are witnesses in this case as to what you should say in evidence against the prisoner?

Answer: No.

Court: Did you feel the prisoner's prick within your body?

Answer: I felt it about an inch within my body.

Court: How long did the prisoner's prick remain in your body?

Answer: Not long. He took it out and in. I would not give him time.

Court: What did you feel in consequence of his prick being in your body?

Answer: Nothing particular.

Court: Did you tell any body of what had been done to you?

Answer: No.

Court: Why did you not tell some body of it?

Answer: The prisoner told me if I told any body of it he would get me flogged.

Court: Was you ever flogged?

Answer: Yes, several times.

Court: Had you any conversation with the other boys about what you or they should say when examined at {two words illegible}.

Answer: No.

Court: To what boy did you first tell that this had happened to you or who did you hear speak of it before you mentioned it?

Answer: The boy, Hopkins, told me it had happened to him, and three other boys said they had been treated so, and I told them that I had been so treated. They told me it before we were had before the captain on the occasion.

The witness withdrew

Thomas Hooper, a volunteer of the 2nd class onboard His Majesty's sloop, *Tisiphone*, aged 11 years. Being examined by the judge advocate as to the nature of an oath and not giving any answers that could satisfy the minds of the members of the court as to his being a competent and {illegible} subject for taking an oath, he was dismissed.

John Davy further examined as follows:

Court: Did you feel the prisoner's prick within your body on the first time?
Answer: Yes, about one inch.
Court: Did you feel his prick within your body the second time?
Answer: Yes, about the same as the first.
Court: Did you feel it so the third time?
Answer: Yes, near about as it was the first and second times.
Court: Did you feel any thing come from the prisoner's prick at either of the 3 times you say you felt it within your body?
Answer: While he was working of it in to and fro there was something like water came running down my thighs.
Court: Did you ever speak to any of the boys about this business or did they or any of them ever speak to you about it?
Answer: One day, just after I came to the ship, Mr. Ambler was going onshore and he desired me to clean a pair of boots for him. Gammicliff said to me, if I was you, I would not go down for if you do he will serve you as he has served us. I asked him what he did to them, and he told me that he used to take them down in his cabin and roll them atop of the bed and put his cock in their hands. So I sent down and told Mr. Ambler that I could not clean his boots because I was going to clean the gunroom knives and forks, and he said never mind, I shall surely get you flogged. I went away.
Court: Have you ever been told to give this evidence that you have given about the prisoner or ever been threatened with any sort of punishment or pain if you did not give such evidence?
Answer: No, by no person at all.
The witness withdrew.

John Wilcott further examined as follows:

Court: Did you feel the prisoner's prick within your body the first time you was in the cabin with him as you have stated?

Answer: Yes, about one inch and half.

Court: Did you the second time?

Answer: No.

Court: Did you the third time?

Answer: No.

Court: When you felt the prisoner's prick within your body did you feel any thing come from it?

Answer: No.

Court: Have you ever been told to give the evidence that you have given about the prisoner or ever been threatened with any sort of punishment or pain if you did not give such evidence?

Answer: No, nobody at all.

Prisoner: Have your master or mistress ever encouraged you to say any thing of this kind against me?

Answer: No, never.

Court: Did your master or mistress ever say any thing whatever to you about the prisoner?

Answer: No, never spoke about him.

The witness withdrew.

The evidence in support of the charge being finished, the prisoner was called upon to make his defense, who requested half an hour to prepare the same, which being granted, the court was cleared. The required time being expired, the prisoner signified that he was prepared with his defense, whereupon the court was opened, the prisoner brought in, and the audience admitted. The prisoner put into the hands of the judge advocate a written paper, signed by himself, which was read to the court as follows:

Defense:

Mr. President and Gentlemen of this honorable court:

All that I have to say in my defense on this occasion is, in the most solemn manner, and in the face of heaven and this honorable court to declare that I am completely and entirely innocent of the charges alleged against me. And I beg that evidence may be examined on my behalf.

B. Ambler

Evidence in behalf of the prisoner:

Joseph Dowman, ship's corporal of His Majesty's sloop, *Tisiphone*, sworn and examined as follows:

Prisoner: Did you ever know me guilty of the crime alleged against me?
Answer: Never, nor ever had the least occasion to believe it.
Prisoner: Do you know if the boys who have been examined in support of the charge against me are notorious liars?
Answer: Two of them. Hopkins and Wilcott have been several times punished for lying.
Court: What is the character of the boy Davy?
Answer: He bears a very bad character by the whole ship's company.
Court: Did you know of any quarrel between the prisoner and any officer or others of the ship that might have induced any person to invite, bring forward, or instruct the witnesses against the prisoner?
Answer: I have heard the boatswain, gunner, and carpenter quarrel with the prisoner, but I have not taken particular notice what it was about.
Court: Do you know of any person who at any time heard a boy cry out in the cabin of the prisoner?
Answer: I do not.
The witness withdrew.

Samuel Pester, a seaman belonging to His Majesty's sloop, *Tisiphone*, and servant to the prisoner, sworn and examined as follows:

Prisoner: Did you ever know me guilty of sodomy with any or either of the boys. And do you, from what you have seen of my conduct, believe me inclined to that vice or likely to make such an attempt on you?
Answer: I did not. I do not believe the prisoner inclined to that vice. I do not think the prisoner likely to make such an attempt.
Prisoner: Have you ever seen any of the boys who have been brought as witnesses against me in my cabin?
Answer: No, never.
Court: What are you on board?
Answer: I am servant to the prisoner and have been for 7 or 8 months.

Court: Do you know of any quarrel between the prisoner and any officer or others of the ship that might have induced any person to invite, bring forward or instruct the witnesses against the prisoner?

Answer: No.

The witness withdrew.

Mr. Robert Baker, midshipman onboard His Majesty's sloop, *Tisiphone,* sworn and examined as follows:

Prisoner: Did you ever know me guilty of sodomy with any or either of the boys. And do you from what you have seen of my conduct believe me inclined to that vice, or likely to make such an attempt?

Answer: I did not. I do not believe the prisoner in the least inclined to that vice. I do not think him likely to make such an attempt.

Prisoner: Do you know of any persons who may be so much my enemies as to have induced the boys to give untrue evidence against me in this case?

Answer: No.

Prisoner: Did you ever hear any of the officers of the *Tisiphone* or their {illegible} speak disrespectfully of me?

Answer: Yes, very disrespectfully.

Court: How long have you known the prisoner?

Answer: Sixteen months. I have messed with him four months, and all the time I have known him, he always behaved with the greatest decency that man could behave.

Court: Do you know the boys, Hopkins and Wilcott?

Answer: Yes.

Court: Are they of notorious character in the ship?

Answer: Yes, very much so. I heard an old seaman in the ship say two days after the prisoner was put into confinement that he never saw such boys in his life, and that he did not believe what they had said of the prisoner was true, and that he believed they might be induced to say it by some one or other.

Court: Have you known Hopkins or Wilcott punished particularly for lying?

Answer: Yes.

Court: What is the character of John Davy and Thomas Hooper. Are either of them to your knowledge notorious bad characters?

Answer: Davy is a very wicked boy indeed as ever lived. Every one in the ship will say that if it was in his power he would even hang his own father. I heard Hooper's mother say that her son had denied to her all that has been said against the prisoner. He is a very wicked boy. His mother said that the prisoner had always behaved like a father to her boy, and she ever should respect him for what he had done, that he had been particularly kind to him.

Court: Do you know of your own knowledge if any one of the officers have ever complained of the bad character of those boys or either of them to the captain or first lieutenant?

Answer: No.

Court: Did you ever understand that any person had heard a boy cry out in the cabin of the prisoner at any time?

Answer: Never.

Prisoner: Did you ever see me use any improper or indecent freedoms with any of the young gentlemen under my care?

Answer: No, but gave them always the best advice that could be.

The witness withdrew.

Mr. John Waters, boatswain of His Majesty's sloop, *Tisiphone*, sworn and examined as follows:

Prisoner: Did you ever since you have known me see any thing that could induce you to believe me inclined to the vice of which I am charged?

Answer: No, I can't say that I ever did.

Prisoner: Did you ever hear any of the young gentlemen under my care complain of my having made any attempt of that nature on them?

Answer: Never.

Court: How long have you known the prisoner?

Answer: About 2 years. He messed with me a month when he first came to the ship and then went to the mess of the gentlemen where he was caterer till this business happened.

Court: Do you know the boys Hopkins and Wilcott?

Answer: I know Hopkins very well. He was my servant. He was always a very honest boy. I some times found him guilty of a lie on some trivial occasions. I have had him punished for it once or twice. I do not know much about

Wilcott. I have always heard him spoke of as a noisome sort of lad and full of mischief and every thing of this kind that was bad.

Court: Do you know any thing of Davy or Gammicliff?

Answer: No. I only recollect Davy being punished once.

The witness withdrew.

Mr. William Baker of Exmouth sworn and examined as follows:

Prisoner: While I was at your house for months, did any of your children complain of my having taken liberties with them of the nature with which I am charged?

Answer: No.

Prisoner: You having been very frequently onboard the *Tisiphone*, did you ever see any thing there that could induce you to believe me guilty of the crimes with which I am charged?

Answer: No.

The witness withdrew.

Mr. Edward Adam Steel, midshipman of His Majesty's sloop *Tisiphone*, sworn and examined as follows:

Prisoner: Did you ever see me with any of the boys who have given evidence against me on this occasion in my cabin?

Answer: No.

Prisoner: Did you ever see me inclined to the vice with which I am charged or do you believe me inclined to it?

Answer: No.

Prisoner: Did you ever see me take any liberties of that kind with any of your messmates?

Answer: No. Never.

Prisoner: Did you ever hear me use words of that tendency?

Answer: No.

Court: How long have you been in the *Tisiphone*?

Answer: Fifteen months and have messed with the prisoner all that time.

Mr. Thomas Holloway Holman, midshipman of His Majesty's sloop, *Tisi-phone*, sworn and examined as follows:

Prisoner: Did you ever see me with any of the boys who have given evidence against me on this occasion in my cabin?

Answer: No.

Prisoner: Did you ever see me inclined to the vice with which I am charged or do you believe me inclined to it?

Answer: No.

Prisoner: Did you ever see me take any liberties of that kind with any of your messmates?

Answer: No.

Prisoner: Did you ever hear me use words of that tendency?

Answer: No.

Court: How long have you been onboard the *Tisiphone*?

> *Answer:* Eighteen months and have messed with the prisoner the whole time. The witness withdrew.

Captain William Foote of the *Tisiphone* sworn and examined as follows:

Court: State to the court what you know of the characters of the boys Hopkins, Gammicliff, Wilcott, and Davy.

Answer: I never heard a complaint from any officer belonging to the ship that either of those boys acted any way improper or were bad characters until some days after the prisoner was in confinement. Then my first lieutenant informed me that two of them had been punished for improper conduct under the bowsprit. I think those two were Wilcott and Hooper, who is not before named here.

Prisoner: What is my general character since you have known me?

Answer: The prisoner always done his duty very much to my satisfaction, and I had ever a very good opinion of his abilities as an officer.

The prisoner not having any thing further to offer in his defense, the court was cleared and proceeded to deliberate upon and form the sentence.

The court having heard the evidence in support of the charge as well as what the prisoner had to offer in his defense, and the evidence adduced on his behalf, and very maturely and deliberately weighed and considered the same, was of the opinion that the charge had been proved against the prisoner, Mr. Bartlet Ambler, and did in consequence thereof adjudge the said Mr. Bartlet Ambler to be hanged by the neck until he is dead at the yard arm of such one of His Majesty's ships, and at such time as the Right Honorable the Lords Commissioners of the Admiralty shall direct.

The court was opened. The prisoner brought in. The evidence and audience admitted, and sentence passed accordingly.

Robert Liddel

Deputy Judge Advocate.

{Included with the court-martial documents is the following letter from the Earl of Northesk to Mr. William Marsden, at the Admiralty.}

His Majesty's Ship *Salvador del Mundo*

Harmoaze 22nd April 1805

Sir:

By desire of the members of a court martial assembled by me this day to try Mr. Bartlet Ambler, I have to request you will call their Lordships consideration to the hardship the court have labored under in being obliged to condemn a man to death upon the evidence of four boys, the eldest not more than thirteen years of age, and therefore beg to recommend him to mercy.

I am, Sir, your obedient servant,

Northesk

{To:} William Marsden, Esq.

The Court Martial of Hepburn Graham (ADM 1/5376)

Minutes taken at a Court Martial Assembled on Board His Majesty's Ship *Gladiator* in Portsmouth Harbor on the Ninth Day of December, 1806

Present: Sir Isaac Coffin, Baronet, Rear Admiral of the Red and Second Officer in the Command of His Majesty's Ships and Vessels at Portsmouth and Spithead, President

Captain Edward Buller, Captain George Sosack, John Lamphorne, Sir Joseph S. Yorke, Knight, Edward Coderington, Thomas LeMerchant Joselin, John Gwin, the Honorable Courtnay Boyle, George Astle, James Oswald, Michael Seymour, Thomas James Maling

The Prisoner was brought in and the audience admitted.

The President reported to the court that Captain William Hargood was absent on admiralty leave.

The order from the Right Honorable Lords Commissioners of the Admiralty dated the sixth day of December instant and directed to the president to assemble a court martial for the trial of Mr. Hepburn Graham, masters mate belonging to His Majesty's ship, *St. George,* for having been guilty of the sin of sodomy with George Parr, a boy, on or about the afternoon and evening of the twenty-first and twenty-seventh of November last, and for making repeated attempts on the said boy and also making repeated attempts on John Sky, another boy, particularly on the afternoon of the twenty-ninth ultimo {illegible}.

The members of the court and the judge advocate then in open court and before they {illegible} to trial respectively took the several oaths enjoined and {illegible} in and by an act of Parliament made and passed in the twenty-second year of the reign of His Majesty King George the Second entitled An Act for Amending, Explaining and Reducing into Act of Parliament the Laws Relating to the Government of His Majesty's Ships, Vessels, and Forces by Sea.

Then the letter from Captain Thomas Bertie commander of His Majesty's ship, *St. George,* dated the first instant and directed to Admiral Montague, Commander in Chief of His Majesty's ships and vessels at Portsmouth and Spithead, containing the charge was read and is hereto annexed. And the witnesses were ordered to withdraw and attend their examinations separately, which they did {illegible}.

George Parr, a boy of fourteen years of age belonging to His Majesty's ship, *St. George,* called in and sworn:

Captain Bertie asked:

Q: Do you know the prisoner?

A: Yes.

Q: Relate to the court what the prisoner was guilty of with you on the twenty-first of November last, the day after the *St. George* arrived in Torbay, and also on the twenty-seventh of November last.

A: On the twenty-first of November last, Mr. Graham took me into his hammock. He got me on a stool and got hold of me, telling me I must be a good boy. He got hold of my hair, and pulled me into his hammock in his berth on the starboard side, forward on the lower gun deck. It was between eight and nine o'clock in the evening of the first watch. He told me to put down my trousers, and he put them down himself. He pulled his yard out, and put it into my backside. He kept doing backwards and forwards, and made my arse wet. I was laying on my side in his hammock when he committed the act, and immediately afterwards he said you may go to your hammock now, and told me I must not tell any one, and if I did he would get me flogged. He would get me three dozen that it should not be the one dozen, but should be three dozen. I then went away to my hammock on the middle deck on the larboard side. In the morning, I told Symes, a waister, and Williams, a mizzen topman what he had done to me and they would not believe {illegible}. I am not sure as to the date of {the} other time, but it was after Mr. Graham sent me to cook some victuals for him, as I was his servant. It was at night and boys Sky and Taylor and me {illegible} sitting talking together, and the victuals was in the oven. I was on the deck and he sent for {illegible} boy Sky to his berth. He then sent for me by Taylor from the deck, and gave me a spoon to get the victuals stirred about. Mr. Graham came to the galley {illegible} whilst I was cooking his victuals and took me out of the galley {illegible} near the sick bay, and asked me what I had been saying. He said {illegible} would get both him and me {three words illegible}. Then he got hold of me by the neck and put the spoon to my throat and said if it had been a knife he would have cut my throat and jumped overboard himself {illegible}.

Mr. Morris, a midshipman, came past and asked him what he was doing, and he told Mr. Morris I had filled the victuals full of {illegible}. Then I went down, and he told me many times he would cut my throat before morning, and jump overboard himself. This happened between the twenty-first and the {twenty-}seventh. On the twenty-seventh of November at night, between eight and nine o'clock in the {illegible} watch, I was in his berth attending him as his servant. He told me I must be a good boy. He would make me a good boy. He got hold of me and pulled me into his hammock. I did not want to go into it and he kept hitting me on the head while I was in the hammock. I wanted to get out, and he kept hitting me and asked me to stay in and said if I did not, he would get me flogged, he would get me three dozen. He had made me unbutton the buttons before, and he then pulled down my trousers and pulled out his yard and put it into my backside. It went into my backside. He kept moving backwards and forwards, and made my backside wet. He then told me to go to my hammock and get up in good time in the morning and I went away. On the following morning early, I was again in his berth. It was before breakfast, before the hammocks were up. He pulled a hole in my trousers behind with his fingers and told me he would get them mended. He then pulled his yard out, and put it through the hole of my trousers to my backside, but did not enter it, but kept moving backwards and forwards and made my arse wet.

Q: Did he ever make any more attempts than what you have related?

A: Yes he has attempted it five times in all, but only entered me twice.

Q: Was you sent down on the twenty-ninth of November to the surgeon and his mates to be examined?

A: Yes.

The court asked:

Q: Prior to these transactions had Mr. Graham ever punished you?

A: Yes.

Q: How long was it before?

A: I cannot recollect, but I had not been on board the ship above ten months. The ship's corporal gave me six strokes over the hand with a rope.

Q: What was it for?

A: I do not remember.

Q: When Mr. Graham took you into his hammock, did you resist him?

A: I told him I could not bear it and did not wish to go into his hammock. He got me by the arm and pulled me in. I was afraid he would get me flogged.

Q: Was there any other hammock in his berth?

A: No.

Q: Did any body else sleep in it?

A: No.

Q: Was any screen round it?

A: Yes, of loose canvas.

Q: At what distance does any hammock hang from the outside of the screen?

A: I do not think more than a quarter of a yard.

Q: Did you cry out?

A: No.

Q: Why did you not?

A: I was afraid he would get me flogged.

Q: If you had cried out do you think any body would have heard you.

A: Yes.

Q: The first time the prisoner took you into his hammock had you any idea of what he was going to do with you?

A: No, I did not know what he was going to do with me.

Q: How did you lay on your side?

A: Straight down, one thigh was up, and the other down in the hammock.

Q: How long was the prisoner before he entered your body?

A: Not long.

Q: Was it so painful to you that you felt an inclination to cry out?

A: Yes, I could have cried out but I durst not.

Q: Did the prisoner make use of any force to prevent your crying out such as putting his hand to your mouth?

A: No.

Q: How long after you describe the prisoner to be in your body did you feel any wet come from him?

A: Yes it was not long. He made my backside wet before he entered.

Q: Did the wet appear to you to be wet or cold?

A: I cannot tell. I was so frightened.

Q: Did you feel any flow of any liquid from him after he had entered your body?

A: Yes.

Q: Did you feel his yard in your fundament?

A: Yes, twice.

Q: Did it hurt you when it went in?

A: Yes.

Q: When you were in the prisoner's hammock can you recollect {illegible} he desired you to place yourself {illegible} a particular situation?

A: He told me to lie still and {illegible} shout out.

Q: Did he throw your thigh up?

A: He kept shoving my right thigh, which was the uppermost one.

Q: Did you hear any body speak outside?

A: No.

The prisoner asked:

Q: What is your age?

A: Fourteen years of age next New Years Day.

Q: On the twenty-ninth of November in the galley did I ask you what you was saying to some of the men belonging to the ship, especially to Symes?

A: He asked me what I had been saying. He did not mention any body. He said I would get both myself and him hanged.

Q: Did you then inform me that you had a complaint in your head which you did not know what you said at any time?

A: No, he said to me if any one asked me I should say I had {illegible} my senses, that I was trying {illegible} of pantaloons that he had given and he was seeing if ever I had been flogged.

Q: Did ever Symes bribe you or any of the rest of his messmates to {illegible} this story?

A: No.

Q: To whom did you first relate {illegible}.

A: Symes and Williams.

Q: How long was it after?

A: In the morning afterwards.

Q: Did I severely punish you several times before the twenty-first of November for not obeying my orders in not reading your book?

A: He beat me for not getting his victuals in time and made my nose bleed once. He never punished me for not reading my book that I know of. He told me to read it. It was a spelling book he borrowed.

Q: Did I keep you up several times over past hours as long as my light was permitted, which was until half past nine on purpose to learn your lesson?

A: Yes, when the gentlemen have been in, he has told me he would keep me up to read my book, and then when the gentlemen were gone out, he wanted me to come into his hammock.

Q: Were the ship's company in their hammocks at the time you state I took you into my hammock on the twenty-first and twenty-seventh?

A: I cannot pretend to say whether they were all in or not as they keep watch.

John Sky, a boy about fifteen years of age, belonging to the *St. George,* called in and sworn:

Captain Bertie asked:

Q: Relate to the court what the prisoner was guilty of with you on the twenty-ninth of November, last.

A: On the twenty-ninth of November last I was down between decks talking to one of the boys whose name is Taylor. Mr. Graham, the prisoner came to me and {illegible} me he wanted me in his berth. I went in and he told me he would give me a bed. He then took me round the deck and set me down on a stool {illegible} of him. He began kissing me and told me he must feel my cock. I told him to leave it alone. If he did not, I would sing out. He was at this time going to unbutton the flap of my trousers. Mr. Miller, a midshipman, came in and he asked Mr. Miller to take down a great coat that {illegible} on the gun to give him more light. He said it gave him light. Whilst Mr. Miller was taking down the coat, he took me by the arm and hoved me out of the berth. I told the boy, George Parr, if he did not complain, I would. He then said that he would complain, and I told him to mention my name. He did complain to the first lieutenant, and mentioned my name. I told Mr. Graham that I could not stand it, and would complain. About a fortnight before, Mr. Graham {illegible} me in his berth and had my trousers down and pulled out his private parts. He tried to get these into my backside, but could {illegible}, but got them between my thighs. Before he had had his turn, someone came and disturbed him. I told him I would go out of the berth, and he put me out of the berth. He never succeeded with me in what he wanted to do.

Q: Did the prisoner ever make any further unnatural attempts upon you?

A: He did once the cruise before, but I cannot recollect what he said or did then.

Court asked:

Q: Did the prisoner promise you any money?

A: No, only a bed, as I had lost my bed.

Q: At what time was it on the twenty-ninth?

A: Between four and five in the afternoon.

Q: Did you call out?

A: No, I could not.

Q: Did you tell any body of it?

A: Only his own boy.

Q: Did the boy, Parr, make known to you what the prisoner had done to him?

A: No, not till the twenty-ninth. I was just come out of the berth, and I believe he had a suspicion and asked me what the prisoner had been doing with me. I told him that he had been having me on the stool and kissing me, and wanted to make free with my backside. He told me that Mr. Graham had been wanting to do the same with him, and that he had done it. I told him if he did not complain, I would, and he said that he would complain. I told him if he did to mention my name too, and he did complain.

The prisoner asked:

Q: Were the screens of my berth {illegible}?

A: Yes, they were.

Q: Were the posts up at the time?

A: The posts in his berth were down, but the scuttle was open.

Q: Did you inform me you had {illegible} a bed some time previous to the twenty-ninth of November {illegible} did I then inform you that I would endeavor to get you {illegible}.

A: I do not recollect that I did tell {illegible} so previous to the twenty-ninth.

Q: Did you report it on the quarter deck to the first lieutenant that you had lost a bed?

A: I told the master of arms of it and reported it to the first lieutenant.

Q: Did I on the twenty-ninth of November at half past five o'clock in the evening take you for {illegible} to the boatswain's storeroom to inquire if there were any {illegible} beds in the storeroom?

A: Yes, when I was getting my {illegible} butter and cheese he came down into the after cockpit and had a lantern and candle alight and told me if I came forward with him, he would speak to the boatswain's yeoman, and {illegible} get me a bed. I had some suspicion of him, but went forward with him. When I went forward {illegible} the wing, he told me to stand {illegible} while he went and asked the boatswain's yeoman if he had any beds in the store room. I heard him ask, and the yeoman said no. Then he went on the other side of the cockpit and blowed out his light. My suspicion of him was then stronger, and I ran away.

The Court asked:

Q: What induced you to suspect him?

A: I suspected he wanted to do the same with me as he had attempted in his berth.

The prisoner asked:

Q: Were there lights at the time in the after cockpit?

A: Yes, the sentries'.

Q: Were there also lights in the fore cockpit and main hold?

A: Yes, but none of them shewed a proper light in the wing to shew if any person was there doing any thing.

Q: What wing was it?

A: The midship wing, abreast of the sail room.

Q: Did you pass by a sentinel with a light when you was with the steward for your bread and butter?

A: Yes, when Mr. Graham fetched me into the wing we passed the sentinel with a light in the after cockpit.

Q: Did you in passing see any person in the hold at the main hatchway?

A: I did not.

Q: Did you when you came forward see a sentinel in the fore cockpit with a light?

A: I saw the light but not the sentinel.

Q: At what time of the night was it?

A: I think it was between five and six o'clock.

Q: Did you see me afterwards?

A: After I came on the lower gun deck about half an hour afterwards, I saw him, and told him that I was going to complain of him, that I could not stand his attempts any longer.

Q: Did you see or speak to me afterward?

A: No, I did not until he was fetched to the quarter deck.

Q: Do you imagine that any {illegible} could have been committed in the wing without its being seen there by some person?

A: I could not have been seen {illegible} without there was {four words illegible}.

Q: Do you recollect exactly the time previous to the twenty-ninth of November that you say that transaction happened?

A: No, I cannot, as near as I can recollect it was a fortnight.

Q: Was I there in the same berth on {illegible} cruise before as on the twenty-ninth of November?

A: Yes he was.

Q: Did any of the rest of the gentlemen mess with me?

A: I do not know.

Q: Did I then mess in that berth?

A: I am not certain, but believe he did. James Enise attended on {illegible}.

Mr. Hugh Hughes, surgeon of the *St. George,* called in and sworn:

Captain Bertie asked:

Q: On the twenty-ninth of November was the boy, George Parr, sent to you to undergo a certain examination?

A: Yes.

Request: Relate to the court the result of your examination.

A: About seven o'clock in the evening of the twenty-ninth of November I was sent for by Lieutenant Caulfield on the quarter deck, and when I appeared, he said that Captain Bertie desired that I should examine the two boys, Parr and Sky. I immediately took them down to the sick bay accompanied by my two assistants, and there examined them immediately and found the anus of George Parr inflamed and not excoriated at all. I also examined Sky, and found no appearance of inflamation in the anus, as in the former boy. In order to corroborate what I have now stated I requested both my assistants to examine them also and begged that they would give me their opinion, and it corresponded with my own.

The court asked:

Q: Did you ask the boy, Parr, what had occasioned this appearance in his anus?

A: I did. He answered that two nights before, the twenty-seventh, that Mr. Graham had connection with him and gave him an infinite deal of pain. I asked him whether the anus was very painful at the time he was examining. He said, no, not very painful just then.

Q: Was it your opinion that the appearance was occasioned by the insertion of an instrument similar to a man's yard?

A: I could not ascertain that.

Q: Would such an insertion cause a similar appearance in your opinion?

A: I think it would.

Q: As a professional man, do you think that the crime of which the prisoner stands charged could be committed upon a boy so young as George Parr?

A: Yes, I do.

Q: From your knowledge of instruments could you imagine that the crime could be committed with a passive obedience on the part of that boy?

A: I do think he must have been placed in a particular position and he must have been a passive instrument.

Q: If the offense had been committed on the boy, Sky, do you {illegible} his anus would have had the same appearance?

A: Certainly.

The prisoner asked:

Q: Did the boy, Parr, at any time previously to the twenty-ninth of November come to you with any complaint?

A: Not to my recollection. Not as to that part.

Q: Do you {illegible} as a professional man that the cause of the boy's illness was done on the twenty-ninth or at any time before?

A: The boy was not ill on the twenty-ninth. The injury appeared to be recent. He did not complain. The parts appeared to be inflamed.

Mr. George Geilbraith, surgeon's assistant of the *St. George*, called and sworn:

Captain Bertie asked:

Q: Was you present on the twenty-ninth of November when the boy, George Parr, was examined by the surgeon?

A: Yes.

Q: Relate to the court the result of your examination.

A: On examining Parr, the anus appeared to be slightly inflamed, and it was our opinion it might have been induced by the commission of the crime with which the prisoner is charged.

The court asked:

Q: What did you hear the boy, Parr, state to the surgeon as having been the cause of that appearance?

A: The boy stated to the surgeon that the soreness was owing to Mr. Graham having had an improper connection with him. It was to that import.

Q: What were the words he used?

A: The boy told the surgeon in my presence that Mr. Graham had had him in his hammock. I think he said at two or three different times, and that Mr. Graham had {illegible} had connection with him. I do not recollect the words that was {illegible} impart.

Q: How far up the rectum did it appear to be inflamed.

A: We did not so particularly examine it.

Q: Upon your oath as a professional man, do you think the crime was committed on Parr?

A: My opinion is that the appearance of the boy's anus might have been produced by other causes, but taking it with the boy's story it appeared to me that such a thing had been attempted, but whether it had been completed or not, I cannot say.

The prisoner asked:

Q: Did the boy, Parr, previous to the twenty-ninth of November {illegible} any complaint to you?

A: No.

The prosecution being closed, the prisoner was called on for his defence, and said that he had little to state in his defence. That he had been in the service since 1793, and he had sailed with Admiral Pringle, Sir Thomas Graves, and with Captain Prine, and discovered the mutiny in the *Hope,* sloop of {illegible}.

George Parr called in again:

Prisoner asked:

Q: Did you inform me before I was made prisoner on the twenty-ninth of November that a certain gentleman gave you a guinea to have connections with him, and then offered his watch?

A: No, he told me, if any one asked me, to say that a gentleman promised me a guinea to do as he did. He did not mention a watch.

Q: Did you inform me in coming from your work that a gentleman met you about a mile from your own house?

A: He told me to say that a gentleman met me in a field.

Q: Did you inform me that he gave you a guinea?

A: No.

The court was cleared and agreed that the charge had been proved against the said Hepburn Graham, and did adjudge him to suffer death by being hanged by the neck onboard such ship of His Majesty and at such time as the commissioners for executing the Office of Lord High Admiral of the United Kingdom of Great Britain and Ireland, etc. or any three of them for the time being should direct.

The court was again opened, the prisoner brought, {illegible} audience admitted, and sentence passed accordingly.

{illegible} Greentham {illegible}

Deputy Judge Advocate of the Fleet

{Note at the bottom left corner of a document accompanying the minutes of Mr. Hepburn Graham's court-martial.}

17 Dec. Warrant to be prepared for his execution on board the *St. George* at Portsmouth on Saturday next.

CHAPTER 6

Nineteenth-Century Americans
at War

❧

The Mexican War in the late 1840s and the Civil War a dozen years later wrenched over a million of America's young men from their homes and families and sent them off to serve under arms. The life they discovered as soldiers and sailors was, for most of them, far removed from what they had known before. Familiar restraints imposed by society, community, and the forces of religion vanished, but the military discipline they endured dominated only parts of their daily routine. In the many spare hours these men spent on board ships, garrisoning forts, on furlough, or in army encampments, they were left to their own devices. The absence of organized recreational activities, pervasive loneliness, and idleness were all elements of a constellation certain to encourage dissipation. Gambling, bawdy songs, lewd conversation, drawing or ogling obscene pictures, drinking, and sexual adventuring when possible helped alleviate the days and weeks of boredom endured by the men and boys sent off to fight.

There is no way to gauge the extent or nature of sexual activities indulged in by these young Americans. Few among the legion of authors who have written on the social history of either the Mexican War or the Civil War have even speculated on the chance that homoerotic relationships formed a part of life for some of the hundreds of thousands of men who lived for the most part in a same-sex environment. Neither in the volumes of letters and firsthand accounts that survive from the conflicts nor in other documentary sources are there many overt references to sex. Only the 180,000 cases of gonorrhea and syphilis in Union army medical records provide any quantitative intimation of the extent of sexual activity. There are apparently no records of punishment or dismissals from either the Union or the Confederate army for homoerotic activities. Characterizations such as that made by one soldier, who described the Union bases at Norfolk and Portsmouth as "Sodom and Gomorrow," are exceedingly rare.

Two of the men who sailed on board America's warships during the middle decades of the century wrote of male love: Philip Van Buskirk and Herman Melville. The former, a son of a Maryland secretary of state, joined the United States Marine Corps as a drummer boy in 1846, after his father's financial failure and his own deficient performances as a scholar at Georgetown College in Washington, D.C., and St. John's College in Annapolis. He served as a marine until 1870, with intervening stints as a deserter from the Pensacola Navy Yard, a guard at the United States Naval Academy, a Confederate infantryman, and a vagrant. As the following selection amply illustrates, Van Buskirk kept a careful diary that recorded his own loves and the lovemaking among sailors and marines on ship and on shore. Melville was far more circumspect, writing as he did for publication. In *White Jacket*, he provided only obscure references to the all-male sexuality of the crewmen of the fictional U.S.S. *Neversink*.

Although the selection from the memoirs of General Philip H. Sheridan offers a tantalizing glimpse of what was very likely a lesbian relationship, the only sustained and generally acknowledged link between the Civil War and homoeroticism comes from Walt Whitman, whose preference for male partners is well established. Whitman was over forty and too old for soldiering in 1861, but he spent a large portion of the war in Washington's military hospitals, nursing wounded men and boys, providing small luxuries to brighten their convalescence or their last days, and, on occasion, bringing them into his sexual orbit. Many of those whom Whitman nursed and befriended remembered him when they left the hospital for home or to return to their units, and he remembered them as well. A large correspondence grew during the war and afterward between the poet and his friends, both those he knew in New York and his soldier boys, and a considerable portion of it survives. Many of Whitman's letters are overtly erotic in implication and expression, far more so than those he received in return.

B. R. Burg

"Ganymede at Sea," from *An American Seafarer in the Age of Sail: The Erotic Diaries of Philip C. Van Buskirk, 1851–1870*

{When Marine Corps drummer Philip C. Van Buskirk served with the United States Navy's East India Squadron in the early 1850s, he regularly recorded his masturbations in his diary. At the same time he made his tabulations, and on some of the same pages, he wrote lamenting the deficient willpower that left him unable to resist his autoerotic inclinations. Masturbation was not a new activity for him when he first noted it in his diary. He had in fact become a regular practitioner of the solitary vice some years before during a sojourn at the Pensacola Navy Yard in 1848. While at the yard, Van Buskirk also received an offer to be masturbated by a member of the garrison, but he refused so emphatically that the man never repeated the proposition. (In the diary Van Buskirk referred to such activity as "unseemly tricks.") At another time, during a tour of duty in the Pacific in late 1851, he recorded shock when a man he described as an old reprobate made overtures toward him.

Van Buskirk's hostile reactions to the solicitations are deceptive, however. His innocence had actually been compromised long before the propositions were made. By the time he served at Pensacola, he had already engaged in sex with several men and boys.} His first homoerotic encounter occurred several years before he enlisted in the Marine Corps. During {a} winter he spent as a runaway in Cumberland, Maryland, the ten-year-old Van Buskirk met a man whom he characterized as a "loafer." He described what followed: "One evening [he] . . . promised me a cent if I would do something for him. I assented and the fellow invited me to accompany him to the barn. Here in a secret place he taught me to perform *the act of masturbation upon himself!* It was a strange phenomenon to me. I did not feel that I was committing a great sin. I was wretched and miserable. I had no pride. I never repeated this act upon the loafer, and never thought of practicing it upon myself."

His second experience followed a few years later . . . at Georgetown College. He wrote: "A schoolmate of mine used to familiarize himself with me to a degree and in a manner that would have condemned us both to infamy if we had ever been discovered. . . . We were too young, and knew not of what was sin, and were totally ignorant both of the real infamy and the destructive tendency of our conduct." It is likely that at the time Van Buskirk engaged in these unspecified acts with his classmate he was almost as innocent as he had been when he met the loafer in Cumberland. He did not refer to the destructive tendency of his conduct with a fellow student until ten years later, eight of which were spent in military service. At the time of the relationship, when he was eleven or twelve years old, he thought of his partner as well-bred, handsome, gentle, and amiable in manner, the same characteristics he would seek in the boys he loved throughout his career in the marines.

{When he arrived at the Marine Corps Headquarters music room as a recruit in 1846, Van Buskirk} became strongly attracted to some of the young drummers and fifers but was not sexually involved with any of them. An old crippled soldier named Scott provided him with his only sexual experience during this period. One evening Scott persuaded him to stand against a tree and used him for what Van Buskirk described as "the abusing of himself." During {a cruise the next year on the U.S.S. *Cumberland*, blockading the port of Vera Cruz during the Mexican War,} he wrote proudly that he had not "once consented to participate in sodomy with any one." His pride in his celibacy may have been well earned if his description of the *Cumberland* was correct, that is, a Sodom of a ship on which ten good men could not be found among a crew of four hundred. He explained that "no boy can ever remain a year on board of an American man-of-war without being led or forced to commit this crime (which, by the way, is not regarded as a crime in a man-of-war)."

After he deserted from Pensacola, Van Buskirk learned to profit from homoerotic activity. The recollection of the events surrounding this discovery evinced neither rage nor shame. Instead, he wrote of them in a laconic and unperturbed manner. One night in New Orleans a Spaniard had offered the fugitive lodging. Van Buskirk explained that "he had a fancy to handle my person indelicately—more plainly to play with my pene—which I had to submit to; in the morning he gave me a half-dime or a dime to buy something to eat."

{After his initial assignment to the Marine Corps Headquarters in 1846, his war service on board the *Cumberland*, his six-months stay at Pensacola Navy Yard, and his return to the marines after deserting, Van Buskirk's second tour of duty at sea from 1851 to 1855 offered no surprises.} Already aware of homoerotic relations among seafarers, he claimed that all his acquaintances on board {his ship, the East India Squadron's U.S.S.} *Plymouth*, engaged in sexual contacts with other men, and that no one saw much harm in it. The testimony of other early nineteenth-century seafaring authors supports his observations. Samuel Leech claimed sodomy hardly merited serious attention, even on one of the brutal ships on which he served. Another diarist, Lieutenant Henry B. Watson, the commander of the marine detachment of the {U.S.S.} *Portsmouth*, explained that one of the midshipmen on board was simply allowed to resign after committing "a most unnatural, and diabolical crime." Watson added that the accused was charged with "Arson [which] in nautical parlance . . . is called buggering." A man who sailed on the {U.S.S.} *Ohio* ten years before Van Buskirk served on the *Plymouth* wrote of a Swede and a black who were discharged and sent home for engaging in homoerotic acts. They were neither flogged nor court-martialed, although in this same navy "hallooing" on the gun deck, drunkenness, or insolence could earn the perpetrator a dozen stripes.

{The tediousness and boredom of cruising the Pacific with the East India Squadron was as stultifying for Van Buskirk as the blockade of Mexican ports had been in 1847 and 1848. He} wrote that during the long hours of idleness there was little to pass the time except tobacco, the regular ration of grog, "and the occasional indulgence of unnatural commerce with boys." The trinity of pleasures fulfilled many of the men, and they hardly regretted their confinement to the ship, he commented.

Tradition, convenience, love, and lust all controlled sexual encounters among the crew of the *Plymouth*. Boys seeking relationships with other boys could find them under the boom cover. Van Buskirk lodged there regularly and had ample opportunity to learn the intricacies of what men and boys called the "boom cover trade." Yet more than the desire for sexual gratification induced young sailors to crawl in under the boom cover. Marine sentinels posted on deck sought shelter there, and others found it a convenient place to exchange the considerable gossip they collected on their cruises.

In these secret and secure sessions they learned the whereabouts of old friends and sex partners, discussed the looks of various boys, and found out who was available on their own and other ships. Van Buskirk discovered that a handsome boy named Hurdle, whom he had known from the *Cumberland*, now served with the East India Squadron and practiced mutual masturbation on board the {U.S.S.} *Susquehanna*. The {U.S.S.} *Vandalia* had on board a John

C. Wilson, reputed to be one of the most notorious boys in the navy. His nickname was "Baltimore Lize," and Van Buskirk learned to his horror that Wilson was one of those who exchanged notes with {his own favorite boy,} John Hibbs. The news so distracted him that he implored another boy to obtain the notes so he could learn what was transpiring between them.

Van Buskirk claimed repeatedly that the most wicked boy on board the *Plymouth* was George Coleman. The hope of Coleman's father that a life at sea would reform George had obviously failed. He was once confined to the ship for insubordination and twice convicted of theft. *Plymouth* crew members considered him a notorious sodomite who seduced the chaplain's boy and engaged the young Chinese who worked as officers' servants on the ship. He made little secret of his sexual proclivities. His trinity, according to the drummer was "rum-*-and tobacco."

Part of Van Buskirk's ire against Coleman may have been justified, but much of it undoubtedly resulted from jealousy. The {lad stole young Andrew Milne's affections from Van Buskirk after the drummer labored for months to dissuade Milne from masturbating.} Later, Coleman separated Van Buskirk from another boy, George W. Reever. The drummer and Reever regularly slept together under the boom cover on the port gratings, using the same coat and the same sailor's ditty bag for a pillow. On January 15, 1853, Coleman moved into the nest created by the two boys. Following his practice when sorely agitated, Van Buskirk entered details of what took place in his diary. Coleman and Reever lay close together and in due course their conversation stopped. Van Buskirk then perceived a slight trembling of Reever's head and he reached over and placed his hand upon it. With clearly sarcastic intent he asked, "What's the matter—have you the fever and ague?" The shaking stopped abruptly, and Reever replied to the question in the same spirit. "A *palsy* in his right hand caused the motion," he replied. Van Buskirk congratulated himself, thinking his intervention before emission prevented "a dreadful crime," but his satisfaction was unwarranted. Coleman then proceeded to unbutton his trousers, showed the stains, and proclaimed with a touch of humor that they were the effects of Reever's palsy.

Van Buskirk's anger was directed at others {beside Coleman.} After Andrew Milne rejected the efforts to reform him and abandoned their shared sleeping arrangements, he became the paramour of a lieutenant. The drummer denounced the perfidious Milne, accusing him of cursing, using tobacco, and engaging in sodomy as well as mutual masturbation. Nothing could effect his moral reformation, Van Buskirk claimed. The drummer grumbled that his sailor boy now shared the privileges of rank, in this case the rank of the lieutenant. The "'little slut' . . . exercises the freedom of the Main Deck," Van Buskirk complained, adding later that the timid "Miss Milne" possessed every characteristic of a girl.

Like Milne, fifer William McFarland was broadly defamed in the diary. Van Buskirk reported that he once offered to give Midshipman Lester Beardslee a good "drubbing off," adding that Beardslee wisely refused. McFarland had engaged the doctor's steward in sodomy and then kept him in fear that he would tell what had happened. Van Buskirk had no doubt that the fifer would do the same to the midshipman.

McFarland exasperated Van Buskirk at least as much as Coleman. The diary contains a litany of his sexual involvements. Not only did he offer to masturbate Beardslee and actually sodomize the doctor's steward, but he occasionally engaged in sexual activity with a yeoman, the black steward of the officers' mess, and the black wardroom cook. The fifer frequently sold himself to men on board for money or favors. "A quarter and a good opportunity and Bill will oblige anyone," Van Buskirk complained, adding the information that McFarland committed sodomy not only on board the *Plymouth*, but also in Washington, D.C., New York, and on board the U.S.S. *St. Lawrence* in Norfolk. The drummer claimed that he, too, had once been importuned by McFarland but had rejected the overture.

Attempts to involve Van Buskirk in sexual activities were frequent enough on board the *Plymouth* to become troublesome. Although the drummer continually bemoaned his physical appearance and unengaging personality, he was, according to one man who described him, "a beautiful boy." On one occasion a sailor particularly aggravated him by trying to unbutton his pants while he slept. He tried to grow a beard to make himself look older, but, he complained, the effort failed to discourage "the unnatural lust of the wretches who are disposed to pay me court as a boy."

After two years on board the *Plymouth*, Van Buskirk had {become quite sophisticated about sailors' relationships,} but even then he remained confused by the terminology for some sex acts. He first encountered the word "pederasty" in *Decline and Fall of the Roman Empire*. Gibbon called it the crime of the bishops of Rhodes and Diospolis. In spite of his smattering of the classics, the drummer erroneously understood it to mean the hand of one man being used to "pollute the other," either serially or simultaneously. Illiterate mariners rarely used classical terminology to identify sex acts. Unencumbered by formal education, they learned nomenclature from their peers. Mutual masturbation to them was "going chaw for chaw."

Regardless of his dislike of shipboard solicitations, Van Buskirk occasionally indulged in sex with crew members of the *Plymouth*. He and a boy named Daley went "chaw for chaw" at least one time. Thomas Atkinson, ten years older than Van Buskirk and a yeoman on board the ship, probably engaged him in mutual masturbation, although because the diary does not specify the act they may have exchanged positions for anal intercourse. He once awoke to find himself being masturbated by a quarter-gunner, a man Van Buskirk had never expected to have sexual interests in other men. "My astonishment was great! . . . but mute," he wrote, "I did not move." Just before he reached orgasm, Van Buskirk turned away from the gunner, but in his view, the crime was done. He disengaged too late to prevent emission.

One of Van Buskirk's chief informants on matters nautical and sexual was Charley Berry, captain of the *Plymouth*'s afterguard. Berry was an old salt and well acquainted with love among seafarers. He had tales of sexual activity on board naval ships that went back as far as 1842, during his service on the {U.S.S.} *Constitution*. Before boarding the *Plymouth* he had captained the afterguard of a sister ship, the *Portsmouth*, at the time of a sex scandal. The drummer learned from Berry that {his former school,} Georgetown College, was not the only educational institution where boys had homoerotic relationships. At the School for Moral Discipline in South Boston the cleric in charge, the Reverend Eleazar Mather Porter Wells, regularly importuned his scholars. Berry received his information from a friend on board the *Portsmouth*, Charles Gilbertson, who attended the school and regularly received solicitations from Wells. Gilbertson claimed he had rejected all offers, but Berry did not believe him, even though the ex-scholar declined to participate in sex on board the *Portsmouth*. Another of Berry's acquaintances from the *Portsmouth* attended Wells's school and admitted to being a regular partner for the cleric.

The drummer listened wide-eyed to the sexual tales and supplied at least one of his own. He told of another drummer of his acquaintance who sold cigars to the men of his ship at the outrageous price of thirty or forty cents apiece. After tattoo he distributed favors in return for what in daylight hours seemed an extortionate rate for tobacco. When he finished telling the story, his listeners surprised him by revealing they already knew the tale, including the youth's nickname, "The Little Cigar Boy."

The men and boys of the *Plymouth* talked about sexual activities not only on other ships but on their own as well. Someone on the *Plymouth* {at one time circulated} a rumor about Van Buskirk that dated back to the time of his service in the {Mexican War.} He did not record the substance of the story but wrote only that it was untrue, as was the tale of a gunner's mate on board the *Cumberland* doing laundry for him. He concluded by accusing a "devilishly" handsome marine of spreading the rumor of the gunner's mate washing his clothes. In conversations dealing with the *Plymouth*'s crew, the sailors probably discussed "Old Dhu," a crew member who brewed and sold coffee to the men in addition to his official duties. Billy Dhu admitted loving boys, employing them as prostitutes on board ship, and paying them with free coffee; he also served as a matchmaker, arranging long-term relationships between mariners and boys of their choice. He tried to recruit Van Buskirk, but in spite of his taste for coffee, the marine declined.

Berry was not the only experienced mariner with whom Van Buskirk discussed sexual activities. He recorded a conversation with a seasoned sailor, a mainmastman identified only as "Old White":

Van Buskirk: Well, White, what's your opinion of those men who have to do with boys? If you were King, wouldn't you kill every one of 'em?

White: Yes; Every feller that lives ashore and does *that*, I'd shoot him—yaas, by—, I'd shoot him.

Van Buskirk: And if you had a navy, wouldn't you kill every man in it found guilty of *that*?

White: No;—what can a feller do?—three years at sea—and hardly any chance to have a woman. I tell you, drummer, a feller *must do so.* Biles and pimples and corruption will come out all over his body if he don't.

White's assertion of the benefits to health derived from illicit commerce with boys ran wildly contrary to everything Van Buskirk had read and knew to be true. Responding in a manner that might be expected of a man from polite levels of society, he offered to provide White with a book proving him wrong. Will you read it? he asked. "Thankee—I'll read it," the old sailor said. The pronunciation registered, because Van Buskirk transcribed White's answer with the two Es. Few in the home of a Maryland secretary of state said "thankee," except perhaps the servants. Van Buskirk gave no indication he ever succeeded in forcing his book-learned truths down the social scale to supplant the contrary truths Old White had learned from family and friends. The diary contains no record of a further conversation or of White's having received the book.

Sexual associations on board the *Plymouth* flourished as formalized relationships between either men and boys or older and younger boys. The junior partners in these pairings were called "chickens," and the arrangement was known as "chickenship." The age differential within each dyad, and even the terminology, implies a superior-inferior relationship. Old White and Old Dhu, two crew members Van Buskirk identified as involved in shipboard homoerotic relationships, were both undoubtedly the elder members in their sexual partnerships, as indicated by their nicknames. Although members of these pairings clearly understood the nature of their junior-senior relationship, chickenship did not necessarily imply exploitation. To the contrary, the younger partners often benefited greatly. Not only did mentors frequently ply their boys with gifts and cash, but they customarily provided them with treats to vary the monotonous shipboard fare. Mariners even commented on boys taking advantage of their older partners.

The terms *chicken* and *chickenship* were used on many other ships of the United States Navy. Joseph T. Downey, in his accounts of service on board the *Portsmouth* and with the navy in California, referred to one young man as his chicken. Although Downey did not specify if he was using the word in the sexual sense, a number of *Portsmouth* officers and crewmen believed him to be involved in sexual activities with boys. He was court-martialed on charges of having had unnatural relations with Jonas Rhodes, one of the boys on board, but was acquitted. His only punishments were a demotion for failing to keep the storeroom locked and the surrender of his key.

Downey's loss of access to the storeroom quite likely disrupted any liaisons planned for the future, because storerooms were as notorious as boom covers for trysts. Van Buskirk once referred to the one on the *Plymouth* as a "Sodomy den." Herman Melville described the storeroom of the *Neversink* as a den of "tarry perdition" superintended by a little, goggle-eyed old man with "bachelor oddities" and a taste for the company of faultless young men. If Downey did engage in sexual involvements with Rhodes or any of the boys, he was probably among kindred spirits: the muster roll of the vessel for 1846 listed Billy Dhu as a quarter-gunner.

Regular physical proximity between pairs of boys did not go unnoticed on board the *Plymouth*. A quartermaster once teased Van Buskirk after observing him sleeping on deck with Andrew Milne. Van Buskirk recorded the dialogue:

Quartermaster: Well! You lays alongside o' boys now o' nights, do you?

Van Buskirk: Of late days I rate a chicken—to be sure! What next?

Quartermaster: Why ain't you ashamed of yourself to have a boy alongside you all night.

Van Buskirk: Not exactly, considering who the boy is, and that nothing bad results from our sleeping together.

Quartermaster: Who the boy is! Why that boy would _ _ _ _ a jackass [this and subsequent four-letter omissions appear in the original].

Van Buskirk: I don't care if he would _ _ _ _ a jackass—I know that he don't _ _ _ _ me. Every night passed with me by the boy is a night spent in innocence—when he sleeps with me, he is out of harm's way, and if he didn't sleep with me, he'd certainly sleep with somebody else, and, in that case bad consequences might indeed result.

Quartermaster: Oh Hell! now do you mean to say that you sleeps alongside o' boys o' nights and don't do nothing?

Van Buskirk: Well, you may as well drop the subject—I see you are a little more interested than you ought to be—You are jealous.

The quartermaster evidently erred in accusing Van Buskirk of engaging Milne in sex acts, even though his suspicions were well based. But in addition the dialogue between the two men indicates another of the many disparities in outlook, values, and perceptions between the middle class and the social levels that produced sailors. Many of Van Buskirk's school friends and college associates grew up in large families where siblings regularly shared beds. Brothers slept with brothers, and sisters with sisters, often until maturity or marriage. At boarding schools and colleges the shortage of beds often necessitated sharing, and at inns throughout the nation guests frequently slept next to total strangers. The practice was regarded as economical and, in colder areas of the country, practical because of the added warmth. The more in the bed, the warmer the sleepers. For affluent landsmen, there was no implied meaning or sexual titillation associated with the activity.

Seafarers, however, considered spending the night under a coat with a shipmate a different matter. As the quartermaster informed Van Buskirk, it looked like chickenship to him. If the oral traditions of those from the lower end of the social spectrum did not make explicit the link between sleeping arrangements and homoerotic sexuality, boys learned to make the association once they went to sea. Poor families, with less opportunity for privacy than the more comfortable classes, undoubtedly shared bed, pallet, or straw pile, as opposed to a single bedstead. Furthermore, their marginal living conditions often required siblings, parents, and even members of extended families to sleep together. Given the lack of privacy inherent in such situations, youths of this class had firsthand evidence of the connection between sleeping arrangements and sexual activity and may even have participated in it, in addition to watching and listening. When these boys joined the navy, their experiences and associations went with them. Any young seaman who failed to recognize the immutable link between sex and the pallet or straw pile quickly learned that bedding down with a friend on the gratings or under the boom cover implied more than convenience or friendship.

Van Buskirk knew precisely what occurred on board the *Plymouth*, but his upbringing prevented him from accepting it with the aplomb that others did. He regularly lodged complaints in his diary about the high level of mutual masturbation on board ship. Of the six white boys on the *Plymouth*, he grumbled in an early diary entry, all but one had a reputation tarnished by immorality. He later expanded his estimate of immorality to include the entire United States Navy. Of all the boys he met during his military career, he claimed that only one did not engage in sex with shipmates.

James Keenan was one of the few youths on the *Plymouth* of whom Van Buskirk approved, at least until he came to know him well. Charley Berry once assured him Keenan had no sexual contact with anyone on board the ship. "*He is one of the right sort—one of your sort,*" explained the captain of the afterguard:

"he won't do any thing of that kind." In a confidential moment Keenan admitted to Van Buskirk that he had once been trapped into mutual masturbation but promised never to do it again. Van Buskirk forgave the transgression because of his repentance and soon began bestowing gifts and favors on the boy. Unfortunately, within a matter of weeks the drummer began to suspect that he had been taken in. Keenan probably delighted in telling the tale of his violation to the credulous musician, when he was in fact not only a regular in the boom cover trade but also, Van Buskirk discovered, another man's chicken. Keenan's dubious character soon became apparent to Van Buskirk. An attempt at desertion resulted in Keenan's spending time in double irons on May 26, 1853. On another occasion he deserted while the ship was in port in China, only to be returned, apparently by local authorities. Van Buskirk had also been fooled by the sarcasm of Charley Berry, who, in describing the two boys as "fellows of the right sort," may have been having as much sport with him as had Keenan.

When Van Buskirk returned from liberty during his first months on board the *Plymouth*, other men invariably asked, "Did you get a girl?" The standardized response required him to explain that there was no point in paying three dollars on land for what cost a quarter afloat. By December 1852 he regretted making the casual comment so often in front of impressionable boys. It was a "villainous remark," he reflected, particularly since he was attempting to establish a reputation for unimpeached morality among his cohorts. Van Buskirk assumed he had an unblemished reputation on board the *Plymouth*. He apparently thought that his denial of the story about his activities on board the *Cumberland* and his frequent denunciations of chickenship and other shipboard sexuality made his stand clear.

His reputation for morality may have been widespread, but evidently not all on board the *Plymouth* had received word of his commitment to purity. One winter night while he was on watch at Macao Roads a lad offered to masturbate him. He declined the offer, but the youngster persevered, obviously unaware that Van Buskirk publicly opposed such activity. In this case virtue triumphed and the boy departed, but Van Buskirk gained only a momentary victory. Alone in the darkness, he later confessed to his diary that he then inflicted "the dreadful evil" upon himself.

Van Buskirk may have misled the men on his ship about his motives and past activities, but he could not delude himself. His concern over the immorality of his sexual activities along with a persistent sense of guilt over his perceived betrayal of the family and the Van Buskirk name fill the diary. All his sins were lumped together rather than classified according to level of evil. "I the only son of a Secretary of State, have successively consummated with a vagrant, a soldier, a sailor-boy, a petty-officer of a ship and (over and over again) myself." This list appeared twice in the diary during 1853. On both occasions he neglected to include his school chum at Georgetown or the Spaniard in New Orleans who paid to fondle his penis. The absence of these two males may have been the result of forgetfulness, but more likely it indicated that no seminal emissions occurred. In Van Buskirk's scheme of things, sex acts were sinful only if they proceeded to the point of ejaculation.

Yet with or without his Georgetown friend or the Spaniard, Van Buskirk was sometimes frantic over his sexual engagements. "My title is to a cell or crevice in the bowels of Hell. . . . You were doubly cursed in me," he wrote in a cry to his long-dead father. In the entries for an obviously difficult October weekend, he classified himself as a miserable dog and hell's favorite child, as someone polluted, guilty, unworthy of scorn, criminal, and dreadful. The list of pejoratives continued over the next several years with varying intensity. Like Job, he begged God to rescue him from his agonies while wailing that he was too polluted to pray. Even after washing his "defiled parts" he remained unable to address the Almighty. Meditation on his moral state only moved him to tears.

Van Buskirk's sense of guilt over the disgrace he brought to the family name went far beyond simple agony for sexual transgressions. The failures at Georgetown and St. John's weighed heavily on him, and he may have blamed himself in one way or another for his father's suicide. All of this, coupled with his sexual relationships, made him acutely conscious of having defamed his father's family. "I reviewed, last night the mal-career of my early youth. . . . Water will ever flow freely from my eyes when I reflect upon the fate of my honored Sire, who sunk under the double misfortune of a perverse wife . . . and a son who dishonored his name."

The best analogy he found to illuminate his depravity came from Gibbon's *Decline and Fall of the Roman Empire.* At the capture of Constantinople, the only son of Phranza, the historian, first chamberlain, principal secretary, and close friend of the emperor, was taken prisoner by the Turks. Although Van Buskirk saw the obvious parallel—the only son of a principal secretary and the only living son of a secretary of state—the differences struck him more forcefully. The gulf that divided one son from the other exceeded time and place. Phranza's son chose death rather than a pampered life as a favorite harem boy of Mohammet II, whereas Van Buskirk willingly engaged in sex with sailors and ne'er-do-wells.

Herman *Melville*

"A Peep through a Port-Hole at the Subterranean Parts of a Man-of-War," in *White Jacket*

While now running rapidly away from the bitter coast of Patagonia, battling with the night-watches—still cold—as best we may; come under the lee of my white-jacket, reader, while I tell of the less painful sights to be seen in a frigate.

A hint has already been conveyed concerning the subterranean depths of the *Neversink's* hold. But there is no time here to speak of the *spirit-room,* a cellar down in the afterhold, where the sailor "grog" is kept; nor of the *cable-tiers,* where the great hawsers and chains are piled, as you see them at a large ship-chandler's on shore; nor of the grocer's vaults, where tierces of sugar, molasses, vinegar, rice, and flour are snugly stowed; nor of the *sail-room,* full as a sail-maker's loft ashore—piled up with great top-sails and top-gallant-sails, all ready-folded in their places, like so many white vests in a gentleman's wardrobe; nor of the copper and copper-fastened *magazine,* closely packed with kegs of powder, great-gun and small-arm cartridges; nor of the immense *shot-lockers,* or subterranean arsenals, full as a bushel of apples with twenty-four-pound balls; nor of the *bread-room,* a large apartment, tinned all round within to keep out the mice, where the hard biscuit destined for the consumption of five hundred men on a long voyage is stowed away by the cubic yard; nor of the vast iron *tanks* for fresh water in the hold, like the reservoir lakes at Fairmount, in Philadelphia; nor of the *paint-room,* where the kegs of white-lead, and casks of linseed oil, and all sorts of pots and brushes, are kept; nor of the *armoror's smithy,* where the ship's forges and anvils may be heard ringing at times; I say I have no time to speak of these things, and many more places of note.

But there is one very extensive warehouse among the rest that needs special mention—*the ship's Yeoman's store-room.* In the *Neversink* it was down in the ship's basement, beneath the berth-deck, and you went to it by way of the *Fore-passage,* a very dim, devious corridor, indeed. Entering—say at noonday—you find yourself in a gloomy apartment, lit by a solitary lamp. On one side are shelves, filled with balls of *marline, ratlin-stuff, seizing-stuff, spun-yarn,* and numerous twines of assorted sizes. In another direction you see large cases containing heaps of articles, reminding one of a shoe-maker's furnishing-store— wooden *serving-mallets, fids, toggles,* and *heavers;* iron *prickers* and *marling-spikes;* in a third quarter you see a sort of hardware shop—shelves piled with all manner of hooks, bolts, nails, screws, and *thimbles;* and, in still another direction, you see a block-maker's store, heaped up with lignum-vitæ sheeves and wheels.

Through low arches in the bulk-head beyond, you peep in upon distant vaults and catacombs, obscurely lighted in the far end, and showing immense coils of new ropes, and other bulky articles, stowed in tiers, all savoring of tar.

But by far the most curious department of these mysterious store-rooms is the armory, where the pikes, cutlasses, pistols, and belts, forming the arms of the boarders in time of action, are hung against the walls, and suspended in thick rows from the beams overhead. Here, too, are to be seen scores of Colt's patent revolvers, which, though furnished with but one tube, multiply the fatal bullets, as the naval cat-o'-nine-tails, with a cannibal cruelty, in one blow nine times multiplies a culprit's lashes; so that, when a sailor is ordered one dozen lashes, the sentence should read one hundred and eight. All these arms are kept in the brightest order, wearing a fine polish, and may truly be said to *reflect* credit on the Yeoman and his mates.

Among the lower grade of officers in a man-of-war, that of Yeoman is not the least important. His responsibilities are denoted by his pay. While the *petty officers,* quarter-gunners, captains of the tops, and others, receive but fifteen and eighteen dollars a month—but little more than a mere able seaman—the Yeoman in an American line-of-battle ship receives forty dollars, and in a frigate thirty-five dollars per month.

He is accountable for all the articles under his charge, and on no account must deliver a yard of twine or a tenpenny nail to the boatswain or carpenter, unless shown a written requisition and order from the Senior Lieutenant. The Yeoman is to be found burrowing in his under-ground store-rooms all the day long, in readiness to serve licensed customers. But in the counter, behind which he usually stands, there is no place for a till to drop the shillings in, which takes away not a little from the most agreeable part of a storekeeper's duties. Nor, among the musty, old account-books in his desk, where he registers all expenditures of his stuffs, is there any cash or check book.

The Yeoman of the *Neversink* was a somewhat odd specimen of a Troglodite. He was a little old man, round-shouldered, bald-headed, with great goggle-eyes, looking through portentous round spectacles, which he called his *barnacles*. He was imbued with a wonderful zeal for the naval service, and seemed to think that, in keeping his pistols and cutlasses free from rust, he preserved the national honor untarnished.

After *general quarters,* it was amusing to watch his anxious air as the various *petty officers* restored to him the arms used at the martial exercises of the crew. As successive bundles would be deposited on his counter, he would count over the pistols and cutlasses, like an old housekeeper telling over her silver forks and spoons in a pantry before retiring for the night. And often, with a sort of dark lantern in his hand, he might be seen poking into his furthest vaults and cellars, and counting over his great coils of ropes, as if they were all jolly puncheons of old Port and Madeira.

By reason of his incessant watchfulness and unaccountable bachelor oddities, it was very difficult for him to retain in his employment the various sailors who, from time to time, were billeted with him to do the duty of subalterns. In particular, he was always desirous of having at least one steady, faultless young man, of a literary taste, to keep an eye to his account-books, and swab out the armory every morning. It was an odious business this, to be immured all day in such a bottomless hole, among tarry old ropes and villainous guns and pistols. It was with peculiar dread that I one day noticed the goggle-eyes of *Old Revolver,* as they called him, fastened upon me with a fatal glance of good-will and approbation. He had somehow heard of my being a very learned person, who could both read and write with extraordinary facility; and, moreover, that I was a rather reserved youth, who kept his modest, unassuming merits in the background. But though, from the keen sense of my situation as a man-of-war's-man, all this about my keeping myself in the *back* ground was true enough, yet I had no idea of hiding my diffident merits *under* ground. I became alarmed at the old Yeoman's goggling glances, lest he should drag me down into tarry perdition in his hideous store-rooms. But this fate was providentially averted, owing to mysterious causes which I never could fathom.

Herman *Melville*

From "The Social State in a Man-of-War," in *White Jacket*

What too many seamen are when ashore is very well known; but what some of them become when completely cut off from shore indulgences can hardly be imagined by landsmen. The sins for which the cities of the plain were overthrown still linger in some of these wooden-walled Gomorrahs of the deep. More than once complaints were made at the mast in the *Neversink,* from which the deck officer would turn away with loathing, refuse to hear them, and command the complainant out of his sight. There are evils in men-of-war, which, like the suppressed domestic drama of Horace Walpole, will neither bear representing, nor reading, and will hardly bear thinking of. The landsman who has neither read Walpole's *Mysterious Mother,* nor Sophocles's *Œdipus Tyrannus,* nor the Roman story of *Count Cenci,* dramatized by Shelley, let that landsman guardedly remain in his ignorance of even worse horrors than these, and forever abstain from seeking to draw aside this veil.

"Collecting Forage," from volume 1 of *Personal Memoirs of P. H. Sheridan, General, United States Army*

Corn was abundant in the region to the south and southwest of Murfreesboro', so to make good our deficiences in this respect, I employed a brigade about once a week in the duty of collecting and bringing in forage, sending out sometimes as many as a hundred and fifty wagons to haul the grain which my scouts had previously located. In nearly every one of these expeditions the enemy was encountered, and the wagons were usually loaded while the skirmishers kept up a running fire. Often there would occur a respectable brush, with the loss on each side of a number of killed and wounded. The officer in direct command always reported to me personally whatever had happened during the time he was out—the result of his reconnoissance, so to speak, for that was the real nature of these excursions—and on one occasion the colonel in command, Colonel Conrad, of the Fifteenth Missouri, informed me that he got through without much difficulty; in fact, that everything had gone all right and been eminently satisfactory, except that in returning he had been mortified greatly by the conduct of *the two females belonging to the detachment and division train at my headquarters.* These women, he said, had given much annoyance by getting drunk, and to some extent demoralizing his men. To say that I was astonished at his statement would be a mild way of putting it, and had I not known him to be a most upright man and of sound sense, I should have doubted not only his veracity, but his sanity. Inquiring who they were and for further details, I was informed that there certainly were in the command two females, that in some mysterious manner had attached themselves to the service as soldiers; that one, an East Tennessee woman, was a teamster in the division wagon-train and the other a private soldier in a cavalry company temporarily attached to my headquarters for escort duty. While out on the foraging expedition these Amazons had secured a supply of "apple-jack" by some means, got very drunk, and on the return had fallen into Stone River and been nearly drowned. After they had been fished from the water, in the process of resuscitation their sex was disclosed, though up to this time it appeared to be known only to each other. The story was straight and the circumstance clear, so, convinced of Conrad's continued sanity, I directed the provost-marshal to bring in arrest to my headquarters the two disturbers of Conrad's peace of mind. After some little search the East Tennessee woman was found in camp, somewhat the worse for the experiences of the day before, but awaiting her fate contentedly smoking a cob-pipe. She was brought to me, and put in duress under charge of the division surgeon until her companion could be secured. To the doctor she related that the year before she had "refugeed" from East Tennessee, and on arriving in Louisville assumed men's apparel and sought and obtained employment as a teamster in the quartermaster's department. Her features were very large, and so coarse and masculine was her general appearance that she would readily have passed as a man, and in her case the deception was no doubt easily practiced. Next day the "she dragoon" was caught, and proved to be a rather prepossessing young woman, and though necessarily bronzed and hardened by exposure, I doubt if, even with these marks of campaigning, she could have deceived as readily as did her companion. How the two got acquainted I never learned, and though they had joined the army independently of each other, yet an intimacy had sprung up between them long before the mishaps of the foraging expedition. They both were forwarded to army headquarters, and, when provided with clothing suited to their sex, sent back to Nashville, and thence beyond our lines to Louisville.

To Nathaniel Bloom and John F. S. Gray from Walt Whitman, March 19–20, 1863, from *The Collected Writings of Walt Whitman*, I, No. 40

Dear Nat and Fred Gray,

Since I left New York . . . have struck up a tremendous friendship with a young Mississippi captain (about 19) that we took prisoner badly wounded at Fredericksburg—(he has followed me here, is in Emory hospital here, minus a leg— he wears his confederate uniform, proud as the devil—I met him first at Falmouth, in the Lacy house, middle of December last, his leg just cut off, and cheered him up—poor boy, he has suffered a great deal and still suffers—has eyes bright as a hawk, but face pale—our affection is quite an affair, quite romantic—sometimes when I lean over to say I am going, he puts his arm round my neck, draws my face down, etc., quite a scene for the New Bowery). . . . I miss you all, my darlings and gossips, Fred Gray, and Bloom and Russell and every body. I wish you would all come here in a body—that would be divine. (We would drink ale, which is here of the best.) My health, strength, personal beauty, etc, are, I am happy to inform you, without diminution. . . . My beard, neck, etc., are woollier, fleecier, whiter than ever. I wear army boots, with magnificent black morocco tops, the trousers put in, wherein shod and legged confront I Virginia's deepest mud with supercilious eyes.

To Nathaniel Bloom from Walt Whitman, September 5, 1863, from *The Collected Writings of Walt Whitman*, I, No. 74

Dear Nat,

I wish you were here if only to enjoy the bright and beautiful weather we are having here now for about two weeks—then it is sufficiently cool, and the air buoyant and inspiriting. . . . I tell you, Nat, my evenings are frequently spent in scenes that make a terrible difference—for I am still a hospital visitor . . . I spend the evenings in hospital—the experience is a profound one, beyond all else, and touches me personally, egotistically, in unprecedented ways—I mean the way often the amputated, sick, sometimes dying soldiers cling and cleave to me as it were a man overboard to a plank, and the perfect content they have if I will remain with them, sit on the side of the cot awhile, some youngsters often, and caress them etc.—It is delicious to be the object of so much love and reliance, and to do them such good, soothe and pacify torments of wounds etc.—You will doubtless see in what I have said the reason I continue so long in this kind of life—as I am entirely on my own hook too. . . . Dear Nat, your good and friendly letter came safe, and was indeed welcome—I had not thought you had forgotten me, but I wondered why you did not write—what comfort you must take out there in the country, by the river—I have read your letter many times, as I do from all my dear friends and boys there in New York—Perkins lately wrote me a first-rate letter, and I will reply to it soon—I wish to see you all very much—I wish you to give my love to Fritschy, and Fred Gray—I desire both to write to me—Nat, you also, my dear comrade, and tell me all about the boys and everything, all the little items are so good—should Charles Russell visit New York, I wish you to say to him I send him my love—I wish you the same to Perk, and to Kingsley and Ben Knower—so good bye, my comrade, till we meet, and God bless you dear friend—

Walt

Alonzo S. Bush to Walt Whitman, December 22, 1863, from *Drum Beats: Walt Whitman's Civil War Boy Lovers*

Friend Walt,

Sir, I am happy to announce the arrival of your kind and very welcome epistle, and I can assure you that the contents were perused with all the pleasure imaginable. I am glad to know that you are once more in the hotbed city of Washington so that you can go often and see that friend of ours at Armory Square {Hospital}, L[ewis] K. B[rown]. The fellow that went down on your BK, both so often with me. I wished that I could see him this evening and go into the ward master's room and have some fun for he is a gay boy. I am very sorry indeed to hear that after laying so long that he is about to lose his leg. It is too bad, but I suppose that the Lord's will must be done and we must submit. . . .

I remain your true friend, Alonzo Bush

Alonzo Bush to Walt Whitman, March 7, 1864, from *Drum Beats: Walt Whitman's Civil War Boy Lovers*

Friend Walter,

Your kind favor of 22nd came to hand all O.K., and I was glad to hear from you and the Hospital Boys and learn that you were getting along fine. I should like to have been out to the front with you and seen the old army of {the} Potomac once more for since we left them we have had no fight or skirmish in that line. Every thing is dull down here. You say you have had some hard weather of late. We experienced some of it I dare say—

I am glad to know that the boys had such good quarters this winter and hope that they may be able to whip the rebs in the coming contest. I was much pleased to hear that Lewis Brown had recovered so much as to go out on pass. Tell him to go slow and all will be well in the outcome. And tell him that I still look for his and Benedict's photographs. Bartlett's I have. . . . There is a large dance house and pleasure garden about 1/4 {mile?} from here. They are fixing it up for the summer. So you must come down. When it gets in full blast a boat will play between here and Washington so it will be handy and I shall expect many of the boys to come. John Strain is in pretty good health, but his leg has never been of much service to him since he is expecting his discharge at this time, he will get it. . . . I gave that note to Larr, and he was much pleased to hear from you, and will reply to it in person. They both wish to be remembered to you and the boys of Hospital. Please remember me to Miss Lowell, Brown, Benedict, Bartlett, and Charles Cate—also to all others of my acquaintance—and don't forget to reserve a due portion for yourself. I will now close. Hoping to hear from you soon. Good bye.

To Lewis K. Brown from Walt Whitman, August 1, 1863, from *The Collected Writings of Walt Whitman*, 1, No. 60

Both your letters have been received, Lewy—the second one came this morning and was welcome as any thing from you will always be, and the sight of your face welcomer than all, my darling—I see you write in good spirits, and appear to have first rate times—Lew, you must not go around too much, nor eat and drink too promiscuous, but be careful and moderate, and not let the kindness of friends carry you away, lest you break down again, dear son—. . . . You speak of being here in Washington again about the last of August—O Lewy, how glad I should be to see you, to have you with me—I have thought if it could be so that you, and one other person and myself could be where we could work and live together, and have each other's society, we three, I should like it so much—but it is probably a dream.

To Elijah Douglass Fox from Walt Whitman, November 21, 1863, from *The Collected Writings of Walt Whitman*, 1, No. 98

Dear son and comrade,
I wrote a few lines about five days ago and sent on to Armory Square, but as I have not heard from it I suppose you have gone on to Michigan. . . . Dearest comrade, I only write this lest the one I wrote five days ago may not reach you from the hospital. I am still here at my mother's, and feel as if [I] have had enough of going around New York—enough of amusements, suppers, drinking, and what is called *pleasure*—Dearest son, it would be more pleasure if we could be together just in quiet, in some plain way of living with some good employment and reasonable income, where I could have you often with me, than all the dissipations and amusements of this great city—O I hope things may work so that we can yet have each other's society—for I cannot bear the thought of being separated from you—I know I am a great fool about such things, but I tell you the truth, dear son. I do not think one night has passed in New York or Brooklyn when I have been at the theater or opera or afterward to some supper party or carouse made by the young fellows for me, but what amid the play or the singing, I would perhaps suddenly think of you—and the same at the gayest supper party, of men, where all was fun and noise and laughing and drinking, of a dozen young men, and I among them, I would see your face before me in my thought as I have seen it so often there in Ward G, and my amusement or drink would be all turned to nothing, and I would realize how happy it would be if I could leave all the fun and noise and the crowd and be with

you—I don't wish to disparage my dear friends and acquaintances here, there are so many of them and all so good, many so educated, traveled, etc., some so handsome and witty, some rich etc., some among the literary class—many young men—all good—many of them educated and polished, and brilliant in conversation, etc.,—and I thought I valued their society and friendship—and I do, for it is worth valuing—but Douglass, I will tell you the truth, you are so much closer to me than any of them that there is no comparison—there has never passed so much between them and me as we have—besides there is something that takes down all artificial accomplishments, and that is a manly and loving soul—My dearest comrade, I am sitting here writing to you very late at night—I have been reading—it is indeed after 12, and my mother and all the rest have gone to bed two hours ago, and I am here alone writing to you, and I enjoy it too, although it is not much, yet I know it will please you, dear boy—If you get this, you must write and tell me where and how you are. I hope you are quite well, and with your dear wife, for I know you have long wished to be with her, and I wish you to give her my best respects and love too.

Douglass, I haven't written any news, for there is nothing particular I have to write. Well, it is now past midnight, pretty well on to 1 o'clock, and my sheet is written out—so, my dear darling boy, I must bid you good night, or rather good morning and I hope it may be God's will we shall yet be with each other— but I must indeed bid you good night, my dear loving comrade, and the blessing of God on you by night and day, my darling boy.

Nicholas Palmer to Walt Whitman, June 24, 1865, from *Calamus Lovers: Walt Whitman's Working-Class Camaradoes*

Mr. Whitman, dear friend,
I concluded I would talk a few words to you through this instrument. I am well and hope the safe arrival of this may find you the same. There is not much talk of the veterans getting out. Yet if you have anything in the way of advice to give concerning my employment when I am discharged, names talk plain to me, Mr. Whitman. I have been over the world more perhaps than you would imag-

ine. There are a great many cruel turns and there are a variety of ways of making a living. Leaving hard work out of the books, I'd have thought that there were bigger fools than me making a living very easy. Although I admit my education is limited, name anything you please, and if I do not propose to accept: that is as far as it will go. I will *blow* no one. What about such houses are we were talking about? {*sic*} And [what?] if it could be made agreeable for me to take up lodging in close proximity with yours? I should be pleased in the superlative degree. Please write immediately after you receive this and give me some advice, no matter what sort. I conclude hoping to hear from you soon. Until then, I remain your friend, as ever.

Nicholas D. Palmer

Note in Walt Whitman's Hand

June 28th, '65. I have received many curious letters in my time from one and another of those persons (women and mothers) who have been reading "Leaves of Grass"—and some singular ones from soldiers—but never before one of this description—I keep it as a *curiosity*. The writer was one of the soldiers in Sherman's army last of [May]—one of the hundreds I talked with and occasionally showed some little kindness to—I met him, talked with him some.—He came one rainy night to my room and stopped with me—I am completely in the dark as to what "such houses as we were talking about," are—

—upon the whole not to be answered—(and yet I itch to satisfy my curiosity as to what this young man can have really taken me for).

To Bethuel Smith from Walt Whitman (draft), September 16?, 1863, from *The Collected Writings of Walt Whitman*, 1, No. 79

Dear Comrade,
I thought I would write you a few lines and see if they would reach you—I was very much disappointed when I went to Armory {Square Hospital} that evening to find my dear comrade was gone so sudden and unexpected.

[Deleted: Thuey, I think about you often and miss you more than you have any idea of—I hope you will. . . .]

Thuey, did you take the envelope you had with my address?—if you did why have you not written to me, comrade?

What kind of accommodations have you at Carlisle, Thu, and how is the foot? I want to hear all about it—if you get this you must write to me, Thu, you need not mind ceremony—there is no need of *ceremony* between dear friends for that I hope we are, my loving boy, for all the difference in our ages.

There is nothing new with me here—I am very well in health and spirits, and only need some employment, clerkship or something, at fair wages to make things go agreeable with me—no, there is one thing more I need and that is Thuey, for I believe I am quite a fool, I miss you so. . . . Well I will not write any more at this time—so good bye for present, Thuey, and I pray God bless you, my dear loving comrade, and I hope he will bring us together again—good bye, dear boy, from your true friend—

Thuey, I enclose an envelope but will write my address here too for future—

Thuey, you went away without getting paid, ain't you broke? I can send you a little, a few 10ct bills, my darling—you write to me, Thu, just how it is—you need not be afraid, my darling comrade—it is little, but it may be some use—Thuey, you write to me just as you would to your own older brother—

Bethuel Smith to Walt Whitman, September 17, 1863 (first letter), from *Drum Beats: Walt Whitman's Civil War Boy Lovers*

Friend Walt I take my pen in hand to let you know where I am. I am at Carlisle Barracks in the hospital. I am getting along very well now. We stop in tents here and it looks very lonesome here to me.

Write soon. Direct your letters to Bethuel Smith, Carlisle Barracks, Pennsylvania.

Bethuel Smith to Walt Whitman, September 17, 1863 (second letter), from *Drum Beats: Walt Whitman's Civil War Boy Lovers*

Dear friend Walt,

I received your kind letter and was very glad to hear from you and to hear that you was well. I left the Armory Hospital in somewhat of a hurry. I went in the ambulance to the depot and took the cars north at 11 o'clock and we got to Philadelphia about 2 o'clock. There we got some bread and ham and coffee. We stayed there till three, and then we started to Harrisburg. We got there about dark, and stayed there all night. The next day we started for Carlisle. We got to Carlisle about 10 in the morning. We went in to hospital tents. We have rather poor accommodating here. The foot is getting better fast. I can get around quite smart on it. I think in a few days I can put on my boots and not hurt me much of any. There is lots of fruits here and cakes, pies etc., but it don't do me much good for I have not got any money to buy it with. I wish that you would send me a few of them ten cents notes if you please. It is very lonesome here to me.

I hope that I shall soon go to my regiment, for I don't like to stay here very well. I would like to see you very well.

Well, Walt, I don't know as I have any more to write at present, so good bye for this time. Write soon, please.

Benton H. Wilson to Walt Whitman, November 11, 1865, from *Drum Beats: Walt Whitman's Civil War Boy Lovers*

Mr. Whitman, Dear Friend,

I suppose you will think that I have forgotten you long before this time, but I have not, your kindness to me while in the hospital was never to be forgotten by me.

I have entirely recovered from my wounds long since and have been at work part of the time attending commercial school. I have been at work about six weeks, consequently my hand is not in very good condition for writing. . . . I would like to know what chance I would have to go into business with a few hundred dollars capital. If I can not go into anything then what do you think of my going further south, say to Savannah.

I want you when you write to tell me just what you think about it. I do not know as you will be much interested by receiving this letter from me but I would like to hear from you very much. Yours with respect,

Benton H. Wilson to Walt Whitman, January 27, 1867, from *Drum Beats: Walt Whitman's Civil War Boy Lovers*

Your letter of the 10th of January was received more than a week ago and should have been answered before this time but I have not been in the humor of writing and have kept putting it off till some more convenient season but I will try to be more punctual in the future. . . . You say you wish me to write how I am situated what I am doing etc. I wrote you a year and more ago that I was married but did not receive any reply so I did not know but you was displeased with it. . . . If you come to New York next summer on a visit I shall expect you to take a short trip up here to see me (if I am still here) and I will pay your fare and take as good care of you as we possibly can. Now if you come to New York, you must not fail to let me know it. . . . I remain as ever Your Boy Friend with Love.

Benton H. Wilson to Walt Whitman, April 7, 1867, from *Drum Beats: Walt Whitman's Civil War Boy Lovers*

Dear Friend and Comrade,
I can not make any other excuse for my delay in answering your welcome letter of March 15 than negligence for I have had time for it but have kept putting it off from day to day because I have not heard much news that I thought would interest you. . . . I spoke of going to South America but I have given that idea up for I do not believe a man can do as well any where else as he can in the

United States the greatest country in the world, but I will tell you why I thought of going there. I am poor and am proud of it but I hope to rise by honesty and industry. I am a married man but I am not happy for my disposition is not right. I have got a good woman and I love her dearly but I seem to lack patience or something. I think I had ought to live alone, but I had not ought to feel so.

I would like very much to see you for I have so much to tell you, and to talk about, but I fear I shall wear you with such a letter as this so I will close it with my love to you.

To Benton H. Wilson from Walt Whitman, draft letter of April 12, 1867, from *The Collected Writings of Walt Whitman*, 1, No. 230

Dear boy,

Your letter has come to hand. According to request, I send you immediately a few hurried lines in response. My dear loving boy, I wish things were situated so you could be with me, and we could be together for a while, where we could enjoy each other's society and sweet friendship and you could talk freely. I am sure it would do you good, and it would be a great pleasure to me. But we must take things as they are. I have thought over some passages in the letter but will not at present say much to you on the subject, in writing. One or two things I will say briefly at present—One is, that it is every way the best and most natural condition for a young man to be married, having a companion, a good and affectionate wife—and another is, that contentment with one's situation in life does not depend half so much on what that situation is, as on the mood and spirit in which one accepts the situation and makes the best of it.

But these are bits of cold wisdom. I must put something to you better than that in my letter. So I will cheer my boy [and] tell you again, Benton, that I love you dearly, and always keep you in mind, though we are separated by hundreds of miles. Remember this dearest comrade, when things are cloudy with you, for it is true—and such thoughts are often a balm and comfort to the mind.

Write to me often as you can. Don't mind because we are separated now, as things are. We will meet one day, I have no doubt. Try to keep up the same brave heart in the affairs of peace, that I know you did when you were a soldier. A young man's life is a battle any how. Noble—thrice noble is he who steadily carries throughout the march, through defeat or whatever happens, a gay, unconquered spirit.

CHAPTER 7

The U.S. Navy after World War I

✤

The U.S. military had not been particularly concerned with the homoerotic practices of its soldiers or sailors during the late eighteenth or the early nineteenth
century. One of marine drummer Philip Van Buskirk's most frequent laments
during his service in the 1840s and 1850s was that the officers and noncommis-
sioned officers cared little about the vice and immorality he observed, chronicled,
and reported to them. Even the strains of the Civil War produced no move to
protect either Union or Confederate warriors from covert sodomites who might
be lurking in their tents or sleeping close by in shipboard hammocks. The continuous need for personnel by both Northern and Southern forces may have
made officers unenthusiastic about eliminating able-bodied men for any reason,
but it is unlikely that the lack of sodomy prosecutions resulted from the desper-
ate manning needs of either army or navy. The British, after all, pursued those
accused of homoerotic offenses with considerable vigor at the height of the
Napoleonic Wars. It is more likely that American military officers did not consider same-sex sexual activity among their men as a problem. Not until some
months after the end of World War I, when there were no longer threats to
democracy from any quarter, did the United States Navy generate its first homosexual scare. It is not entirely clear why, in a time of restored peace and continuing prosperity, the navy launched an offensive against homosexuals. Perhaps
national leaders who at the time were attempting to crush radical political movements inspired other men to cleanse the land of sexual subversives. More likely,
however, the well-established homosexual community in Newport, Rhode Island

had simply become more flagrant after the war, and the high visibility of the many sailors known to be among its members persuaded authorities to take action. Franklin Delano Roosevelt, then the assistant secretary of the Navy, authorized the probe and provided the investigators with administrative cover and support.

The enthusiasm demonstrated by the investigators and prosecutors in the Newport cases may or may not have reflected Roosevelt's own determination to root out homosexuality from the navy. He never revealed his own sentiments on the subject. The overzealous pursuit, perhaps, represented only a case of bureaucracy run amok. Later, during World War II, Roosevelt not only took considerable political risks to protect Sumner Welles, a high State Department official, from charges of homosexuality but may also have used his wartime censorship powers to shield Massachusetts senator David A. Walsh from public disgrace after his arrest in a police raid at all-boy brothel in New York City.

Ted Morgan
"The Newport Scandal," from *FDR: A Biography*

In 1919, reports began to come into the Navy Department about conditions at the Naval Training Station in Newport, Rhode Island. Apparently, there was a group of homosexuals among the sailors who called themselves the "Ladies of Newport" and who attended the socials at the Army and Navy YMCA. The Newport military chaplain, Episcopalian minister Samuel N. Kent, was often at the socials. Dressed in his officer's khaki uniform with a cross on the cap, the forty-six-year-old Kent was reported to pick up sailors, tell them they looked lonesome, and invite them back to the parish house on Spring Street, where he had a spare room.

Ervin Arnold, a forty-four-year-old chief machinist's mate stationed in Newport, who had once worked as a detective for the state of Connecticut, reported on the situation on February 27 to the training station's welfare officer, Lieutenant Erasmus Mead Hudson, Medical Corps.

Together, they took the matter to the station commander, Captain Edward H. Campbell, who had recently been instructed by {Secretary of the Navy}

Josephus Daniels to "clean the place up." Campbell asked Arnold how he would proceed, and Arnold said that conditions in Newport were so rotten that the only way would be to recruit a vice squad of enlisted men and send them out to be solicited. They might have to commit homosexual acts in order to obtain evidence, but there was no other way.

On March 15, 1919, a four-man court of inquiry was appointed to investigate the immoral conditions in Newport, with Lieutenant Commander Murphy J. Foster as president and Lieutenant Hudson as one of its members. The court asked Arnold to form a squad to help secure evidence. He recruited thirteen newly enlisted sailors, and was given office space in the Newport Red Cross headquarters.

Arnold told his men to go to Newport bars and other hangouts and mingle with homosexuals. "You people will be on the field of operation," he said. "You will have to use your judgment whether or not a full act is completed. If that being the fact, it might lead into something greater. You have got to form that judgment at the time you are on that field with that party."

Arnold was very insistent that his men be legally protected when they allowed immoral acts to be performed on them. He was told by Stewart Davis, the aide for information in the second naval district, that they would be protected provided they did not take the leading part. The volunteers were warned that they might be placed in embarrassing positions, and that the work was of a very nasty nature.

On March 22, 1919, Franklin {D. Roosevelt, the assistant secretary of the Navy,} who was acting . . . in Daniels' absence, was informed about the conditions at Newport, and at once wrote Attorney General A. Mitchell Palmer a confidential letter: "The Navy Department has become convinced that such conditions of vice and depravity exist in and around Newport, R.I., as to require a most searching and rigid investigation with a view to finally prosecuting and clearing out those people responsible for it. This department, through its local representatives, can indicate certain persons in the Army, Navy, and Marine Corps, and others who are civilians, who, our information leads us to believe, are not only engaged in traffic in drugs, but also are fostering dens where perverted practices are carried on. In view of the fact that the conditions involve others than those in the naval service, and of the further fact that the practices are carried on outside the places under the jurisdiction of the Navy

Department, it is impossible for this department through its own efforts to handle the situation. As the facts so far indicate that the combination is working beyond the limits of Newport, even to Providence, New York and Boston, it is evident that the situation is one that is even above the state authorities to handle. Newport is the home of several naval activities, one of which is a training station where thousands of young men are under training for the Navy. It is also one of the bases from which the Atlantic Fleet operates. This department, eager for the protection of its young men from such contaminating influences, desires to have the horrible practices stopped, and therefore requests that the Department of Justice put its most skilled investigators to work."

While waiting for the Justice Department to root out this sinister network with its tentacles stretching up and down the eastern seaboard, Arnold's Newport squad was busily catching "perverts." As Lieutenant Commander Foster remarked to Lieutenant Hudson: "If they don't stop Arnold right away he will hang the whole state of Rhode Island." The "Ladies of Newport" ring was broken up. Eighteen sailors were arrested between April 8 and April 14, fourteen of whom were court-martialed in August (two deserted and two were given dishonorable discharges). In its report, the Foster court of inquiry named the Arnold squad operatives upon whom completed homosexual acts had been performed, and recommended that a notation be entered in their service records "in recognition of their interest and zeal in their work in assisting the Judge Advocate, and in the best interests of the naval service." Surely this was the first time in the history of the U.S. Navy that sailors were officially commended for committing homosexual acts.

In the meantime, Roosevelt was called by his old friend, Governor R. Livingston Beekman of Rhode Island, who told him he was sending the Reverend Charles P. Hall, field director of the Newport Red Cross, to tell him what was going on. Hall said conditions were worse than ever. "What do you mean by that?" Roosevelt asked. "Everything," Hall said, "drugs, prostitution and perversion."

"What do you think we ought to do?"

"I think you should start a new investigation."

"Why can't we go ahead with the Court of Inquiry that is already sitting in Newport?"

"Because all the people they have got working for them are thoroughly well known in Newport."

"Why can't we employ civilians?"

"Because a civilian coming to a little bit of a place like Newport is spotted before he leaves the station platform."

Hall suggested that Roosevelt send for Lieutenant Hudson, who was familiar with conditions and could suggest ways to proceed with the investigation.

On May 1, Hudson and Arnold were summoned to Washington for temporary duty under the office of the assistant secretary of the Navy. Roosevelt was pleased to see that Hudson was from Plattsburgh in upstate New York and had gone to Harvard (class of 1913). Arnold handed him a detailed report on the completed homosexual acts performed by his operatives. Included in the report were accounts of homosexual acts with the Reverend Kent.

On May 5, Roosevelt sent a confidential memo to the director of Naval Intelligence, Rear Admiral Albert P. Niblack: "The conditions in and around one of our naval training stations is very serious indeed, insofar as moral perversion and drugs are concerned. . . . I wish Lieut. E. M. Hudson . . . and Chief Machinist Mate Ervin Arnold . . . be placed in your office for work in connection with suppressing these practices. . . . It is requested that this be the only written communication in regard to this affair, as it is thought wise to keep this matter wholly secret."

Niblack did not like the idea of a vice squad. You couldn't handle pitch without getting some on your hands. It would be extremely difficult for a young man in a U.S. Navy uniform, without any experience as a detective, to engage in work of this character without subjecting himself to the danger of suspicion as to his real motives, and as to the method which he would necessarily have to adopt to get evidence that would hold up in a court of law and lead to conviction. He told Roosevelt that the suppression of vice was outside the jurisdiction of Naval Intelligence.

Since the Justice Department was dragging its feet and Naval Intelligence wasn't interested, Roosevelt decided to take the Hudson-Arnold unit under his wing. On May 9, he signed the order detaching Lieutenant Hudson to new duty. On May 15, he gave Hudson a "To whom it may concern" letter, a highly unusual procedure in the Navy, which said: "Lieutenant E. M. Hudson, Medical

Corps, U.S. Navy, is engaged on important work in which I am interested, and any assistance you can render him will be appreciated."

On June 6, Hudson was back in Washington, complaining that nothing had been done because no orders had been issued and they still couldn't figure out where to attach him. Someone suggested the naval district in Hawaii, but that seemed ridiculous, so Roosevelt attached him directly to his own office. The order that he signed on June 11 read: "You are hereby designated as Commanding Officer of a group of officers and enlisted (or enrolled) men and women who have been assigned or may be assigned certain confidential special duties as agents of the Assistant Secretary of the Navy. This group, or unit, will bear the name: 'Section A—Office of the Assistant Secretary,' or simply: 'Section A—OASN.'"

As commanding officer of the mysterious Section A, Hudson was given the authority to promote his men, which as a lieutenant he would not normally have had. Since the Bureau of Navigation leaked like a sieve, all the orders and the correspondence would go out through Roosevelt's confidential stenographer. All the orders including the "Transfer of Personnel to Special Duty," were signed by Roosevelt. In all he signed at least twenty orders relating to Section A, including one on June 9 attaching Arnold to the assistant secretary's office for "duty of such a nature that he does not have written orders and will be out of the district most of the time." Thanks to Roosevelt, both Hudson and Arnold were given Naval Intelligence cards as special agents. Section A was financed out of the Contingent Navy Fund, with which the secretary of the Navy paid for unforeseen needs, such as banquets for distinguished foreigners or oil paintings of war actions.

When he had been in Washington on June 6 and 7, Lieutenant Hudson had expressed his concern to Roosevelt about the legal status of the operatives, whose unusual methods of investigation might make them vulnerable to criminal charges. Roosevelt directed Hudson to seek {legal} advice. . . . He was told that the methods he proposed to use constituted no criminal offense under the law, although {one attorney} did raise the moral question of whether the end justified the means. Section A recruited a total of forty-one enlisted men, ten of them between the ages of sixteen and nineteen. They were quite active in July, obtaining cases against sixteen Newport residents.

One of the sixteen was the Reverend Kent, who on July 30 was arrested, handcuffed, thrown into prison, and charged with being a lewd and wanton person. One of his fellow ministers put up the $400 for his bail. At his trial in Newport district court on August 22 and 23, before Judge Hugh Baker, two members of Section A testified that Kent had performed homosexual acts upon them. Thus it came out in open court that young men, some of them still in their teens, confided by their parents to the care of the U.S. Navy, had been ordered to submit to immoral acts in order to obtain evidence. This caused great indignation among the citizens of Newport. It was felt that Kent's possible guilt was less odious than the methods used by the Navy Department.

It was in this climate of wrought-up public opinion that Kent was acquitted, to the consternation of Roosevelt, who was informed by Hudson that Baker was a crooked judge who had been pressured by the Newport political and religious establishment.

On September 3, two Newport clergymen, Hamilton Fish Webster and Stanley C. Hughes, came to Washington to complain to Franklin about the methods of entrapment used by the Hudson squad. They presented him with a transcript of part of the trial testimony and asked that the Navy Department make a statement exonerating Kent. Professing to be greatly surprised that such orders had been given to enlisted men, Roosevelt said: "If anyone has given orders to commit immoral acts, someone will swing for it."

Then he added that "Newport has always been a very bad or immoral place."

"Why then do you arrest a clergyman from Massachusetts?" asked Reverend Hughes.

"Well, your courts are corrupt and untrustworthy," replied Roosevelt, "and I am informed that the judge who presided in this trial is accustomed to give his decisions for political reasons."

Reverend Webster rejoined that he knew the judge to be a man of the highest rectitude and character.

"I haven't time to go through all this matter that you have brought here," Roosevelt said. "Please lay it before Captain Leigh and I will give you a note to him and let him consider what ought to be done."

The two ministers went to see Captain Richard H. Leigh, acting chief of the Bureau of Navigation, who felt that the Hudson operatives had gone too far, that it could be embarrassing for the Navy, and that Section A should immediately cease its activities. The order to that effect, confirmed by Roosevelt, went out on September 4. Captain John D. Wainright was chosen to conduct an internal investigation of Section A. He interviewed the operatives and found that most of them had either been sodomized or had committed acts of sodomy in the course of their work.

On September 22, James De Wolf Perry, the Episcopal bishop of Rhode Island, came to Washington to see Josephus Daniels, who passed him on to Admiral Niblack of Naval Intelligence. Niblack, who had been opposed to Section A from the start, said: "Bishop, I know these facts very intimately and have been following the thing very closely. We placed these investigators in Newport and gave them wide range and I have reason now to investigate the investigators and to disapprove of the whole proceeding, and I have decided that it should come to an end, and I am making that recommendation."

That afternoon, Niblack spoke to Captain Leigh, who expressed his distress and disgust that methods had been used that would discredit the personnel of the Navy and adversely affect recruiting. When Niblack questioned Hudson and Arnold and read some of their reports, however, he felt that he had done them an injustice in having doubted the sincerity and merit of Section A. It seemed outrageous to him that the YMCA had been used as a recruiting ground for homosexuals. He was so convinced of the Reverend Kent's guilt that he took Hudson and Arnold to see Daniels on September 25. Daniels was horrified by their disclosures and agreed with Niblack that the Navy should press for a retrial. All the evidence the Navy had collected was turned over to the Justice Department, which decided to try Kent before the U.S. district court in Providence.

When the federal trial opened in Providence on January 5, 1920, Kent claimed entrapment. Four days later, he was again acquitted. The trial had somehow shifted from the issue of Kent's guilt to whether the sailors of Section A were right in obeying Hudson's orders. As Judge Arthur L. Brown put it: "There is no provision of law in the United States which compels any man to receive orders from any government official through the whole length of executive, judicial, military or naval authorities, which compels him to subject his person to indignity."

Indignity was what the Newport clergy felt it had been subjected to after the Reverend Kent's two acquittals. On January 10, Bishop Perry and twelve other clergymen took their grievance to the highest authority, writing President Wilson that ". . . a score of youths enlisted in and wearing the uniform of the

United States Navy [had been] instructed in the details of a nameless vice and sent through the community to practice the same in general and in particular to entrap certain designated individuals; and this in spite of the fact that prominent citizens of Rhode Island made in person strong and continuous protest directly to the Secretary and Assistant Secretary of the Navy against this iniquitous procedure." The clergymen asked the president to take "such measures as will eliminate from the Navy all officials, however highly placed, who are responsible for the employment of such execrable methods."

At the time when Roosevelt was being mentioned as a possible vice-presidential candidate, the Section A mess was turning into a dangerous political scandal. Acting quickly to keep the situation under control, Daniels appointed a court of inquiry on January 17, 1920. Heading it was Admiral Herbert O. Dunn, commandant of the first naval district, with whom {the assistant secretary} was on particularly cordial terms, having just done him a favor. He had written Representative Henry D. Flood of Virginia to recommend a nephew of Dunn's wife for a Naval Academy appointment, which the young man obtained.

On January 22, the Senate Naval Affairs Committee appointed Senators L. Heisler Ball (R., Del.), Henry W. Keyes (R., N.H.), and William H. King (D., Utah) to determine whether the Newport matter should be investigated.

When Hamilton Fish Webster, one of the two clergymen who had come to see Franklin in September, wrote to ask "in view of this second acquittal do you still feel that the evidence given in the Newport Court did not warrant acquittal, that the Chaplain was guilty, and that an apology was not due him by your Department?" Roosevelt replied angrily that "I did not feel that the Chaplain was guilty or not guilty. . . . Now, my dear Mr. Webster, I want to keep my temper, just as long as I possibly can, but I will not stand idly by and have rotten statements made, as they have been made in Newport, by people who cannot prove them, by people who know them to be false, and I shall not only welcome just as much publicity as you may want to give to it, but I will go just as far, and probably farther, than you will in seeing that the Navy gets a square deal."

The Dunn court of inquiry convened in Washington on January 27, and met for eighty-six days, collecting 4,800 pages of testimony. By the time Roosevelt was called to testify, on May 20, the Senate Naval Affairs Sub-Committee had also launched its investigation.

Questioned by Judge Advocate Henry L. Hyneman, Roosevelt denied all knowledge of the Arnold squad's activities before it had been turned into Section A.

Q. "Mr. Secretary, did you know that in nine instances, between the 18th of March and the 14th of April, that certain naval operators had permitted sexual perverts in the naval service to suck their penis for the purpose of obtaining evidence to be used before the court of inquiry, which evidence resulted in a recommendation by that court to try by general court-martial sixteen enlisted men and to give two men undesirable discharges?"

A. "The answer is no. I knew absolutely nothing about the court or its methods or its personnel. . . . In view of the fact that the Acting Secretary is called upon each day to pass on anywhere from 20 to 100 court-martials, courts of inquiry, and boards of investigation cases, to go into details would require ten lives instead of one day."

Roosevelt further denied all responsibility for or knowledge of the methods of the secret section he had organized and led.

Q. "Who would be responsible for the acts of the men in an organization so constituted?"

A. "The officer in command."

Q. "Did you give them [the men] any instructions or orders as to how the details should be carried out?"

A. "Naturally not."

Q. "Would that not have been your duty, since these men were attached to your office?"

A. "Absolutely not."

Q. "Whose duty would that have been?"

A. "The commanding officer."

Q. "Did not Hudson report to you from time to time what progress he was making?"

A. "Several times during the summer Dr. Hudson either telephoned me or came to my office and told me, in general terms, that the investigation was proceeding very satisfactorily."

Q. "And on none of these occasions you asked him what methods he was using?"

A. "Absolutely not."

Q. "Why not?"

A. "Because I was interested merely in getting results. I was not concerned any more in finding out about their methods than I am concerned in finding out how the commanding officer of a fleet takes the fleet from New York to Newport. What I want to know is that he gets the fleet over to Newport."

Ervin Arnold, however, testified that on May 1 he had given Roosevelt the operatives' report in the Kent case, that he had seen the report in Roosevelt's hands, and that Roosevelt had taken it and other reports to his office and "went over them in a rough way."

Roosevelt was then cross-examined by Mr. {Claude} Branch, a Newport lawyer representing the clergymen, who asked whether he had said that the judge in Kent's Newport Trial was incompetent: "You are aware, are you not, that mere repetition of this serious charge, is often as serious as the original statement?"

A. "That is impossible to answer any more than this: Have you stopped beating your wife? And you cannot answer it either way, yes or no."

Q. "You were aware of the fact that one of the subjects of investigation was unnatural crime?"

A. "One. Sodomy was one of four or five other vices which were to be investigated."

Q. "As a lawyer, how did you suppose that evidence of such a crime could be obtained?"

A. "As a lawyer I had no idea. That is not within the average lawyer's education."

Q. "Did you give that matter any thought whatsoever?"

A. "Not any more than how they were going to close the whore houses or the sale of drugs."

Q. "Did you realize as a lawyer . . . that investigations in such matters often lead to improper actions on the part of the investigators?"

A. "I never had such an idea. Never entered my head. No, sir."

Q. "Were you aware that unnatural crimes are not commonly committed in the open?"

A. "Neither is prostitution nor the selling of drugs committed in the open."

Q. "How did you think evidence of these things could be obtained?"

A. "I didn't think. If I had I would have supposed they had someone under the bed or looking over the transom."

The Dunn court was a whitewash. The one man who could have testified that he had kept Roosevelt informed about the methods of Section A, Lieutenant Hudson, was excused from appearing on account of illness.

Roosevelt had repeatedly said that if immoral methods had been used "someone should swing for it," but Hudson was let off with a letter of censure. A court-martial would have implicated the secretary and assistant secretary of the Navy. Hudson was allowed to resign from the Navy in January 1921.

The Dunn court report, released in March 1921, said: "This court is of the opinion that it was unfortunate and ill-advised that Franklin D. Roosevelt, Assistant Secretary of the Navy, either directed or permitted the use of enlisted personnel to investigate perversion."

"Unfortunate and ill-advised" was pretty mild, hardly even a slap on the wrist. There the matter would have ended had it not been for the Senate investigation. When the subcommittee released its report in July 1921, a strong case was made that Roosevelt had known about the methods used by Section A from the start, and had lied to the Dunn court under oath, committing perjury.

This was as shocking a matter as had ever been found in the annals of the U.S. Navy. It was shocking to the American standard of morality, and flagrantly at variance with the example that should be set by a military department. Young boys, immature and inexperienced, who because of their patriotism and the patriotism of their parents had responded to the call of their country to defend their flag and their homes, had been sent out to have their bodies polluted, which they would remember and regret to their dying day. It was particularly shocking that Josephus Daniels, who was such a Bible-thumping moralist, who had banned wine from officers' messes and condoms for the enlisted men, was the ultimate authority who had permitted young men under his care to commit sordid acts with homosexuals.

The Senate subcommittee {that later investigated the matter} concluded: "That such orders, instructions, or suggestions could have been given . . . is most reprehensible and beyond comprehension. . . . The committee is of the opinion that Secretary Daniels and Assistant Secretary Franklin D. Roosevelt showed an utter lack of moral perspective when they allowed men in the uniform of the United States Navy . . . to publicly testify to the beastly acts that had been performed on them.

This was the majority report drafted by the two Republican senators, Ball of Delaware and Keyes of New Hampshire. A minority report written by the subcommittee's only Democrat, King of Utah, said that "the attacks upon Mr. Roosevelt I consider unjust, entirely unwarranted and not supported by the record."

But the majority report, with its scandalous revelations, would get press coverage, and Roosevelt would be branded as guilty of gross abuse of high office. All the years he had spent in the Navy Department, guiding its fortunes through a world war, trying to infuse energy and decision into his vacillating chief, were culminating in public censure. His political career, already at a standstill after the 1920 campaign, would receive a terrible, perhaps a fatal blow. In the Senate report, he was described in nauseating terms, not as a distinguished public servant, but as the mastermind of one of the most shameful episodes in the history of the U.S. Navy. . . .

On July 21, 1921, having learned that the majority report was about to be released to the newspapers, Roosevelt was in Washington, in a Navy Department office with his friend Steve Early, going through the 6,000 pages of testimony. It was like emptying the sea with a child's pail. They went through volume after volume as a fan buzzed overhead, working on the statement that Roosevelt would give to the press.

"Damn it, Steve," he said, "this whole business is nothing but dirty politics. That's the point we've got to emphasize."

"We'll make that subcommittee look sick," Early said.

At four that afternoon, reporters called to say that the majority report had been released. Senator Ball had declined to hold it back. That alone proved the futility of trying to get any fair treatment. Well, he would make his statement anyway, and he would ask for an open hearing before the full Senate Committee on Naval Affairs.

The statement was finished by eight, and Early took it across the street to the Senate Office Building.

It was a spirited defense, but the *New York Times,* on July 23, told the real story: "Lay Navy Scandal to F. D. Roosevelt—Details Are Unprintable."

Refusing to concede that there was any validity to the report, Roosevelt felt that he had been smeared. He seemed to have convinced himself that he really hadn't "officially" known about the methods until September, that his "unofficial" knowledge didn't count, that there was a difference between the "official" knowledge of an assistant secretary and knowledge in the accepted sense, as the ordinary person has it.

Roosevelt was hurt as he had never been before. All his life he had succeeded, as president of the *Crimson,* as state senator, as assistant secretary— even his defeat on the Cox ticket was a disguised success, for he had run on a national ticket before he was forty and secured a national reputation. With his charm and good looks and trenchant intellect, he had until now escaped wounding criticism. He was accustomed to praise, a habit formed at his mother's knee.

Now for the first time there was an attack to which he could not respond, because it was largely true. The Senate subcommittee's majority report described his conduct as dishonorable, and said flatly that he had abused the authority of high office . . . he had strayed from the model of the "Good Roosevelt." He had done something that was truly disgraceful, which he could only excuse by claiming that the majority report was a partisan hatchet job.

Publicly, Roosevelt said he was the innocent victim of Republican calumny. He pretended not to be bothered by the report, and wrote Daniels: "In the long run neither you nor I have been hurt by this mud-slinging . . . what is the use of fooling any longer with a bunch who have made up their minds that they do not care for the truth and are willing to say anything which they think will help them politically?"

Privately, he was in pain, the pain of someone who has been tried and convicted, for whom there was no appeal, and whose sentence was the besmirching of his good name. The extent of that pain could be measured in a letter he wrote on the day after the first newspaper stories appeared, July 21, to Republican Senator Henry Keyes, coauthor of the majority report and an alumnus of Harvard. "I have had the privilege of knowing many thousands of Harvard Graduates," Franklin wrote. "Of the whole number I did not personally know one whom I believed to be personally and willfully dishonorable. I regret that because of your recent despicable action I can no longer say that. My only hope is that you will live long enough to appreciate that you have violated decency and truth and that you will pray your Maker for forgiveness." On the back of the envelope were a few scrawled words: "Not sent—what was the use? FDR."

From "Alleged Immoral Conditions and Practices at the
Naval Training Station, Newport, R.I.," from *Report of the
Committee on Naval Affairs,* United States Senate,
Sixty-seventh Congress, First Session, 1921

The subcommittee of the Committee on Naval Affairs of the Senate, which was directed in January, 1920, to investigate alleged immoral and vicious practices at the naval training station at Newport, R.I., and to report to the full committee thereon, has concluded its investigations.

In the outskirts of the city of Newport, R.I., within 10 minutes ride of the center of the city, is located what is known as the Newport Naval Training Station. From all over the country boys who enlist for service in Uncle Sam's Navy are sent to this station for preliminary training and instruction before being assigned to duty in the Navy itself. They are given instruction in seamanship, etc., and in naval practices, rules, and regulations. One of the first ideas instilled in the mind of the newly enlisted man is prompt, unquestioning, and implicit obedience of orders from a superior officer of whatsoever rank.

It was natural, under the circumstances, that among these thousands of boys who had come from all parts of the country there should have been some whose moral character was not of the highest. It is true that because of the great number of young men who were thus gathered in and about Newport many persons of low morals, both male and female, congregated in the city for the purpose of plying their nefarious trades. Conditions became so serious that both naval officials and the city authorities of Newport realized the necessity of some action to prevent wholesale demoralization among the enlisted personnel. Several indifferent and incomplete investigations were made by civil authorities and one or two by minor naval authorities, but without apparent result.

Suddenly there appeared upon the scene a petty naval officer, Ervin Arnold by name, holding the rank of chief machinist's mate. Arnold had at this time served for 15 years in the Navy, and for 9 years previous thereto had been a state detective in the employ of the State of Connecticut. His duties as state detective had been those of trailing and running down murderers, and more particularly the securing of evidence against sexual perverts. He was aggressive, uneducated, and of the bulldog type. Immediately upon his arrival at Newport he was sent to the naval hospital on account of rheumatism, and in less than 12 hours after being placed in the ward in the hospital claims to have discovered and made copious notes of the existence of sexual perversion among the enlisted personnel then in the hospital. He immediately reported these conditions to the welfare officer at the training station, Lieut. Erasmus M. Hudson, Medical Corps, United States Navy, who was attached to the hospital at the time.

Through his aggressiveness, insistence, and persuasiveness, Arnold succeeded in having detailed under his own command a number of newly enlisted boys, who were to go forth into Newport and vicinity and associate and mingle with the alleged sexual perverts, whose names were furnished by Arnold from his own personal investigations. These boys, as the evidence discloses, were to allow certain immoral acts to be performed upon them for the purpose of securing evidence.

Subsequent to this the seriousness of conditions in Newport were brought to the attention of both Secretary Josephus Daniels and Assistant Secretary Franklin D. Roosevelt. Mr. Daniels ordered a court of inquiry to be convened (hereinafter referred to as the Foster court of inquiry), and Arnold together with the men under his command, was assigned to the judge advocate of this court for investigation work. Later, on June 6, 1919, a special investigating squad was organized, known as Section A, O.A.S.N. (Office of the Assistant Secretary of the Navy), by order of and under the direct supervision of Assistant Secretary Franklin D. Roosevelt. This squad was immediately in command of Lieut. Hudson, who received his orders from Assistant Secretary Franklin D. Roosevelt.

Arnold acted as Hudson's chief assistant, and at various times, while the organization was in existence, had under his charge some 41 enlisted men. Previous to the formation of section A, conferences were held at the Navy Department between Assistant Secretary Franklin D. Roosevelt, several officers of the department, and Hudson and Arnold. At the first conference, which took place between May 1 and May 5, 1919, it was decided that it was necessary to proceed with the investigation under consideration, and this was in charge of Hudson, Arnold, and their men. The second conference took place between the same men on June 6 and 7, 1919, at which time ways and means were discussed and the matter fully gone into.

Immediately after this conference Hudson was given his confidential orders by Assistant Secretary Franklin D. Roosevelt. During the time the organization was under the direct supervision of Franklin D. Roosevelt, and particularly between the dates of May 5 and July 20, 1919, the enlisted men who acted as operators or detectives were instructed by both Hudson and Arnold to go forth into Newport and to allow immoral acts to be performed upon them, if in their judgment it was necessary for the purpose of running down and trapping or capturing certain specified alleged sexual perverts.

The committee knows that the immoral conditions which existed in Newport at this time were a menace to both the health and the morale of the men in the naval training station, and some method should have been conceived whereby those conditions could be eliminated; but to send out into Newport young men, some of them mere boys, practically on their own responsibility and under instructions to use their own "discretion and judgment" whether they should or should not actually permit to be performed upon them immoral acts, is in the opinion of the committee utterly shocking to the American standard of morality, and that any civilian or naval officer in charge of young men and boys to be trained for service in the United States Navy should permit such a thing is absolutely indefensible and to be most severely condemned.

The attention of the committee was directed to these vicious and immoral practices at Newport by various clergymen of Newport and by . . . John R. Rathom, editor of the *Providence Journal.*

Pursuant to a request made by the committee to the editor of the *Providence Journal,* Arthur L. Fairbrother, representing that publication, appeared before the committee on January 24, 1920, and submitted data in the possession of that paper which was so serious and startling in character and so convincing as to the truth of the allegations . . . that a full and thorough investigation was ordered.

His attention having been brought to conditions alleged to exist in Newport, Secretary Daniels, on January 20, 1920, appointed a naval court of inquiry, of which Rear Admiral Herbert O. Dunn was president to investigate methods employed by Hudson, Arnold, and others in their investigation of conditions in Newport. . . .

The record of testimony and exhibits of the Dunn court of inquiry consist of approximately 5,000 pages of closely typewritten matter, of which this committee have a certified copy and of which they have taken judicial notice, thus saving the committee the labor and expense of calling before them approximately 100 witnesses where only duplication would have resulted. The findings of fact, opinion, and recommendations of the Dunn court of inquiry (comprising approximately 150 typewritten pages, together with Secretary Daniels's 11-page typewritten memorandum thereto annexed) have not been made public by the Navy Department, but the committee have been furnished with an official copy and take judicial notice thereof. . . .

On the moral question involved the Dunn court was of the opinion that "the use of enlisted personnel in the uniform of the United States Navy by any bureau of the Navy Department whatsoever is to be condemned and disapproved. Therefore this court is of the opinion that it was unfortunate and ill-advised that Franklin D. Roosevelt, Assistant Secretary of the Navy, either directed or permitted the use of enlisted personnel to investigate perversion. . . ."

On this particular feature the committee not only agrees with the court of inquiry that the use of enlisted personnel for this purpose "is to be condemned," but is of the opinion that it is to be most severely condemned; that Franklin D. Roosevelt's action was not only "unfortunate and ill advised," but most reprehensible. . . . While the boys who participated in these immoral acts may, from a technical standpoint, be protected from prosecution for taking part in them, nevertheless the naval officials who at any stage of the proceedings ever permitted or approved of the use of enlisted personnel for such purposes can not be too severely criticized and condemned from a moral standpoint.

Various charges and allegations with reference to conditions at the training station at Newport were made by the leading clergymen of Newport. These were followed by seven separate and distinct allegations (in substance similar to those of the clergymen) made by the *Providence Journal*, as follows:

First Allegation

That young men, many of them boys in the naval service, have been compelled, under specific orders of officers attached to the Office of Naval Intelligence, to commit vile and nameless acts on the persons of others in the Navy service, or have suggested these acts to be practiced on themselves. . . .

The evidence shows that members of this squad of young men and boys, known as section A, O.A.S.N., permitted the basest of vile acts to be performed upon them at the suggestion, instigation, instruction, or order, it matters not the designation, of Lieut. Hudson and Chief Machinist's Mate Arnold, immediately in command of them. . . . The instructions given to these young men were: To frequent places where immoral practices were suspected of being carried on; to place themselves in a position where an alleged sexual pervert might make improper advances upon them; that they were at all times to remain passive and not take the initiative or solicit, and were to use their own judgment and discretion as to how far the improper advances of the alleged sexual pervert should be permitted. . . . Such were the acknowledged official instructions issued to boys, some of whom were not over 19 years of age. It is unfortunately necessary to state that in some cases the men used their "judgment" and "discretion" and allowed to be committed upon themselves the most vile and unnameable acts.

Second Allegation

That the victims selected for traps of this character have been picked out in every case by Lieut. Erasmus Mead Hudson, of the Medical Corps, and Ervin Arnold, machinist's mate, both of whom have declared that they were able to recognize degenerates by the way they walk along the streets. . . . Arnold testified before this committee: "I can take you up on Riverside Drive at night and show them [perverts] to you and if you follow them up nine times out of ten you will find it is true."

Hudson testified before the Dunn court of inquiry that he could recognize degenerates by their "looks and actions. . . ."

Third Allegation

That the orders given to young men, 20 in all, to commit offenses of the character outlined with the men selected for this prosecution were given officially. . . .

The evidence referred to {above reveals} that orders were issued to Hudson direct by Assistant Secretary Franklin D. Roosevelt.

Fourth Allegation

That both Secretary of the Navy Josephus Daniels and Assistant Secretary Franklin D. Roosevelt have known of these methods for several months and have not only been deaf to all appeals for the breaking up of such practices but have either directly ordered, or with full knowledge permitted, a recommendation for citation to these men for "their interest and zeal in their work. . . ."

The original court of inquiry, of which Lieut. Commander Murphy J. Foster was president, completed its report on or about May 1, 1919, and it was forwarded to the Navy Department for approval through the proper channels, reaching the final reviewing authority, Admiral William H. Benson, Acting Secretary of the Navy, August 26, 1919, who placed his endorsement of approval on the document. In this report 18 men were recommended for general court-martial, their unnatural offenses were named, and the operators upon whom these acts were permitted were named. Although the operators were not designated as such, the testimony of the men who secured the evidence was clearly set forth.

So carefully was this testimony read by the reviewing authorities that the recommendations for the trials of two of the men under arrest were disapproved because the time and place of the alleged acts were not sufficiently clear. The others, 14 in all (2 men having deserted), were ordered before a general court for trial. It is incredible that in reviewing the findings of the Foster court of inquiry no one realized that the immoral acts for which 18 men had been recommended for general court-martial had been performed upon other enlisted men, and the question most naturally must have arisen in any thoughtful man's mind why the men upon whom the acts were committed were not also recommended for trial. The committee believes, as did the Dunn court of inquiry, that both Hudson and Arnold had authorized and had knowledge, on May 1, 1919, that members of the squad of enlisted men investigating vice were allowing immoral acts to be performed upon them. . . .

On May 1, and from then until May 5, several conferences were held at the Navy Department, at which were present at various times Assistant Secretary Franklin D. Roosevelt, several officers of the department and Hudson and Arnold, the final result of the conference being that a further investigation into the alleged vice conditions at Newport was directed ordered to be made by Hudson and Arnold. . . .

On June 6 and 7, 1919, a two days' conference was held in the office of the Assistant Secretary of the Navy at which were present Assistant Secretary Franklin D. Roosevelt, several officers of the department and Hudson and Arnold. At this conference the plans were completed for a further investigation, and a full discussion of the subject took place including "ways and means for immediately proceeding." . . . On June 11, 1919, Assistant Secretary Franklin D. Roosevelt, "acting for the Secretary of the Navy," issued an order creating section A, O.A.S.N., and assigning Hudson to command with Arnold as chief assistant. . . .

Fifth Allegation

That the records attached thereto of the courts-martial held to consider the guilt or innocence of the victims of these practices, the court proceedings before the district court in Newport, and the testimony given by representatives of the Naval Intelligence in the Federal court at Providence prove conclusively that (we quote from a letter sent to the President of the United States on January 10, 1920, by Bishop {James DeWolf} Perry, of Providence, and 13 clergymen of Newport):

> Two men who claim to possess the unusual power of detecting sexual degeneracy at sight were given charge by the Navy Department of over a score of youths enlisted in and wearing the uniform of the United States Navy. These boys they then instructed in the details of a nameless vice and sent them through the community to practice the same in general, and in particular to entrap certain degenerated individuals, and this in spite of the fact that prominent citizens of Rhode Island made in person strong and continuous protests directly to the Secretary and the Assistant Secretary of the Navy against this iniquitous procedure. . . .

Sixth Allegation

That . . . testimony revealed the existence in the Naval Intelligence of a secret organization authorized by the Navy Department and known as section A, O.A.S.N., to prescribe certain "third degree" methods to use against prisoners in order to compel confessions of nameless crimes, and that the Naval Intelligence representative who testified to the existence of this secret body declined to enter into any details with regard to its power or its methods. . . .

The Dunn court of inquiry was of the opinion that although "third degree" methods were recognized as customary civilian police methods, they should have no part in naval discipline. The committee believes that any naval officer, of whatsoever grade, who in any way makes use of the "third degree" as testified to by Arnold should be tried by general court-martial and at least be dismissed from the Navy if not otherwise more severely punished.

Seventh Allegation

That boys arrested on these charges in April, 1919, were kept in confinement for many months without trial, in spite of the continued pleadings of relatives and friends and in spite of the demands made for speedy action by Capt. Edward R. Campbell, in command of the training station, who declares that he was finally compelled to make official requests regularly at intervals of every 10 days for some action on these cases and that all of these requests were ignored. . . .

The testimony before this committee is very clear, and official records of the Navy Department show that 17 enlisted men charged with unnatural acts were arrested during the month of April, 1919 at the naval training station at Newport. These men, some of whom were less than 21 years of age, were kept in close confinement for many months before they had any knowledge of the charges against them. Many months elapsed before the great majority of the enlisted men were brought to trial. Capt. Edward H. Campbell, United States Navy, in command of the naval training station at Newport, frequently protested in writing through official channels, and State Senator Max Levy, attorney for many of the boys, vigorously protested against the dilatory methods and the unjust proceedings of the Navy Department in not expediting the trials. No attention was paid for months even to official protests of Capt. Campbell. . . .

The committee feels that great injustice was done to these men at the naval training station who were under confinement, that the Navy Department was lax and its personnel inhuman in requiring men in confinement to remain for months without trial, and even without knowledge of the charges under which they were held in confinement. So strongly does the committee feel in regard to this particular charge, which is clearly proven, that it will discuss it at length in later paragraphs and make full recommendation in the hope that such brutal acts may never be repeated.

Conclusions

The committee has reached the following conclusions:

1. That immoral and lewd acts were practiced under instructions or suggestions, by a number of the enlisted personnel of the United States Navy, in and out of uniform, for the purpose of securing evidence against sexual perverts, and authorization for the use of these enlisted men as operators or detectives was given both orally and in writing to Lieut. Hudson by Assistant Secretary Franklin D. Roosevelt, with the knowledge and consent of Josephus Daniels, Secretary of the Navy.

2. That instructions issued to members of the Navy personnel who permitted lewd and immoral acts to be performed upon them were given by officers of the United States Navy, Lieut. Erasmus N. Hudson and Ervin Arnold immediately in charge, and because of these orders or instructions, the men so instructed permitted lewd and immoral acts to be performed.

3. That the orders, instructions, or suggestions given to the enlisted men by their immediate superiors were "to frequent places where immoral practices were suspected of being carried on, to place themselves in a position where an alleged sexual pervert might make improper advances upon them; that they were at all times to remain passive and not take the initiative or solicit and were to use their own judgment and discretion as to how far the improper advances of the alleged sexual perverts should be permitted;" and the men were advised that those acting under these instructions as operators or detectives were not

liable to prosecution by civil authorities even though an immoral act was completed.

4. That such orders, instructions, or suggestions could have been given, express or implied, in any manner, for any cause, by a commissioned or petty officer of the United States Navy is most reprehensible and beyond comprehension. That Secretary Daniels or Assistant Secretary Franklin D. Roosevelt should have allowed enlisted men to be placed in a position where such acts were even liable to occur is, in the opinion of this committee, a most deplorable, disgraceful, and unnatural proceeding.

5. 6. The committee is of the opinion that Secretary Daniels and Assistant Secretary Franklin D. Roosevelt showed an utter lack of moral perspective when they allowed men in the uniform of the United States Navy to take the witness stand at the trial of Mr. Kent in the Federal court, Providence, and publicly testify to the beastly acts that had been performed upon them. This was done notwithstanding the protest of Capt. {Richard H.} Leigh that such testimony in public would necessarily injure the Navy and have its effect upon recruiting.

7. That Franklin D. Roosevelt, Assistant Secretary of the Navy everpermitted or directed as he did, according to the opinion of both the Dunn court of inquiry and of this committee, the use of enlisted personnel for the purpose of investigating perversion is thoroughly condemned as immoral and an abuse of the authority of his high office.

8. Anyone in an official capacity in the United States Navy who should direct, permit, or suggest that enlisted personnel under their command, acting as operators or detectives, allow their bodies to be used immorally for the purpose of securing evidence, which was done according to the Dunn court of inquiry, and in the opinion of this committee, is not a safe person to have charge of the enlisted personnel of the Navy.

9. It is inconceivable that anyone in the Naval Establishment could countenance such proceedings as took place in Newport. That the men were acting as operators or detectives and had strict instructions not to take the initiative in the acts, is immaterial and not worthy of discussion; that while acting to secure evidence they were within the civil legal code does not alter the moral aspect of the case. The moral code of the American citizen was violated by instructions of certain Navy Department officials, and the rights of every American boy who

enlisted in the Navy to fight for his country were utterly ignored. It is doubtful, in the minds of the committee, if such an immoral condition as presented can be found in the annals of the United States Navy.

10. Lieut. Hudson and Ervin Arnold had knowledge at the time the acts were performed, that boys were lending their physical bodies for immoral purposes under the screen that they were acting for the good of the service. Official and semiofficial authority protected these lads from civil prosecution. They went forth into Newport and vicinity as a sacrifice to, and the prey of every degenerate and sexual pervert, male and female, in the city and at the training station.

11. The details of this work, according to their own statements were left to the arbitrary ideas of a totally unknown Navy doctor and an equally unknown petty officer. Neither of these men had any practical experience fitting him for an investigation of this character, nor apparently any sense of moral obligation. Hudson was a full-fledged physician and knew something about finger-print methods of crime detection. Arnold's experience as a detective in Connecticut did not qualify him for the position he occupied as the officer immediately in charge of and directing the activities of these young and inexperienced men, and the committee is of the opinion that he is in no manner fitted to be in charge of men in any capacity.

12. Many of these boys were immature in mind and experience. Their first instruction in the service was that orders were to be unhesitatingly and implicitly obeyed. Orders, to them, either expressed or implied, were orders in the strictest sense of the word. Before they were told what acts they were to perform, Arnold showed them the order of Capt. Campbell, detailing them to his (Arnold's) command. Then he explained the nature of the work. It matters not, in the minds of the committee, that not one boy declined the assignment. Under the circumstances, it is reasonable to believe that none refused the duty simply because he hesitated to decline in the face of the order signed by Capt. Campbell, detailing him to Arnold's command. One might argue that each boy who accepted the assignment was himself a pervert. This, the committee does not believe. It does believe that these lads were practically forced into this duty because of their ignorance of naval procedure and civil law and their mental perspective regarding the obedience of any order given them by a superior.

13. It is to be regretted that one connected with the Naval Establishment should have allowed such a situation to develop. Better far that perversion in

Newport should have been stamped out by the arbitrary wholesale discharge of suspected perverts in the service, as at first suggested by Capt. Campbell, and the arbitrary running out of town by the Department of Justice of every suspected civilian pervert, male or female, as could have been done under the emergency war laws, than that one innocent boy in the naval service should have been placed in the position of allowing his body to be polluted—a crime perpetrated upon him which he will remember and regret to his dying day.

14. The committee can not express in too strong language its condemnation of the methods of investigations at Newport from the time the Foster court of inquiry was organized in March, 1919, to the time when orders were given to Hudson to discontinue the work of section A, O.A.S.N., on September 20, 1919. Assistant Secretary Franklin D. Roosevelt, to whose office section A was attached, is, in the opinion of the committee, morally responsible for the orders issued by Hudson and Arnold.

15. Although denial is made by both Hudson and Arnold that at any time during the conferences of May 1 to 5 and June 6 and 7, any mention was made of the methods to be pursued in the investigation under supervision of Franklin D. Roosevelt, the committee is of the opinion that those present knew and realized that enlisted men were to be used for the purpose of investigating sexual perversion. It is not reasonable to believe that a man of the wide experience of Assistant Secretary Franklin D. Roosevelt should have discussed an investigation for several days without any mention being made of the methods by which evidence had been and was to be obtained. Prior to the conference there had been many completed acts performed upon the men under Hudson and Arnold and it is unbelievable that such acts should not have been referred to by one or both of them.

16. It is impossible for the committee to conceive of discussion lasting this length of the time concerning a subject of such unusual gravity without some mention of the methods Hudson had in mind for the rounding up of the sexual perverts in Newport. It is incredible that at no stage of the discussion Franklin D. Roosevelt or anyone else present asked Hudson or Arnold how he intended to proceed and what duties he had in mind for the men under his command to perform. If the "ways and means" for rounding up sexual perverts in Newport were discussed at all during the two days' conference it is beyond comprehension of this committee how the methods to be used could have been

entirely eliminated and apparently forgotten. The committee is not of that opinion, and believes that at this time Franklin D. Roosevelt and the others present had knowledge that enlisted personnel had been and were to be used to investigate perversion and must have realized that in previous investigations under the charge of Hudson and Arnold men had allowed lewd and immoral acts to be performed upon them and that a similar plan was being adopted.

17. If, during the conferences of May 5 and June 6 and 7, Assistant Secretary Franklin D. Roosevelt did not inquire and was not informed as to the proposed methods theretofore used and to be used by the men attached directly to his office and under his supervision, then it is the opinion of this committee that Assistant Secretary Franklin D. Roosevelt was most derelict in the performance of his duty. The committee, however, can not believe so. Franklin D. Roosevelt was a man of unusual intelligence and attainments, and after three days of conversation on the subject must have known the methods used and to be used to secure evidence.

18. In the opinion of the committee Hudson's expression of a desire for legal advice and his subsequent visits to attorneys . . . under suggestion of Mr. Roosevelt, substantiate the committee's belief that Franklin D. Roosevelt knew of the methods Hudson and Arnold used and intended to use, realized that the operations to be conducted were out of the ordinary and were fraught with legal danger for the men who actually performed the acts. It is not probable than any man with ordinary intelligence, and who had not previously known what procedure was contemplated, would have advised the visit of Hudson to the attorneys without knowing why such legal advice was necessary. Franklin D. Roosevelt appeared solicitous of the legal welfare and status of the men in section A, but apparently for the moment overlooked the important moral obligation he owed the Navy and the country.

19. The fact that Franklin D. Roosevelt made the unusual request in {a} confidential letter of May 5, 1919, to Admiral {Albert P.} Niblack "that this be the only written communication in regard to this affair as it is thought wise to keep this matter wholly secret" would seem to indicate knowledge on Roosevelt's part of the seriousness of the situation and of its astonishingly unusual character, as otherwise he would not have gone to such extreme and unusual length to keep it "wholly secret" and have no written communications regarding it; this, too, in spite of the fact that the whole matter had been gone into by the

Foster court in extended hearings and that on May 1, four days previous to the writing of this letter by Franklin D. Roosevelt, 18 men had been arrested as a result of the Foster court. Even the phraseology of the letter in reference to Hudson's and Arnold's qualifications for this particular line of work shows a knowledge on Roosevelt's part of the methods used and to be used by them.

20. Nevertheless, it is probably true, as contended by both Secretary Daniels and Assistant Secretary Franklin D. Roosevelt, that they were not "officially" informed regarding the acts of operators or detectives until September 19 and 22, 1919, respectively. The official red tape of the Navy unwinds slowly, and all through the records before this committee strenuous and strained efforts were made by naval officers to differentiate between "official" knowledge and knowledge as the ordinary layman has it.

21. The committee deplores the fact that anyone in the naval service of the United States should have been guilty of such a moral wrong as to conceive the idea of using men in the uniform of the United States Navy to investigate perversion, with the added instruction that they were to allow immoral acts to be performed upon themselves if necessary to secure evidence. It therefore condemns the acts of Lieut. Erasmus M. Hudson, Medical Corps, United States Navy, who must stand responsible for all orders issued to enlisted men under his command. The fact that he was notified that the men under his command were protected legally does not mitigate the responsibility he assumed. Such acts may have their part in the running down of sexual crime by civil authorities, but that any enlisted man in the United States Navy should be used for such a purpose, is shameful and disgraceful. Anyone whose moral standard is no higher than to permit such acts by men under his command is, in the opinion of this committee, better out of the naval service than in it. In the opinion of the committee, Lieut. Hudson should have been ordered before a general court-martial. The Dunn court of inquiry is of the opinion that Hudson used good judgment in assuring himself that his men were protected legally, but that he used bad judgment for countenancing the use of enlisted men for such purposes, which were not in accordance with the best traditions of the Navy. The committee is of the opinion that Lieut. Hudson showed an utter lack of moral responsibility from the beginning to the end of the entire investigation.

22. The committee is of the opinion that Ervin Arnold may be a first-class machinist, but has no qualifications to command young men in any capacity

whatsoever. His moral perspective appears to be entirely warped, and his attitude while testifying before this committee showed that while he had a full realization of the immoral acts he had forced on young men by his own instructions or suggestions, yet he was perfectly willing to sacrifice them morally to gain his ambitious end, apparently to be known as a great detective, a modern Sherlock Holmes. His whole attitude invited the belief that he thought that as long as the men were protected from arrest because of their acts nothing else mattered. The moral responsibility for giving such instructions to men, in some cases young enough to be his son, did not appear. His whole course impressed the committee with the belief that had the investigation resulted otherwise than as it did he would have claimed the credit and the glory for its outcome; but that he so conducted himself and so protected his own interests throughout that if it should turn out as it eventually did he could place the blame upon others. His attempt to clear himself by shifting the responsibility of orders to another but emphasized the belief of the committee that he is not a fit man upon whom to place any responsibility whatsoever. It is the sense of this committee, after hearing Arnold testify, that he is not the character of a man which adds to the high standing of the personnel of the United States Navy, and because of this belief the committee is of the opinion that the Navy personnel would be much benefitted were Ervin Arnold's name stricken from the roster of the Navy.

23. In the opinion of the committee the judge advocate of the Dunn court of inquiry went to great length to prove that various statements made in the charges before it were not technically accurate, and that there was no evidence specifically to prove the statements. The authors of the charges, who appeared before the Dunn court and the committee, were not trained lawyers. Neither were they preparing a legal technically worded indictment that might be scrutinized with a judicial microscope for errors in wording that would or would not throw the case out of court on a technicality or reverse it on appeal; they were not even undertaking to frame or submit charges as such upon which any man was to be tried for his life or liberty. They were merely, as public-spirited citizens, calling attention in a general way to conditions which it was believed existed and the methods used and events which took place, for which they had an ample justification. Yet the judge advocate spent several days in a vigorous, searching, grueling cross-examination of these men, not so much to ascertain

if they had knowledge of any specific facts to which they could testify but to show that the statements in their charges were general and that they were without specific facts upon which to base such statements, all the while the judge advocate having before him the testimony of the Foster court of inquiry and other evidence which amply proved all the charges made. . . . Yet the judge advocate's effort was to prove that they were without justification making a general attack upon certain naval officials. For instance, finding . . . that Arnold and Hudson "made no claim to possess the unusual power of detecting sexual degenerates at sight," while finding . . . that "Hudson stated he was able to form an opinion as to whether or not a man was a degenerate, which statement was corroborated by Arnold." This is one of the many instances of the judge advocate of the Dunn court of inquiry straining to differentiate between tweedledee and tweedledum.

24. There is, in the opinion of the committee, too much apparent studied effort on the part of the members and judge advocate of the Dunn court of inquiry to at times observe what may be termed petty red tape procedure and preserve the dignity of the court, resulting in a lack of real justice, while at other times gravely waving aside all recognized rules of evidence in order to admit something against the parties involved.

25. No department of the Government has the right to ask an enlisted man to volunteer to do such things as would take away his self-respect, even though it is to convict some one who has committed a crime.

26. The responsibility for the deplorable situation created at Newport rests not only with those immediately in charge of the squad, but with civilian officials of the Navy Department because they by their own acts showed they were familiar with the methods being used.

27. It is a regrettable fact that the great length of time taken to complete the record of the Dunn court of inquiry necessitated the signing of the document by Secretary Daniels just before he turned over the office of Secretary of the Navy to his successor. Whatever criticism there may be of former Navy Department officials or others of the Navy in either the court of inquiry report or the report of this committee, {it} is in no matter directed, nor does it apply to anyone attached to the Naval Establishment of today. All four of the principals discussed in this report are now out of the service. They left it either before or on March 4, 1921, and therefore no reflection from this report can in any man-

ner touch or affect the personnel of the department or the naval service as at present constituted.

Before making its recommendations, the committee desires to point out that the abnormal practices at the Newport Naval Training Station had their origin with a few men of bad character who came there among the many thousands concentrated there under the emergency of war. The responsibility for mishandling the resulting situation rests principally with the former Assistant Secretary of the Navy Franklin D. Roosevelt, a petty officer named Ervin Arnold, and a medical officer of recent appointment to the Navy, Lieut. Erasmus M. Hudson (whose resignation was accepted after the Dunn court of inquiry made its report and he was reprimanded as recommended by that court), and whose conduct evidenced an absence of any appreciation of the high standards characteristic of regular naval officers.

The committee desires to point out that no regular commissioned naval officer indoctrinated with the high standards that result from the regular training of naval officers was involved in the obliquities to which the subcommittee has had occasion to direct attention.

CHAPTER 8

World War II

♣

Large gay communities were well established in major American cities by the early twentieth century. Physicians, academics, and investigators of human sexuality had, by then, already adopted the term *homosexual* to describe men who belonged to what was widely recognized by both participants and observers as relatively stable confraternities of individuals with similar sexual preferences and an aggregation of overlapping interests, many of which were unrelated to their sexual practices.

The expanding awareness of homosexuality was not shared by the United States military forces. They continued to regard sexual activity between members of the same sex as a crime, much as it was regarded during the reign of Henry VIII four hundred years earlier. Army and navy regulations, to be sure, did not attribute satanic features to sodomy, nor were they much concerned with defining it as a crime against nature. It was sufficient to classify it as a violation of regulations, less frequent than desertion but certainly more serious for the damage it could do to morale and fighting capability. Still, sodomy prosecutions were rare in the period between the post–World War I Newport scandal and the Japanese attack on Pearl Harbor in late 1941.

World War II was a signal event for the American military not only because conscription brought large numbers of gay men into the armed forces but because neither the army nor the navy was prepared to deal with a large influx of recruits who in previous times would have been classified as sodomites or

sodomists. The difficulties were compounded in the 1940s by conflicting considerations: the expanded authority of psychologists and psychiatrists, the medical
model of homosexuality that defined sexual attraction between members of the
same sex as a disease, the desire to be rid of afflicted soldiers and sailors, and the
pressing need for more men in uniform to defeat the enemy. As a result of an-
tipathetic and sometimes irreconcilable imperatives, the policies adopted were
often erratic; they were applied unevenly in different locations at different times,
and the fates of gay men and lesbians in the military during the war varied considerably. Many, and probably most, were able to hide their homosexuality
throughout their terms of service; others known to be gay were allowed to do
their jobs without official harassment or interference; and still others were de-
graded, prosecuted, incarcerated, ejected, and given dishonorable discharges that
damaged or destroyed their prospects once they returned to civilian life after the
war was over.

One of the selections in this chapter represents the efforts of a military psychiatrist to establish a policy for dealing with homosexuals in the armed forces.
The study grew out of research conducted during the war, and while his recommendations exerted some influence, when the U.S. military established policies
for dealing with homosexuals in the peacetime army and navy after 1945, the plea
for understanding and compassion in the report was ignored. The sort of brutal
treatment experienced by many homosexual men and women during the war was
institutionalized in the postwar armed forces for the next half century.

Allan Bérubé

"Why We Fight," from *Coming Out under Fire*

When German tanks and bombers invaded Poland in September 1939, the
United States was not prepared to enter a war in Europe. Years of isolationism,
neutrality acts, military budget and pay cuts, and competition from New Deal
social welfare programs had left the peacetime Army and Navy backward, neglected, and unable to fill their ranks with volunteers. The Army (which included the Air Corps) was a small organization that between the wars did not
exceed two hundred thousand soldiers and officers; the Navy (which included

the Marine Corps) barely reached an active-duty strength of one hundred thousand. In 1939 the U.S. Army still had to rely on surplus weapons and uniforms from World War I, the Navy's Atlantic Fleet was weak (relying on the Royal Navy to defend Atlantic waters), and most airplanes were not fit for combat. Military service itself was an unpopular, low-status occupation. Judges sometimes sentenced young male offenders to Army service as punishment; Army privates received half the pay of men in the Civilian Conservation Corps. Even slight decreases in the high unemployment rates of the late depression hurt Army enlistments.

But in 1940, after Germany's continuing victories in Europe and air bombings of Britain, public opinion—still deeply divided over conscription and any possible declaration of war—slowly turned away from isolationism, allowing the still-neutral United States to start a limited mobilization. President Roosevelt called for the nation to become an "arsenal of democracy" that would provide arms for Britain's war against Germany. After much national debate, Congress in September 1940 passed the nation's first peacetime conscription act and set the maximum number of draftees called to active duty at nine hundred thousand. Conscripts now began to fill the Army's ranks.

Before the peacetime mobilization of 1940–41, the Selective Service System and the Army and Navy had not concerned themselves with sexual orientation when screening men for military service. But when more than 16 million men between the ages of twenty-one and thirty-five registered for the draft in October, 1940, Selective Service officials felt free to set strict qualification standards for military service. With so many men available, the armed forces decided to exclude certain groups of Americans, including women, blacks in the Marines and Army Air Corps, and—following the advice of psychiatrists—homosexuals. The rationale for disqualification was the same for each of these groups. Officials believed that they made poor combat soldiers, their presence in units would threaten morale and discipline, and their integration would turn the military into a testing ground for radical social experimentation rather than a strong fighting force.

Traditionally the military had never officially excluded or discharged homosexuals from its ranks. From the days following the Revolutionary War, the Army and Navy had targeted the act of sodomy (which they defined as anal and sometimes oral sex between men), not homosexual persons, as criminal, as had their British predecessors and the original thirteen colonies. Any soldier or officer convicted of sodomy, whether he was homosexual or not, could be sent to prison.

But in World War II a dramatic change occurred. As psychiatrists increased their authority in the armed forces, they developed new screening procedures to discover and disqualify homosexual men, introducing into military policies and procedures the concept of the homosexual as a personality type unfit for military service and combat—a concept that was to determine military policy for decades after the war. Their success in shifting the military's attention from the sexual act to the individual had far-reaching consequences. It forced military officials to develop an expanding administrative apparatus for managing homosexual personnel that relied on diagnosis, hospitalization, surveillance, interrogation, discharge, administrative appeal, and mass indoctrination.

The bombing of Pearl Harbor in December 1941, however, and the ensuing declaration of war, denied the military the luxury of disqualifying large groups of Americans from the manpower pool. By the end of the war in 1945, the armed forces had enlisted not 900,000 but more than 16 million citizens and residents, 10 million of whom were draftees. Most soldiers {here defined as enlisted personnel, male and female, in all branches of the service} were unmarried white young men—35 percent of the Navy personnel were teenagers—but other groups filled the military's ranks as well. Seven hundred thousand were black (4 percent), 350,000 were Mexican American, 275,000 were women (2 percent each), and 30,000 were Japanese American. In addition, Selective Service drafted 48,000 Puerto Rican, 19,000 American Indian, and 12,000 Chinese American soldiers. No census was taken of the number of gay men and lesbians who entered the military. But if Alfred Kinsey's wartime surveys were accurate and applied as much to the military as to the civilian population, at least 650,000 and as many as 1.6 million male soldiers were homosexual.

Among the American soldiers of World War II who were privately homosexual were many with familiar names. Tyrone Power started as a private in the Marine Corps in 1942, achieved the rank of first lieutenant, and was sent to the South Pacific with a Marine Transport Command, and was among the first pilots to fly supplies into Iwo Jima under artillery fire. Rock Hudson enlisted in the Navy after graduating from high school and served as an airplane mechanic in the Philippines. Photographer Minor White served from 1942 to 1945 with the Army Intelligence Corps in the South Pacific, where he was wounded in jungle combat. Novelist and essayist Gore Vidal enlisted in the Army in 1943 after high school, serving as first mate on an Army transport ship in the Aleutians. Novelist John Cheever was drafted in May 1942 and served in the Army Signal Corps making training films. Merle Miller, who later became a biographer of presidents Truman and Johnson, served in the Army as an editor of *Yank*, the enlisted men's magazine, in both the Pacific and Europe. Novelist John Horne Burns entered the Army as a private right after Pearl Harbor and served in North Africa and Italy.

As these and other men went off to war, women filled jobs in heavy industry and other defense work, widely expanding their presence in the paid labor force and increasing their ability to live independently. Although relatively few women entered the military, their inroads into such a traditionally masculine institution symbolized how dramatic were the wartime changes, and led the military to adopt its first policies regarding the screening, discharge, and management of lesbian personnel.

With so many gay Americans entering the military to meet their country's call, their presence and the expanding antihomosexual policies and procedures came into increasing conflict. Military officials, even as they developed a rationale for why homosexuals could not function in the armed forces, knew that they could not afford to exclude most gay recruits. At the same time, the gay men who were drafted or enlisted, and the lesbians who volunteered, began to realize that the military was prepared to discharge them as undesirables if their homosexuality became known. Since most were eager to do their part for the war effort, their awareness of the military's antihomosexual policies placed them in a double bind.

When Pearl Harbor was bombed, Stuart Loomis and his gay college pals together faced the dilemma of how to serve their country while escaping the military's widening antihomosexual net. That Sunday afternoon, they gathered at a soda fountain in downtown Omaha where they listened to a rebroadcast of President Roosevelt's speech to Congress and argued, over malted milks and peanut butter sandwiches, about what they were going to do. "We were already hearing stories of people who had been caught in gay activities and dishonorably discharged," Loomis recalled, "and we had friends in the service who were telling us 'Don't go in!'" Some of the boys in his crowd sought medical deferments, even though they faced the stigma of being classified 4-F (unacceptable) during the war. Others tried to get deferrable jobs in defense plants. But most, like Loomis himself, didn't want to avoid military service as they responded to their president's call for national unity and heard him declare December 7, the "day that will live in infamy."

Thousands of patriotic gay men and lesbians faced similar dilemmas as they weighed the sacrifices and opportunities of military service against those of remaining civilians during a national emergency. For many the desire to join their peers in serving their country was too powerful to ignore. Bill De Veau was inducted when he was a freshman at Boston University in 1943 after Congress passed the Teenage Draft Act. It seemed to him that "everyone in my age group went into the service that year—and you would have been ashamed if you didn't go in." Against the wishes of his family, Vincent Miles dropped out of college in 1943 and in his hometown of Davenport, Iowa, enlisted in the Army, which assigned him along with other black trainees to the 92nd Infantry Division. When Jacquelyn Beyer was an undergraduate at the University of Colorado, she decided to enlist in the Army after a recruiter came to the campus and made the Woman's Army Corps sound inviting. Her mother, who raised her to be independent, wouldn't let her enlist until she received her degree, so she went to summer school, took extra courses to finish in three years, and then became a Wac.

Some gay teenagers were so eager to enlist that they signed up before they finished high school. Their motives were varied. In February 1943 seventeen-year-old Tom Reddy was still too young to be drafted, but he quit high school, said good-bye to his family in New Jersey, and joined the Marine Corps. He wanted to "find out about myself all by myself. I knew pretty much that I was gay. I was engaged to marry a girl when I left, and I knew that wasn't exactly what I wanted. I think one of the reasons I enlisted was because everybody told me the Marine Corps was going to make a man out of me." Maxwell Gordon also left home to join the armed forces. His mother had single-handedly raised him and his older brother on an income that was "hand to mouth," and had told them that they had to support themselves as soon as they turned seventeen. Gordon chose the Navy in 1942 because his brother had already enlisted and because "there was a lot of naval activity in Southern California. It just seemed to me a natural thing."

Betty Somers was one of many gay Americans who separated from their partners to enlist. She left college and a "lovely romance" with a woman student to join the Marines because she didn't think she could live with herself unless she joined the fight. "I really wanted to serve my country," she recalled. "I expected to make the kind of sacrifices and I expected to go overseas." Bob Ruffing also left his lover, as well as his job as a high school English teacher on Long Island. Their relationship was breaking up anyway, he recalled, and "I didn't like teaching and suddenly Pearl Harbor happened. I went out immediately and joined the Navy. I started out having good thoughts about World War II because it got me out of this dilemma that I was in." Charles Rowland tried to enlist in Cleveland with his boyfriend, who had heard rumors (which were untrue) that the Marine Corps "had the buddy system and you could stay together forever throughout the service." When the couple went down to enlist, his boyfriend was accepted but Rowland was rejected because of poor vision. "So that ended our affair," he recalled. Late in 1942 Rowland was drafted into the Army.

As these and other young people entered military service, they became part of a massive wartime migration of Americans. Along with the 16 million men who left home to become soldiers were nearly as many civilians—most of them women—who left home to find war work. Black men and women in the South moved north and to the West Coast where defense jobs were plentiful; Japanese Americans were "relocated" from the West Coast to internment camps inland; millions of others moved from small towns and rural areas into the booming port cities and industrial centers. The uprooting of so many Americans during the war disrupted the everyday lives of a generation of young men and women, exposing them to the power of the federal government and the vast expanse of the United States, the great variety of its people, and ways of life they had not imagined.

Once they left the constraints of family life and watchful neighbors, many recruits were surprised to find that military service gave them opportunities to begin a "coming out" process. The meaning of the phrase "coming out" itself expanded as the war began to change gay life. In the 1930s, "to come out" or "to be brought out" had meant to have one's first homosexual experience with another person. But by 1941 gay man and women were using "coming out" to mean that they had found gay friends and the gay life, and were saying that circumstances in their lives, not just their first sexual partner, had brought them out. A person could come out to others part way by "dropping hairpins" to hint that one was "queer" rather than "normal"—the most common words used both by gay people and the general public in the war years. But when one felt safe or daring enough, one could come out all the way by pulling out every last pin and "letting one's hair down," a phrase that by World War II already had migrated into popular slang from gay culture.

During the 1930s and 1940s, young men and women who grew up feeling homosexual desires had little help coming out. They were likely to lead isolated lives, not knowing anyone else like themselves, with no one to talk to about their feelings and often unsure of who or what they were. There were no publicly gay leaders or organizations to act on their behalf, no press to acknowledge their existence or the problems they faced, no discussions of homosexuality on the radio, and only a few tragic novels with characters who were called "sexual inverts." In the cities, gay men and women who had found each other were able to form their own private social circles or to patronize a small number of gay bars and nightclubs. But these were hard to find, often disreputable or illegal, and attracted only a small minority of all people who were gay.

The massive mobilization for World War II relaxed the social constraints of peacetime that had kept gay men and women unaware of themselves and each other, "bringing out" many in the process. Gathered together in military camps, they often came to terms with their sexual desires, fell in love, made friends with other gay people, and began to name and talk about who they were. When they could get away from military bases, they discovered and contributed to the rich gay nightlife—parties, bars, and nightclubs—that flourished in the war-boom cities.

But the military's expanding antihomosexual policies also forced many citizen-soldiers and officers to come out against their will. Draftees were brought out whenever induction examiners publicly rejected them for military service as homosexual, or when they were caught or "declared themselves" to escape harassment and received undesirable discharges. Their self-declarations began to add a political dimension to the previously sexual and social meanings of coming out. Those veterans who fought to upgrade their undesirable discharges for homosexuality began to define their struggle with the government as one for justice and equal rights, ideas that became a prerequisite for a political movement. Twenty years later, lesbian and gay male activists stretched this political meaning even further, so that coming out became a public statement that one was both gay and proud—the cornerstone of a political movement.

As the military's management of homosexuals grew in importance during the war, three groups of personnel—administrators, psychiatrists, and GIs—found themselves engaged in conflicts with one another. The social and political changes that grew out of their confrontations must be examined not so much as the story of how the military victimized homosexuals, but of how a dynamic power relationship developed between gay citizens and their government and how it transformed them both. From draft boards and induction stations to the battlefields of Europe and the Pacific, members of the armed forces lived out daily tensions between the expanding antihomosexual policies, the need for the efficient use of all personnel, and their private sexual lives. In the process gay male and lesbian soldiers discovered that they were fighting two wars: one for America, democracy, and freedom; the other for their own survival as homosexuals within the military organization.

Lt. Col. Lewis H. Loeser

"The Sexual Psychopath in the Military Service (A Study of 270 Cases)," from *American Journal of Psychiatry*

While the number of sexual offenders in the military service is small, it is generally agreed that they present administrative problems out of proportion to their actual numbers. There appears to be considerable disagreement in attitudes, criteria and disposition of these cases by those responsible. The following study is offered as an attempt to bring about more uniformity and greater understanding in this field.

This study is based upon experience with and statistical data of 270 cases of sexual offenders who have been discharged from the 36th Station Hospital (NP) after varying periods of observation. Of this group 210 or 78% were, after careful study, diagnosed as true homosexuals; 60 or 22% were diagnosed administratively as "No disease," although accused of various types of sexual offenses.

The exigencies of the military situation have been such as to preclude certain aspects of research which would have been desirable. We were unable to perform biological and endocrine studies, owing to lack of critical materials and laboratory facilities. However the cases were, from the neuropsychiatric point of view, carefully studied and evaluated, and the data resulting therefrom should be of value.

1. Reasons for Hospitalization

Of the total 270 cases, 100 or 37% entered the hospital of their own volition and voluntarily disclosed their psychosexual disturbance to the medical officers. The greater number represented cases of homosexuals who were making efforts to control their sexual drives and in whom mounting tension and anxiety, or fear of being detected, led to voluntary hospitalization. A smaller number entered hospitals for other reasons and while convalescing decided to discuss their problems with the medical officer, or chaplain.

In view of the widespread notion that a large number of soldiers attempt to evade military duties by claiming to be homosexuals, it is justifiable to point out that in the entire E.T.O. during the 18 months' period of February 1943 to August 1944, only 100 soldiers did so declare themselves, and that all of this group were, after careful study, considered to be true homosexuals by the staff of this hospital. Whether the problem of feigned homosexuality is serious elsewhere, or under other circumstances, is not known—certainly it is not a serious problem in this theater.

One hundred seventy cases, or 63% entered the hospital involuntarily for the following reasons: 116 were alleged or reported by others to have participated in homosexual activity, but were not seen in the act by witnesses; 34 were apprehended during a homosexual act, most often during fellatio; 8 were charged with exhibitionism; 5 were accused of sexual play with minors; 5 were accused of bestiality; 1 was charged with fetishism of perverse and unusual nature; 1 was alleged to be abnormally sadistic during sexual intercourse.

Homosexuality and incidents relating to homosexual practices thus constitute the greater proportion of the sexual psychopaths; 93% of all members of this group were either confirmed homosexuals or had indulged in homosexual practices on one or more occasions. Other forms of sexual perversion were relatively uncommon in this series.

The influence of the role of selection on statistical data is well illustrated by contrasting these figures with the data collected. . . . {from} 250 sexual offenders at Bellevue Hospital, New York, 10% {of whom} were homosexual, whereas pedophilia was seen in 30% and indecent exposure in 33% of . . . cases.

2. Medico-Legal Status

Twenty-five of the 210 true homosexuals were tried by general court-martial for sodomy. The remainder (185) were evacuated to the Zone of the Interior for further disposition. No information is available at this time as to their ultimate disposition. Of the 60 cases diagnosed as "No disease" and not considered true homosexuals, all were under general court-martial charges for sodomy; the exact number tried is not known at this time.

The cases diagnosed as "No disease" were predominantly normal heterosexual individuals who were accused of homosexual behavior on a single occasion, usually while under the influence of alcohol. Apparently a single act of sodomy is considered a serious offense. The true homosexual who admitted repeated acts of sodomy was brought to trial infrequently, while the infrequent or first time offender was usually court-martialed. This has resulted in gross inequalities and apparent injustices on many occasions. In civil life this would be parallel to a situation wherein confirmed habitual criminals and repeated offenders are permitted to go free while single or first offenders are punished.

If sodomy is a punishable offense it should be so considered, whether committed by a homosexual or by a heterosexual individual and all offenders should be held equally responsible. There is nothing about the homosexual drive which deprives the sufferer of ability to restrain his sexual actions. The homosexual differs from the heterosexual only in the *direction* of his sexual drive, and he may be expected and usually is able to control, restrain and guide his sexual behavior into socially acceptable channels. While the anti-social and unethical aspects of homosexual practices are obvious and in no way to be condoned, it is not believed that sodomy should be of itself a punishable offense, unless accompanied by coercion, directed toward a minor, or under circumstances which would disgrace the uniform. The sexual offender should be tried for the appropriate offense—impairing the morals of a minor, for example, but not for the act of sodomy. Considered coldly, without emotion or prejudice, the homosexual act is the natural sexual outlet for a numerically small group of otherwise normal people. Alone and by itself it is probably less dangerous to society than sexual promiscuity, adultery or prostitution. In this connection attention is called to the fact that in most urban communities today, punitive action for homosexuality is becoming infrequent, and the medical and psychiatric aspects are receiving increasing attention.

3. Age

No significant findings are noted in the age distribution—the grouping corresponds closely to the normal age distribution of army personnel.

4. Race

Seven percent of the group are of the colored race. Colored admissions to this hospital have averaged about 10%. The rate of sexual offenders is less than expected and bears out the general impression that reported homosexuality is less common in the negro than in the white.

5. Environment

Sixteen percent come from rural homes, 63% from urban, and the remainder, 21%, have lived in both rural and urban communities. The predominance of sexual offenders from urban communities is noteworthy.

6. Status of Families

Forty-one percent of the group come from broken homes. The family histories disclose a high proportion of divorces, separations and early deaths among the parents. The unusually high figure is considered to be significant in the psychopathology of the sexual deviant.

7. Occupational Grouping

Of the 270 cases, only 6 would be placed in the unskilled group, and only 15 are classified as farmers. The remainder are in the skilled, technical, clerical or professional category. The distribution is as follows:

1. Unskilled. 6
2. Semi-skilled (service) 100
3. Agriculture. 15
4. Student 18
5. Clerical 46
6. Skilled (technicians). 38
7. Managers-salesmen 21
8. Executives 3
9. Professional. 20
10. Others (unclassified) 3

The figures would thus indicate a preponderance of skilled trained personnel, and a relative infrequency of the unskilled in this group.

8. Mental Age (Intelligence)

Two hundred thirteen or 79% of this group were classified as normal adults by the psychiatric examiner. Of the remainder, 13 (or 5%) were estimated to have a mental age of 13 years (Binet), 13 (or 5%) a mental age of 11, and 12 (or 4%) to be 10 years, or below. The figures are well above the average of the Army and would indicate that the sexual offender is predominantly a problem of normal intelligence and that mental deficiency plays an unimportant role in the Army in so far as sexual offenses are concerned.

9. AGCT {Army General Classification Test} Grouping

The figures obtained from a study of the AGCT ratings are significant, particularly in view of the preceding paragraph:

Classes I and II	118	(50%)	(110 or above)
Class III	63	(27%)	(90–109)
Class IV	30	(13%)	(70–90)
Class V	25	(10%)	(70 or below)
No information	33		

There were no illiterates in this series. The AGCT ratings would demonstrate a preponderance of the more intelligent and capable, a preponderance of considerable degree when compared to the average normal distribution of army personnel.

10. Educational Level

The educational level of the group is in keeping with the above scores: 232 (86%) had finished the 8th and 77 (54%) had graduated high school; 19 (11%) were college graduates.

11. Personality

Evaluation of basic personality is, of necessity, based upon information obtained from the patient and is therefore highly subjective. On the basis of information available, the examiners characterized 81 (30%) of the group as highly introverted, 31 (or 11%) as being highly extraverted. Only 60 (22%) were considered to be well balanced, well integrated personalities, the remainder, 98 (36%) were considered to have marked personality defects of various types.

12. Family History of Neuropsychiatric Disease

One hundred sixty-two (60%) gave no history of nervous or mental disease in the immediate family; 19 (7%) gave a history of one or more psychoses in the immediate family; 19 (7%) gave a family history of chronic alcoholism; 58 (21 ½%) revealed definite neuroses in the immediate family. The significance of these figures is in doubt since reliable figures for the population as a whole are lacking.

13. Previous Neuropsychiatric History

One hundred thirty-eight (51%) gave no history of nervous or mental disease prior to admission to this hospital. Ninety-six (25%) disclosed the presence of neurotic symptoms of varying intensity but not of sufficient degree to require treatment. Of these the greater number (77) had conscious conflict over their homosexuality as the immediate cause of their neurotic symptoms. Thirty-two (12%) had definite neuroses sufficiently severe to warrant treatment prior to hospitalization. Of this group, homosexuality formed the basis for the neuroses in 25—only 7 had neuroses considered to be separate and distinct from the problem of homosexuality.

14. Marital Status

As might be anticipated, a high percentage of this group—213 (79%)—have never married. Fifty-seven (21%) were married at one time but 9 were living apart from their wives at the time of entry into service, 10 were divorced and 3 were widowers. Of the 35 (13%) currently married, further investigation revealed highly unsatisfactory marital status in many instances. One is correct in stating that homosexuals occasionally marry, but that the marriages are unsatisfactory in a high percentage of cases and frequently end in divorce or separation.

15. Conflict with the Law

Two hundred four (75%) denied any conflict with legal authorities prior to entrance into the Army, 63 (23%) had minor entanglements and only 3 had served more than one 30-day sentence for any criminal act. The group as a whole would thus be classed as a law abiding group with little serious involvement with the authorities in civilian life.

16. Use of Alcohol

While only 5 (2%) were diagnosed as suffering from chronic alcoholism, 95 (35%) admitted excessive use of alcohol, and 125 (46 ½%) were considered to be moderate drinkers. Only 45 (16 ½%) were abstainers. The immoderate use of alcohol by homosexuals has been noted by other investigators. It is usually considered a secondary factor. The homosexual uses alcohol to release his inhibitions and to permit activities which are not socially acceptable. Alcohol is also used to relieve tension and anxiety of diverse sources.

17. Use of Narcotics

Narcotics appear to play an unimportant role in the life history of the sexual psychopath. Only 2 multiple addictions are recorded—7 cases of indulgence in marijuana are noted. Two hundred sixty-one (97%) denied the use of drugs at any time. In view of the important role of alcohol in this group, the absence of drug addiction is of interest.

18. Previous Accidents and Illnesses

The number of serious accidents and illnesses in this group is remarkably low, and the number of repeated or chronic accident cases is likewise low. Only one patient had three or more accidents in his record and 184 (68%) had no record of any serious accident or illness. As a group their health record is likewise impressive.

19. Venereal Disease

Two hundred twenty-nine (85%) denied any history of venereal disease; 27 (10%) had gonorrhea at one time; 18 (6 ½%) had had syphilis and 4 had had both gonorrhea and syphilis. The ratio of venereal disease is not high in contrast to figures of the Army as a whole, and in view of the known sexual promiscuity of the homosexual.

20. Occupational History

Eighty-seven (32%) had, prior to entry into the Army, held more than three jobs. 182 (68%) had held three or less than three jobs—only 8 (5%) had never worked. The amount of job shifting, an accurate index of unreliability and a constant index of psychopathic trends, is less than that of the hospital population in general.

21. Masculine-Feminine Ratio

Of the 210 true homosexuals (male), 112 (53%) were considered after careful study to be masculine in make up and temperament and mannerisms, 98 (47%) were considered to be feminine. Of the 60 designated as "No disease" only 2 were characterized as being of feminine make up. These figures agree in general with other writers who report from 30 to 45% of male homosexuals to be distinctly feminine in personality traits.

22. Associated Diseases

Secondary conditions of sufficient importance to be diagnosed at the time of discharge include the following:

Diseases	Cases
1. Constitutional psychopathic state	17
2. Syphilis	7
3. Psychoses	4*
4. Mental deficiency	4*
5. Injury	1
6. Epilepsy	1

*Cause of admission in 3 cases.

The number of associated diseases in this group, except for the presence of constitutional psychopathic state and syphilis, is relatively low. Minor conditions have not been recorded.

23. Previous Courts-Martial

Two hundred twenty-seven (84%) have had no courts-martial of any kind; 15 (5 ½%) have had summary courts-martial on one occasion; 5 (2%) have had special courts-martial on one occasion; 16 (6%) have had more than one court-martial. Compared to the average of the hospital population, the number of violations of military law is low.

24. Ratings

Of enlisted men in the homosexual group, only 66 had never had a rating. The distribution of grades was as follows:

> No rating 66
> Private first class 31
> Corporal. 29
> Sergeant 28
> Staff sergeant. 19
> Technical sergeant 6
> Master sergeant. 10

The ratings average considerably higher than in the Army as a whole and would indicate that the group is superior in ability and technical skill to the average. Considerable talent in stenographic, musical, clerical and special service activities has been observed in this group. However the group is lacking in temperament and skills necessary to the combat soldier.

Much the same observation could be made of the officers in this group. Of 40 officers, only 5 were with combat troops, the remainder were with various types of service troops or in ground forces of Air Corps.

25. The Role of the Psychiatrist

War Department Circular No. 3, 3 January 1944, clearly defines the role of the psychiatrist in relation to the homosexual. It is the intent of the War Department that homosexuals be discharged from the service, or in the case of officers, be permitted to resign if they are not deemed reclaimable. Homosexuals are to be tried by court-martial when their misconduct has been aggravated by an independent offense such as the use of force or violence or commission of the act with a minor. Certain cases deemed reclaimable, including first offenders, those whose actions were conditioned by alcohol or drugs, or those who have acted under the undue influence of older or superior persons, may be returned to duty, but are not to be returned to their original units.

It is wise to insist that these cases be hospitalized for observation. Out-patient study is likely to be superficial and lead to errors of judgment. Careful histories, particularly of psychosexual development, and adequate physical, neurological and psychiatric examinations are necessary. The patient's behavior on the ward, his reaction to other homosexuals and his knowledge of the homosexual "lingo" often give valuable clues. At the end of the period of observation—usually 10 to 15 days—the psychiatrist attempts to answer the following questions:

1. Is the soldier sane and responsible?
2. What is the nature of his illness or disability?
3. Is he reclaimable to the service? Does he possess sufficient intelligence, morale, character and power of restraint to warrant a trial period by return to duty?
4. Has he committed an independent offense as defined by War Department Circular No. 3 Jan. '44?
5. Is further treatment or hospitalization indicated?
6. Will punishment be of value to the soldier or necessary for the good of the service?

In cases where charges have been or are to be filed, it should be understood that the psychiatrist plays an advisory role and that final disposition is left to the officer exercising general court-martial jurisdiction. In cases wherein no court-martial charges are filed, or where charges have been dropped, disposition is controlled by the commanding officer of the hospital, acting upon the recommendations of the disposition board. In all cases disposition should conform to the policy laid down in the circular referred to.

We have attempted to make our reports and board proceedings as complete and informative as possible. The completed proceedings consist of the report ... signed by all members of the board and the commanding officer. The form used by the board, with alternative recommendations is stereotyped, but variations are permissible in certain cases.

Cases of confirmed sexual psychopaths not deemed reclaimable, and not under court-martial jurisdiction are evacuated to the Zone of the Interior for further disposition. Section VIII proceedings are not carried out in this theater unless specific orders are received from higher headquarters to do so. In general we have not attempted to obtain resignation of officers while in this theater unless so ordered by higher authority. Procedures of this type delay evacuation of patients and it is considered more practicable to obtain resignations of officers and to accomplish Section VIII discharges of enlisted men after arrival in the Zone of the Interior.

26. Diagnosis

The diagnosis of homosexuality in a military hospital is based upon the following points:

1. *The Accompanying Statements, Records, Affidavits or Allegations.*—In general we have found the greater number of cases admitted with fairly complete documentary evidence. An occasional case is seen with insufficient history, in which case, attempts are made to contact the soldier's organization.

2. *This History Given by the Patient.*—The history of psychosexual development is of paramount importance. It is our opinion that the greater number of these cases give accurate, though not necessarily complete histories. The greatest difficulty arises in cases where court-martial charges are pending—here one frequently finds reluctance to reveal information

which might be self-incriminating. It is in this group that inaccurate case histories are seen. The number of patients claiming to be homosexual who truly are not, is considered to be small.

3. *Behavior of the Patient while under Observation.*—Homosexuals tend to group together and it is interesting to observe the speed and certainty with which they are able to recognize one another. Within a few hours after admission to the ward the homosexual will have located others of his type and becomes one of the group. They tend to stay grouped together and rarely include heterosexuals in their activities.

4. *Appearance and Mannerisms.*—About 47% of the homosexual group are distinctly feminine in appearance, mannerisms and movements. There is rarely any doubt in these cases for years of habit and training result in unmistakable earmarks of feminine traits. Movements, gait, voice and attitude are consistently feminine—there are seldom any half measures in the feminine type of male homosexual. The other 53% are, from outward appearances, misleading—they may vary from neutral to extreme pictures of masculinity.

5. *Homosexual Vocabulary.*—Most homosexuals, before they have gone very far in their career, pick up more or less of the extensive homosexual vocabulary. The psychiatrist should be familiar with the more commonly used terms and test each suspect. The presence or absence of awareness of these words is significant in most cases.

6. *Investigation of Dreams and Masturbation Phantasies.*—With good rapport between psychiatrist and patient, considerable understanding of the direction of the psychosexual drive can be obtained by the study of the content of dreams and of masturbation phantasies. The normal heterosexual rarely, if ever, phantasizes homosexual activities. The homosexual will, on occasion have dreams and phantasies of a heterosexual nature but these will be rare, his content being predominantly homosexual.

7. *Use of Narcohypnosis and "Truth Drugs."*—Under mild narcosis, consciously repressed material may be elicited; however it has been our experience that phantasy and untruths may also be produced and that reliable information is not necessarily forthcoming. The material so elicited must be carefully sifted and one cannot be certain that admissions produced under narcosis are valid.

The diagnosis, ultimately, rests upon clinical judgment, utilizing all available information derived from the above sources. In 90% of the cases the staff is usually in accord. In about 10% of the cases, chiefly in the group of offenders who deny complicity, there is occasional disagreement.

27. Terminology

The writer has found the terms "active" and "passive" to be confusing and misleading. At times they are used to indicate aggressiveness or passivity in the role of soliciting or making advances. At other times these terms are used to indicate the masculine or feminine role respectively, in fellatio or anal intercourse. It would be more accurate and would avoid misunderstanding if the terms masculine or feminine role in fellation (etc.) were to be used. The term "latent" is likewise used carelessly, often in lieu of the term "repressed" and seldom in its true reference to unconscious motivating drives.

28. Etiology

It is evident that diverse and multiple etiological factors are at work. A study of these factors reveals four main sub-groups of homosexuals:

1. Endocrine—or constitutional, determined by glandular dysfunction.
2. Psychological—or environmentally determined by factors at work during the formative state of psychosexual development.
3. Regressive—the compulsive obsessional group who are blocked in normal heterosexual function by obsessional reactions of inadequacy and turn to homosexuality as an outlet.
4. Facultative—the psychopath group who may function either as homosexuals or heterosexuals, depending upon circumstances, surroundings and opportunity.

1. *Endocrine.*—These cases bear unmistakable evidence of the feminizing influence of hormone activity. Body build, fat deposit, hair distribution, voice, movements all bear testimony to the basic alteration of endocrine balance. All degrees of involvement are seen—some cases are near the borderline of the nor-

mal, though the greater number are quite distinct. Recent study of this phase by several investigators demonstrating abnormal amounts of female sex hormone in certain male homosexuals is confirmatory. About 30% of the homosexual group would appear to be distinctly of endocrine origin, or at least to have a basic endocrine disorder closely related to etiology.

2. *Psychological.*—This group, with normal endocrine status, presents histories of severe dislocation in the psychosexual field in early childhood. They include the male children brought up as females by mothers; the only son in a large family of females; the Oedipus situation with strong dislike of the father; and other similar mechanisms. Throughout this sub-group one can trace the influence of abnormal environment during the formative years of the child—the end result being a distortion of the sexual drive and failure of normal heterosexual development.

3. *Regressive (Compulsive-Obsessional).*—This group, to a large extent is composed of heterosexuals whose normal sex activities are inhibited by fairly obvious blocking mechanisms. Most frequently seen is the patient with severe reactions of inadequacy in the sexual field based on masturbation guilt complexes. Fearful of failure in the presence of the female, they experiment and develop facilities in the homosexual field with partial satisfaction. This group is likely to manifest evidence of conflict and tension; their adjustment is rarely secure. Other inhibitory mechanisms are seen, and the end result in each case being reactions of inadequacy in the heterosexual field and regression to a homosexual level. Strong compulsive and obsessional trends are seen in this group—they frequently are more properly diagnosed as compulsive-obsessional neurotics with symptoms centering about the psychosexual field.

In civilian practice this group represents the only subdivision in which psychotherapy is of value. Insight and understanding, and the resulting gain in confidence, will result in resumption of heterosexual activity, although the underlying personality deviation is seldom altered.

4. *Facultative.*—This group can and does function on either a heterosexual or homosexual level, depending upon circumstances, surroundings, etc. The facultative homosexual is likely to be a psychopath whose libidinous drives are

devoid of spiritual values. The orgasm however achieved, is the primary goal. This group frequently gives a history of exposure to homosexual experiences as young adults in gymnasiums, Turkish baths, while serving in the Navy, etc. It is the group most likely to resort to violence or coercion in order to obtain sexual outlets, the most unfit from the rehabilitation point of view, and the trouble makers in the military or hospital set-up. They are essentially psychopaths who achieve sexual orgasm in the most available manner, whether normal or perverse is of little import.

29. Treatment

Results are for the most part dependent upon the goals established. Treatment is of little value and there is little that medical science can offer at this time if the goal is to transform the homosexual to heterosexuality. While interesting and promising research is being conducted along endocrine lines, the results so far are of no proven therapeutic value.

Only the small number in the compulsive obsessional group (and they are not true homosexuals) can be offered any definite results by therapy. The psychiatrist however, can be of great value to the others if the goals are set within reasonable limits. The actual psychotherapeutic goals should be:

1. Overall adjustment of the homosexual: a. To his problem, b. To his family, c. Community, d. Occupation.
2. The treatment of the underlying neurosis. Very few homosexuals who do not have a neurosis will ask for or cooperate in treatment. It is the neurosis, the conflict within, and the symptoms thereof which usually motivate the desire for treatment. The homosexual without conflict, who has accepted his status without reactions of guilt or inferiority, is a well adjusted individual who does not require nor benefit from psychotherapy. I would estimate that roughly 50% belong in this category.

30. Method of Handling

The practice of directing all cases of sexual psychopaths to special hospitals has been fully justified by our experience. The numerous medico-legal and administrative problems which surround these cases make them a difficult problem of management for the ordinary station or general hospital. At a center, where the personnel is familiar with the problem, handling and management are facilitated.

31. Utilization of the Sexual Psychopath in the Military Service

The writer feels that intelligent and calm study of the individual homosexual, followed by careful re-assignment would result in conservation of man power and salvaging of a large percentage of this group. The following recommendations would be made:

a. The homosexual should not be subjected to punitive action unless his case is complicated by an independent offense, *i.e.*, coercion, physical violence or tampering with the morals of a minor. Punitive action does not cure or restrain the homosexual, nor does it act as a restraining influence on others.

b. Homosexuals incapable of normal restraint, the mental defective and the inapt should be discharged from the service.

c. Homosexuals capable of normal restraint, possessing normal talents and aptitude should be utilized by careful assignment. They will usually be found of most value in clerical work and do best in large metropolitan areas where sexual taboos and prejudices are less forceful.

d. The question of deferment of the homosexual under the selective service should be reviewed. It is possible that careful study and individual handling might lead to increased utilization of this group.

e. The policy of centralizing the hospitalization of the sexual psychopath is justified by the increased efficiency and facility in handling.

Summary

General characteristics of 270 sexual psychopaths studied at the 36th Station Hospital (NP) are presented on a statistical basis. Outstanding features:

a. The problem of sexual psychopathy in the military service is essentially that of homosexuality. Cases of other forms of sexual psychopathy are numerically infrequent.

b. Feigning homosexual traits in order to avoid military obligations is not a serious problem in this theater. Careful study of 100 soldiers who applied for hospitalization revealed that practically all were true homosexuals.

c. There has been lack of uniformity in medico-legal handling of these cases. There is considerable variation in attempting to decide which cases to try by court-martial, the severity of the sentences and the handling of clemency. In general, cases with single offenses in men of good repute and honorable service, are more often prosecuted and receive more severe sentences than chronic offenders. Since the publication of War Department Circular No. 3, 3 January 1944, there has been more uniformity.

d. There is less reported homosexuality among colored troops than white.

e. The sexual psychopath is largely derived from urban areas.

f. Broken homes form the background of 41% of the sexual psychopaths. This figure is unusually high and is of significance.

g. Homosexuals are predominantly skilled and semi-skilled workers. Less than 2% are classified as unskilled.

h. The average mental age of homosexuals is well above the average for the Army. Only 9% are below the 12 year level; 79% are normal or higher. More than 50% score above 110 in the army AGCT test. There were no illiterates in the entire group studied.

i. The educational level was higher than in the Army in general; 86% had finished the 8th grade, 54% had graduated from high school.

j. Forty percent of the group gave a history of psychoses, chronic alcoholism or neuroses in the immediate family.

k. Neuroses were found present in 35% of the homosexual group, but were sufficiently disabling to require previous treatment in only 7%.

l. Homosexuals are in general a law abiding group. Arrests for minor or serious offenses are infrequent.

m. Homosexuals are likely to use alcohol to excess; 35% were considered excessive drinkers, only 16% were abstainers. However only 2% were considered chronic alcoholics.

n. Drug addiction is infrequent among this group of sexual psychopaths.

o. The accident and illness rate of the group is very low. Their health record is impressive.

p. Fifteen percent of the homosexual group have had venereal diseases prior to or at the time of admission.

q. Forty-seven percent of the male homosexuals were considered to be feminine in general appearance, make up and temperament.

r. The group held higher ratings than the average of the Army: 10 master sergeants, 6 technical sergeants, 19 staff sergeants are among the list. Many ratings were based upon the possession of considerable talent in clerical, musical and dramatic ability.

s. Temperament and skills necessary to the combat soldier were infrequently seen.

Recommendations based on the above conclusions are submitted. The author does not believe that sodomy *per se* should be a punishable offense, that discharge from the military is necessary for most cases, or that deferment in the draft is advisable in all known cases. A large percentage of homosexuals possess sufficient restraint and insight, and have sufficient talents to justify careful examination of the individual case.

The opinions contained herein are those of the writer and are not offered in any official capacity.

CHAPTER 9

The Cold War to the Age of Clinton

♣

The demand for ever-greater numbers of men and women to fill the ranks evaporated with victory in World War II and the subsequent demobilization of the military. In the smaller postwar army and navy, and after 1947, the air force, manpower levels were easily maintained, and the recommendations of military psychiatrists and psychologists were largely ignored, since there was no pressing need to retain men and women in the services.

When the struggle against communism began in earnest during the late 1940s and early 1950s, the government of the United States met the needs of the military by reinstituting a system of conscription that easily kept all branches of the service at authorized strengths. Homosexuals in the ranks were expendable from the point of view of the Pentagon, and their predicament was made even more tenuous by the domestic political milieu. Rabid foes of communism discovered political capital could be had by denouncing homosexuals in government as security risks and characterizing homosexuality as a symptom of the weakening national fiber that would, if unchecked, facilitate the triumph of the Soviets.

The intermittent toleration found in the military during the war ended, and with considerable encouragement from Congress and the press, the pursuit of homosexuals in uniform went forward at full tilt. Investigators no longer sought merely to root out sodomites, as had been the case in the years between the world wars. Under the new regime, homosexual tendencies as well as homosexual acts condemned servicemen and servicewomen. Not only were they expelled, but the policies were some of the most retributive in American history. Regulations in all branches of the service not only contained provisions for ejecting those found guilty but provided for lengthy prison terms in many cases. Discharges given to those unfortunate enough to be caught in the antihomosexual weirs spread by the services most often received dishonorable or undesirable discharges, whether or not they served prison sentences. Such discharges, often with secret codes included in their numerical classification numbers indicating expulsion for homosexuality, carried the punishment of the hapless victims far beyond ejection from the military and their prison sentences. They were usually denied all veterans benefits, prohibited from working for the federal government, and unable to obtain any but the most menial of jobs because employers knew from their discharge papers the reason they were judged unfit for service.

The documents that follow are only a small proportion of a vast number that deal with homosexuality and the military over the past half century. They include instructional materials, appropriate segments from regulations, statements, and public pronouncements. Taken together, they give a sense of the direction the U.S. military has taken over the preceding five decades.

From Lecture for the "Indoctrination of WAVE Recruits on Subject of Homosexuality," [1952]

Line Officer's [Presentation]

Good morning/afternoon! I am _____. The officer on my right/left is Dr. _____. The officer on my left/right is Chaplain _____. We would like to speak to you today about a subject with which, very likely, many of you have never been confronted and on which most of you, perhaps, have never heard a formal discussion. The subject is homosexuality. . . . I shall speak to you as a woman officer because there are some things about homosexuality that concern us as women in the service. This presentation is to tell you the facts concerning homosexuality and most important of all, how to avoid becoming involved with homosexuals. . . .

My purpose today is to: (1) warn you that there are homosexuals; (2) inform you why the Navy doesn't tolerate homosexuals in the Naval service; (3) tell you what can happen if you are foolish enough to commit a homosexual act; (4) and most important of all, to show how any one of you may become involved in a homosexual act unless you understand the circumstances under which the homosexual may make an approach to you.

Let us first review the definition of homosexuality. It is sexual gratification of an individual through physical contact with another person of the same sex. A homosexual, then, is one who gratifies her sex desires by being sexually intimate with another woman.

You may ask, how can a young woman who has always led a wholesome life become involved? There are several techniques which may be used by the practicing homosexual to lure you into involvement in a homosexual act.

One of the most commonly used techniques is for the practicing homosexual to use friendship as a means to secure for herself a partner in her homosexual acts. . . . The practicing homosexual may begin her approach to you as a sympathetic, understanding and motherly person. At first she will present the same appearance as many of your friends. She will have many interests in common with you, but as time progresses you will be aware that she is developing this friendship as much as possible along emotional lines. This person may begin to demand all of your time, and to shower you with expensive gifts, and to pay all the expenses when you are out together. Even though you may never have indulged in alcohol, she may initiate you into the "art of social drinking." She may plan activities that will end in parties where heavy drinking is being done. She may plan more and more time for the two of you to be alone . . . late rides in her car, intimate conversations between the two of you, and physical advances such as embraces. As time goes by, she may propose that you take a week-end trip with her to a near-by city, to sightsee or take in a show. This trip will involve sharing a hotel or motel room. When you are alone . . . she orders drinks . . . , and more and more alcohol is consumed. Then follow the improper physical advances and a homosexual act is committed. . . .

A woman homosexual may use a technique that is the opposite to the one of kindliness, protective sympathy, and understanding. Her approach may be signaled by domineering, severely bossy, mentally cruel or bossy conduct toward the individual approached. This technique is to secure the domination of the sought individual, and to gain mastery and control over her. Just how this dominance is secured, whether through timidity or fear does not matter . . . ; it may lead to seduction.

The "Come-on-and-no-risk" approach is still another technique that may be used, and it fits into the battle against boredom. Navy women may be propositioned to indulge, just a little bit, in homosexuality, "because you can have a lot of fun with no after effects." Frankly, what is being said is that you can experience sexual stimulation and sexual satisfaction in a homosexual act without risk of pregnancy. . . .

It is important that you understand the Navy's policy toward homosexuality. The policy of the Navy is quite positive in that all persons found guilty of so much as one single homosexual act while in the Naval service must be eliminated from the service. The "first timer" or experimenter is just as liable to separation as the confirmed homosexual. A woman is not tried for being a homosexual, she is tried for committing a homosexual act. One thing is certain, she is going out of the Navy and fast. Under certain circumstances she will be given an undesirable discharge, commonly called a U.D. It means she has been discharged from the Navy as an undesirable, and her discharge papers will state that it is under conditions other than honorable and without satisfactory service. In certain circumstances she may face trial by General Court-Martial.

Answer these questions for yourselves . . . if you were discharged from the Navy for committing a homosexual act . . . what kind of a job would you be able to get? The person hiring you would investigate and find out that you were not the type of person who would be a good risk as an employee. Government employment is impossible. You may lose virtually all rights as a veteran under both Federal and State legislation. You would probably be reduced to getting a job of such low level and so undesirable that your employer wouldn't bother to investigate.

What would you tell your family and friends? Or the man you hope someday to marry? Could you tell them that you were discharged from the Navy as an undesirable, or were Court-Martialed for abnormal sex practices? These facts have an unpleasant way of coming out, no matter how much you try to hide them.

The families, parents, and friends of women who have been discharged from the Navy for homosexual acts, write tearful letters to the Navy Department in Washington, D.C., begging for relief from the type of discharge they have received. They claim the Navy has branded them as homosexuals, and because of this they find it difficult to earn a living, or find an acceptable young man for dating, companionship, or possible marriage. Actually, the Navy has not branded these women. They have branded and disgraced themselves, and no relief is possible. Women who engage in homosexual acts cannot and will not be tolerated by the United States Navy. . . .

If a homosexual makes an approach to you . . . , stay away from her. If you have evidence of homosexual acts report them to the proper authorities. . . .

Remember, the fine friendships between normal, decent women is not the thing I'm referring to today. The many wholesome friendships formed in the Naval service are one of the finest influences in barracks and social life. These friendships are of great value to the Navy woman, both while in the service and in civilian life when she has returned to her home. The annual reunion cele-bration of Navy women throughout the United States every year gives some concept of the importance of such friendships. It is good for young women coming into the service to use their petty officers as guides and models of serv-ice life. Be wise in your choice of friends. Be alert and avoid emotional pitfalls.

Finally, all of us should be very proud to be women serving in the United States Navy, but let us be sure that we retain as much of our basic femininity as possible. We are not competing with the men . . . , we are supplementing and complementing them. We must take pride in the kind of things women do well . . . that of setting a high standard of conduct by living in accord with the moral beliefs of our society.

May I now present Doctor _____, Medical Corps, U.S. Navy, who will speak to you on the medical aspects of homosexuality.

Medical Officer's Presentation (WAVE Recruits)

The medical officer, particularly one that specializes in psychiatry, is interested in homosexuality as an abnormal form of human behavior. . . .

Generally speaking, homosexual activity is the manifestation of failure on the part of the individual to grow up sexually, which leads to personality disor-ders in adult life. This is true whether the individual be exclusively homosexual or only a "dabbler." . . . What you have done in your younger and developing life is *not* to be taken as placing you in a position of the person under discus-sion today, or to be in a position of danger. To draw a comparison, it is not that you wet the bed as a child but do you wet the bed today.

By virtue of the fact that you are now in the Navy, you are considered grown-up and adult behavior is expected of you. If such behavior is not forthcoming, you will be held accountable. . . .

Several common misconceptions exist about homosexuality and it is these misconceptions which lead people into trouble. One such misconception is that it is easy to identify a practicing female homosexual by her masculine mannerisms and characteristics. This is not true. Many practicing female homosexuals are quite feminine in appearance and some are outstandingly so. There are probably more female homosexuals who are completely feminine in appearance than there are female homosexuals who are masculine in appearance.

Another common misconception is that those who engage in homosexuality are safe from acquiring venereal disease. This also is not true, as both gonorrhea and syphilis can be readily contracted through sexual relations with females as well as through sexual relations with males. Reports from various clinics reveal one out of every four male and female patients admitted with syphilis acknowledged homosexual contact as the source of their infection. Practicing homosexuals are notoriously promiscuous and not very particular in whom they pick up, infected or otherwise.

A third misconception is that homosexuals are born and not made. This idea leads to the beliefs, first, that an individual who is not born a homosexual can participate in homosexual acts without danger and, second, that nothing can be done medically for the confirmed homosexual. Neither of these beliefs is true. Treatment is available for even the confirmed homosexual but this is not an obligation of the Navy Medical Corps. As to the other belief, repeated dabbling in homosexuality in late adolescence as well as in adulthood can and frequently does constitute the making of a homosexual. Some who start as "dabblers" or "experimenters" progress steadily to become exclusively homosexual in their behavior. Experimentation, therefore, aside from being an infringement on social as well as Navy standards, is dangerous in its own right.

In this entire problem, the medical officer has a two-fold interest: first, and uppermost, he is a naval officer and has an interest in the Navy as a whole. It is his duty to help eliminate disturbing and undesirable factors from the Naval service, such as confirmed homosexuals. In the second place, as a physician and a psychiatrist, he offers his experience and knowledge of behavior disorders in helping those who are concerned about this problem. In this latter capacity, he maintains an open door attitude to all, and he is available for interview at your request.

May I now present Chaplain _____ who will speak to you on the social, moral and spiritual aspects of homosexuality.

Chaplain's Presentation (WAVE Recruits)

The Chaplain's primary concern with the problem of homosexuality is its relationship to the individual's social, moral and spiritual life. . . .

Homosexuality Destroys a Woman's Social Status and Her Social Future

I do not feel I have to emphasize to you how delicate a structure is a woman's good name, or how easy it is to tarnish or destroy it.

A single act, or an association, may brand a woman as a sexual pervert. Society allows women more emotional demonstrations in public than it allows men. Women friends may embrace and kiss each other as they meet in public without causing suspicion or starting a whispering campaign. Such displays of emotion and friendship, however, must always be within good taste.

By her conduct a Navy woman may ruin her chances for a happy marriage. Friends should be chosen with great care. Friendships are best when they are carefully formed on the basis of similar ages and interests. . . .

To get entangled with homosexuality means three things: (1) The woman gambles with the possible destruction of her social life and future marriage; (2) She will become the target of other homosexuals; (3) All normal, decent people who know, or even who strongly suspect the facts will have nothing to do with her.

Homosexuality Destroys a Woman's Character

Homosexuality is a social offense, and is named a felony by law. . . . People who engage in homosexuality fear exposure for there is always a witness (the other person). It is not possible to live under constant tension and fear, without seriously weakening one's moral fiber, mental and emotional stability.

Homosexuality destroys a woman's personal integrity. Little by little, the individual becomes more deeply entangled in the homosexual web. At first she wonders how it all happened. She reacts with confusion, shame and fear. She rationalizes that she was only a passive partner; that she really did not *do* anything. But she knows better. Then she faces the possibility of blackmail. She finds it easier to submit to homosexuality than to fight against it.

Experience indicates that the odds are heavy against her ever quitting. She slowly deteriorates in character, losing her power of will, and her integrity. Thus the deterioration and destruction of character and integrity are the end results of homosexuality. Even such gross crimes as robbery, suicide and murder often grow out of homosexuality.

HOMOSEXUALITY DESTROYS A WOMAN'S SPIRITUAL VALUES AND HER SPIRITUAL LIFE

Moral and ethical codes reaching far back into history are against any form of homosexuality. It is universally condemned by all religions. All nations who have given way to the practice of homosexuality have fallen and it is against the law of all civilized nations. The guilt associated with homosexuality is a barrier between the individual and God.

The Creator has endowed the bodies of women with the noble mission of motherhood and the bringing of human life into the world. Any woman who violates this great trust by participating in homosexuality not only degrades herself socially but also destroys the purpose for which God created her.

IN CONCLUSION

Let me emphasize the following: It is important to recognize danger. It is foolish to expose yourself. Good sportsmanship and courage are never proved by taking unnecessary risks, flirting with danger, or "taking a chance!" Homosexuality is dangerous in all of its phases. The woman who takes any chances with it demonstrates only her own stupidity, never her courage or smartness.

We do not wish to alarm you about homosexuality, nor do we intend anything that we say in this lecture to lead you to believe that an unmarried woman who does not engage in sexual practices with men is homosexual. She is, on the contrary, a sensible person. Sex was created for the married state and true happiness can best be found through marriage and a home. We are confident that you will go on through life using common sense and self-discipline.

We would also like to emphasize again the need of avoiding vicious gossip and rumors accusing or implying that someone is a homosexual or engaging in homosexual acts. Before engaging in such talk or spreading such dastardly gossip about anyone, I would suggest that you think of two things. First, think of the terrible harm that may come to this girl and her family because of you. And secondly, ask yourself—How would I feel if someone were to spread such vicious rumors about me?

If you are actually approached by one of these people or if you strongly suspect something that is out of line, talk the matter over with someone who can do something about it without harming someone who may be innocent. Your WAVE officer, your Medical officer and Chaplain are always available for personal counsel. If you wish to discuss this presentation just given, please feel free to contact any of us who have given it or any of the above mentioned officers. Thank you for your attention.

Army Regulation 600-443, April 10, 1953, Segments 1–9

Separation of Homosexuals

SECTION I

General

1. *Purpose.*—These regulations prescribe procedures whereby homosexual personnel will be investigated and discharged from the Army.

2. *Separation mandatory.*—True, confirmed, or habitual homosexual personnel, irrespective of sex, will not be permitted to serve in the Army in any

capacity and prompt separation of known homosexuals from the Army is mandatory.

3. *Classification.*—Homosexual personnel coming within the purview of Department of the Army policy fall into several categories which may or may not overlap and will be more or less complicated by the facts and circumstances peculiar to the individual cases. Cases, however, generally are classified as follows:

a. *Class I* is defined as those cases accompanied by assault or coercion, as characterized by any act in or to which the other person involved did not willingly cooperate or consent or where the consent was obtained through force, fraud, or actual intimidation, thereby constituting the invasion of the rights of another; or any homosexual action with a child under the age of consent, whether the child cooperates or not. A child under the age of consent is interpreted to apply to all persons under the age of 16.

b. *Class II* is defined as those cases wherein true or confirmed homosexual personnel have engaged in one or more homosexual acts or where evidence supports proposal or attempt to perform an act of homosexuality and which does not fall into the category of class I. It is emphasized that no distinction is made in the administrative handling of the cases of alleged participation in homosexual acts while a member of the Army based upon whether the role of the person in any particular action was active or passive.

c. *Class III* is defined as those rare cases wherein personnel only exhibit, profess, or admit homosexual tendencies and wherein there are no specific, provable acts or offenses, or court-martial jurisdiction does not exist. All persons who confess homosexual tendencies shall not necessarily be discharged merely on the basis of confession of homosexuality. It is essential to distinguish between those who have uncontrollable, perverse tendencies in fact and those who claim such for the purpose of avoiding military service. Evidence of existing psychological or other maladjustment resulting from such tendencies or other circumstances which render the individual inadaptable for military services will be evaluated carefully in making a decision.

4. *Character of separation.*—The character of separation normally to be effected for all classes of homosexuals arising among personnel of the Army

shall be similar and without distinction as to sex (male or female) or status (officer or enlisted) in all components.

5. *Responsibility.*—It is the duty of every member of the military service to report to his commanding officer any facts which may come to his attention concerning overt acts of homosexuality. Commanding officers receiving information indicating that a person in the Army possesses homosexual tendencies or bias engaged in an act of homosexuality shall inquire thoroughly and comprehensively into the matter and ascertain all the facts in the case, bearing in mind the peculiar susceptibility of such to possible malicious charges.

Section II

Disposition

6. *Class I.*—When the investigation clearly indicates that the accused falls within the provisions which classify an individual as class I, trial by general court-martial is mandatory. Charges will be preferred and forwarded to the commander having general court-martial jurisdiction.

7. *Class II.*—When the investigation clearly indicates that the accused falls within the provisions which classify an individual as class II, charges and specification(s) for trial by general court-martial will be prepared and the accused will be confronted with them. The accused then will be offered the following alternatives:

   a. *Officers*

   (1) *Resignation.*—The accused will be informed that a resignation may be submitted for the good of the service in lieu of trial by court-martial.

   . . .

   (2) *General court-martial.*—If the accused officer refuses to submit a suitable resignation, he will be brought to trial by general court-martial. Charges will be preferred and submitted to the commander, having general court-martial jurisdiction.

   (3) *Referral to Headquarters, Department of the Army.*—When the accused submits a resignation in accordance with (1) above or when the evidence indicates that that by court-martial may not result in conviction of the accused, the tender of resignation with supporting documents

or a complete report of the case . . . will be forwarded to The Adjutant General, Department of the Army, Washington, 25, D.C., for referral to the Army Personnel Board. The Army Personnel Board may direct that one of the following actions be taken:

    (a) Acceptance of the resignation. . . .

    (b) Initiate action with a view to trial by general court-martial.

    (c) When the evidence in the case indicates that trial by court-martial is not warranted or that conviction by court-martial is unlikely, change the classification of the case to class III and direct disposition in accordance with paragraph 8.

b. Enlisted personnel

    (1) *Submission of signed statement.*—enlisted persons will be informed that a signed statement in tenor as follows may be submitted:

> I hereby accept an undesirable discharge for the good of the service and to escape trial by general court-martial. I understand that my separation from the Army effected by undesirable discharge will be under conditions other than honorable: that I may be deprived of many rights as a veteran under both Federal and State legislation: and that I may expect to encounter substantial prejudice in civilian life in situations wherein the type of service rendered in any branch of the Armed Forces or the character of discharge received therefrom may have a bearing.

    (2) *Resignation in lieu of signed statement.*—Enlisted personnel serving in an enlistment for an unspecified period who have served at least 3 years therein may tender a resignation for the good of the service . . . in lieu of the statement outlined in (1) above.

    (3) *Action when* (1) *or* (2) *above are not complied with.*—The accused enlisted person will be brought to trial by general court-martial when the evidence so indicates and he refuses to sign a statement as worded in (1) above, or is not eligible or does not desire to submit a resignation as authorized in (2) above. Otherwise, the action specified in (4) below will be taken.

(4) *Referral to Department of the Army.*—When the action specified in (1) or (2) above is taken or when the evidence indicates that trial by general court-martial specified in (3) above may not result in conviction of the accused, the signed statement or resignation, as appropriate, with supporting documents, or a complete report of the case . . . will be forwarded to The Adjutant General, ATTN: AGPO-XD, for referral to the Army Personnel Board. The Army Personnel Board may direct one of the following actions to be taken:

(a) *Acceptance* of the signed statement under conditions recommended.

(b) *Acceptance* of resignation.

(c) Initiate action, with a view to trial by general court-martial.

(d) When the evidence in the case indicates that trial by court-martial is not warranted or that conviction by general court-martial is unlikely, change the classification of the case to class III and direct disposition in accordance with paragraph 8.

8. *Class III.*

a. *Documentation and forwarding of case.*—When the investigation clearly indicates that the accused falls within the provisions which classify a person as class III, the following actions will be taken:

(1) A detailed signed statement will be obtained from each individual concerned relating to his tendencies and any past homosexual actions. . . .

(2) A written report will be obtained from a psychiatrist or other medical officer based upon his study and evaluation of the individual.

(3) Enlisted persons serving in specified term enlistments and enlisted persons serving in unspecified term enlistments who have not served at least 3 years therein will be afforded an opportunity to submit a signed statement accepting discharge, either general or honorable as determined to be appropriate by the Army Personnel Board. Enlisted persons serving in unspecified term enlistments who have served at least 3 years, therein may tender a resignation . . . in lieu of the foregoing statement.

(4) Officer personnel will be afforded the opportunity of submitting an unqualified resignation.

(5) All papers in the case will be forwarded to The Adjutant General, ATTN: AGPO, with detailed comment and recommendations of the commanding officer for referral to the Army Personnel Board.

b. *Action by Army Personnel Board.*

(1) *When separation is warranted.*—When the Army Personnel Board directs separation, The Adjutant General will—

(a) Accept the resignation in accordance with the appropriate regulations governing the submission of resignations, if such resignation is tendered; or

(b) Direct that elimination action be initiated . . . as applicable.

(c) Direct an enlisted person to be administratively discharged from the service and furnished either an honorable or a general discharge certificate, based upon instructions of the Army Personnel Board. The specific reason for discharge shown on these discharge certificates will be "Convenience of the Government." . . .

(2) *When separation is not warranted.*—When the Army Personnel Board determines that separation is not warranted, The Adjutant General will so notify the appropriate field commander and will transmit such special instructions as may be required in such case.

9. *Reports.*—All class II and III cases processed under these regulations will be forwarded to the commander exercising general court-martial jurisdiction, who will endorse his recommendation by the most expeditious means available to The Adjutant General, ATTN: AGPO, with an information copy of the case sent through normal channels to the major command concerned. It is essential that all facts indicating homosexual tendencies or nets {*sic*} be recorded properly and that signed statements of all witnesses be obtained, except when individuals are brought to trial by general court-martial. In all cases, the reports will include the date of the individual's birth; the amount of active service of the individual concerned; the statement required in paragraph 8a(1) {above} from the officer or en-

listed person concerned, or his statement to the effect that he does not desire to make a statement; statements of witnesses; copy of the general court-martial charge and specifications, when indicated; resignation of the officer or agreement by the enlisted person to accept discharge, as worded in paragraph 7 or 8 where appropriate; and the commanding officer's detailed comments and recommendations. The report also will include a medical evaluation and, when feasible, a psychiatric study of the person concerned. An adequate psychiatric study will include as a minimum a—

a. Personal history, including detailed account of development of homosexuality, if any.

b. Report of mental status examination.

c. Psychiatric diagnosis, if any.

d. Statement regarding the existence or not of homosexuality, its degree and type.

e. Statement regarding the mental responsibility of the individual.

f. Medical recommendation regarding the disposition of the case, including comment as to reclaimability of the individual and advisability of restoration to duty or separation from the service.

g. Statement as to whether there are any medical contributions to administrative disposition.

Army Regulation No. 635-89, Section I, July 15, 1966

Personnel Separations

HOMOSEXUALITY

Section I. General

1. *Purpose.* This regulation prescribes the authority, criteria, and procedures for the disposition of military personnel who are homosexuals and military personnel who engage in homosexual acts, or are alleged to have engaged in such acts. This regulation is applicable only to military personnel on active duty.

2. *Policy.*

a. Personnel who voluntarily engage in homosexual acts, irrespective of sex, will not be permitted to serve in the Army in any capacity, and their prompt separation is mandatory. Homosexuality is a manifestation of a severe personality defect which appreciably limits the ability of such individuals to function effectively in a military environment. Members who engage in homosexual acts, even though they are not homosexuals within the meaning of this regulation, are considered to be unfit for military service because their presence impairs the morale and discipline of the Army.

b. The following classes of persons who engage in homosexual acts will not be processed under this regulation.

(1) Individuals who have been involved in homosexual acts in an apparently isolated episode, stemming solely from immaturity, curiosity, or intoxication. This provision does not preclude consideration of the conduct involved, together with other matters, if disciplinary action or administrative elimination under other regulations is deemed appropriate.

(2) Individuals who engage in homosexual acts because of a mental illness which is deemed to incapacitate them for further service, upon a determination that their case should not be processed as Class I. Such individuals will be processed for separation from the service by reason of their primary medical condition. . . .

(3) Individuals who engage in homosexual acts which fall within the scope of Class II and Class III and are determined by a medical evaluation to have a physical or mental condition which incapacitates them for further service but which is unrelated to their homosexual acts, upon a determination by the officer exercising general court-martial jurisdiction over the individual that disposition through medical channels rather than under this regulation is warranted.

c. As an alternative to action pursuant to this regulation, individuals who *engage* in homosexual acts may be brought to trial by court-martial. The disposition of any charges preferred is within the discretion of the appropriate commander. In determining his course of action, he will carefully consider all pertinent factors, including the nature of the acts charged, the surrounding facts, the character of the accused, and any applicable medical condition. Commanders will not take action under this regulation in lieu of disciplinary action solely to spare an individual who may have committed a serious homosexual act (such as a Class I case) the harsher penalties which may be imposed under the Uniform Code of Military Justice.

(d.) In determining the characterization of service to be furnished a member whose separation is provided for in this regulation, due regard will be given to the member's current record of service and the particular circumstances which require his separation. Adverse matters unrelated to his current period of service will not be considered. Such characterization will be determined without regard to component, sex, or status (officer, warrant officer, or enlisted).

AR 635-100, Change No. 4, Section III, 5–9; Section IV, 5–12; Section V, 5–15; January 21, 1970

Personnel Separations

OFFICER PERSONNEL

Section III. Medical Processing

5–9. Medical evaluation when homosexuality is involved.

a. If the officer is being considered for separation . . . medical evaluation including a psychiatric study of the individual will include the following:

(1) Personal history including, if any, a detailed account of development of homosexuality.

(2) Opinion regarding the existence of homosexuality.

(3) The psychiatrist will further render an opinion whether the individual should be:

(a) Eliminated from the service under the provisions of this regulation.

(b) Retained in service. If retention in the service is recommended, then, if considered appropriate, statement of the procedures likely to be of value in the individual's rehabilitation may be included.

(4) Psychiatric diagnosis, including an opinion whether the officer was able to distinguish right from wrong and adhere to the right at the time of the conduct under investigation, and whether he currently has the mental capacity to understand board and judicial proceedings and participate in his own defense. If it is determined that the member is suffering from an incapacitating mental illness, the examiner should indicate whether the illness was probably the cause of the homosexual conduct under investigation.

(a) A copy of the medical evaluation to include the psychiatric study will be filed with the individual's health record. The medical treatment facility commander will forward the original of this evaluation report to the unit commander.

Section IV. Reasons Which Require Elimination

5–12. Moral or professional dereliction or in interests of national security.

a. While not all inclusive, existence of one of the following or similar conditions, unless successfully rebutted, authorizes elimination of an officer due to moral or professional dereliction or in the interests of national security:

(1) Discreditable intentional failure to meet personal financial obligations.

(2) Mismanagement of personal affairs detrimentally affecting the performance of duty of the officer concerned.

(3) Mismanagement of personal affairs to the discredit of the service.

(4) Intentional omission or misstatement of fact in official statements or records, for the purpose of misrepresentation.

(5) Acts of intemperance.

(6) Acts of personal misconduct.

(7) Commission or attempted commission of a homosexual act. (Includes cases in which personnel have engaged in one or more homo-

sexual acts during military service. No distinction is made in the handling of such cases based upon the active or passive participation of the individuals.)

(8) Existence of homosexual tendencies. This category includes cases of personnel who have not engaged in a homosexual act during military service, but have a verified record of preservice homosexual acts.

(9) Intentional neglect of or failure to perform duties.

(10) Conduct unbecoming an officer.

(11) Acts or behavior not clearly consistent with the interests of national security. . . .

b. When one or more of the reasons enumerated in a(1) through (7) or (9) above is alleged, if the circumstances which form the basis thereof indicate that the reason in item (10) also is involved, it will constitute additional reason for requiring elimination.

Section V. Initiation of Elimination Action

5–15. Investigation of homosexuality.

a. A commanding officer receiving information that an individual under his command is a homosexual or has engaged in an act of homosexuality, will inquire thoroughly and comprehensively into the matter and ascertain all the facts in the case, bearing in mind the peculiar susceptibility of such cases to possible malicious charges. Any investigation required, normally, should be referred to the local provost marshal for investigation and recording on DA Form 2800 (CID {Criminal Investigation Division} Report of Investigation (Military Police)). The facts and circumstances of each case will govern the commander's decision as to the appropriate agency of investigation. If the information available is of sufficient stature to warrant investigation the commander will take necessary action to protect the security of his command to include suspension of security clearance, if any, and denial of access to classified defense information pending completion of actions on the case. When the report of investigation substantiates such allegations, the commanding officer will refer the individual for medical evaluation, revoke his security clearance, if any, and prepare a memorandum for the record outlining action taken and forward it with the subject's revoked certificate of Clearance and/or Security Determination . . . to the Commanding Officer, U.S. Army Investigative Records Repository, Fort Holabird, MD 21219. . . .

b. It is essential that all facts indicating homosexual tendencies, or acts, be recorded properly. The file will consist of the following documents in addition to that required by AR 635-120:

    (1) Report of investigation will include but not be limited to:

        (a) Statement of date and place of birth.

        (b) Amount of active service.

        (c) Date and current period of service.

    (2) Statements of witnesses. . . .

    (3) Medical evaluation reports. . . .

    (4) An individual's statement in his own behalf, if it is desired.

Extract from DOD Directive 1332.14, January 28, 1982

Enlisted Administrative Separations

HOMOSEXUALITY (PART 1, SECTION H)

1. Basis

a. Homosexuality is incompatible with military service. The presence in the military environment of persons who engage in homosexual conduct or who, by their statements, demonstrate a propensity to engage in homosexual conduct, seriously impairs the accomplishment of the military mission. The presence of such members adversely affects the ability of the Military Services to maintain discipline, good order, and morale; to foster mutual trust and confidence among servicemembers; to ensure the integrity of the system of rank and command; to facilitate assignment and worldwide deployment of servicemembers who frequently must live and work under close conditions affording minimal privacy; to recruit and retain members of the Military Services; to maintain the public acceptability of military service; and to prevent breaches of security.

b. As used in this action:

(1) Homosexual means a person, regardless of sex, who engages in, desires to engage in, or intends to engage in homosexual acts;

(2) Bisexual means a person who engages in, desires to engage in, or intends to engage in homosexual and heterosexual acts; and

(3) A homosexual act means bodily contact, actively undertaken or passively permitted, between members of the same sex for the purpose of satisfying sexual desires.

c. The basis for separation may include preservice, prior service, or current service conduct or statements. A member shall be separated under this section if one or more of the following approved findings is made:

(1) The member has engaged in, attempted to engage in, or solicited another to engage in a homosexual act or acts unless there are approved further findings that:

   (a) Such conduct is a departure from the member's usual and customary behavior;

   (b) Such conduct under all the circumstances is unlikely to recur;

   (c) Such conduct was not accomplished by use of force, coercion, or intimidation by the member during a period of military service;

   (d) Under the particular circumstances of the case, the member's continued presence in the Service is consistent with the interest of the Service in proper discipline, good order, and morale; and

   (e) The member does not desire to engage in or intend to engage in homosexual acts.

(2) The member has stated that he or she is a homosexual or bisexual unless there is a further finding that the member is not a homosexual or bisexual.

(3) The member has married or attempted to marry a person known to be of the same biological sex (as evidenced by the external anatomy of the persons involved) unless there are further findings that the member is not a homosexual or bisexual and that the purpose of the marriage or attempt was the avoidance or termination of military service.

Table 1, adapted from United States General Accounting Office Report to the Honorable John W. Warner, U.S. Senate, *Homosexuals in the Military: Policies and Practices of Foreign Countries*, June 1993

POLICIES CONCERNING MILITARY SERVICE OF HOMOSEXUALS IN 25 FOREIGN COUNTRIES

Country	Size of active force	Primary source of personnel	Policy allows homosexuals to serve[a]	Applicable laws, regulations, and/or restrictions
Australia	68,000	All-volunteer	Yes	Military policy changed in Nov. 1992.
Belgium	85,000	Both[b]	Yes	No specific law/military reg.
Brazil	297,000	Both	No	No specific law/military reg.
Canada	78,000	All-volunteer	Yes	Prohibition lifted in October 1992.
Chile	92,000	Both	No	Civilian law applies.
Colombia	134,000	Both	No	Military code applies.
France	453,000	Both	Yes	No specific military law/reg.
Germany	476,000	Both	Cons. = Yes, Vol. = No	Civilian laws changed in 1969.
Greece	159,000	Conscript	No	Military reg. applies.
Hungary	87,000	Both	Cons. = Y, Vol. = No.	No specific law/military reg. Restrictions apply to volunteers.
Israel	141,000	Conscript	Yes	Military regulation on restrictions revoked in May 1993.
Italy	361,000	Conscript	No	Codified into law in 1985.
Japan	246,000	All-volunteer	c	No specific law/military reg.
Peru	105,000	Conscript	No	No specific law/military reg. on acceptance. Military code applies regarding discharge.
Poland	305,000	Conscript	d	No specific law/military reg.
Portugal	62,000	Both	Yes	Military laws modified in 1989.
Republic of Korea	600,000	Conscript	Yes	Military law applies.
Romania	201,000	Conscript	No	Civilian law applies.
South Africa	72,000	Both	d	No specific law/military reg.
Spain	257,000	Both	Yes	Civilian laws revised in 1985.
Sweden	53,000	Conscript	Yes	Civilian law/military policy.
The Netherlands	92,000	Both	Yes	No specific law/military reg. Military policy revised in 1974.
Turkey	579,000	Conscript	No	Military law applies.
UK	300,000	All-volunteer	No	Military law applies
Venezuela	75,000	Both	No	Military law applies.

[a]When no specific law or regulation applies, the countries' officials informed us of the policy
[b]The Belgian military is currently transitioning to an all-volunteer force.
[c]Japanese officials indicated the issue is handled on a case-by-case basis.
[d]Officials did not provide detailed information to enable us to make this determination.

Office of the Secretary of Defense, 32 C.F.R. Chapter 1,
Part 41, *Appendix A to Part 41—Standards and Procedures,*
Section H.1.a, July 1, 1993

Part 1—Reasons for Separation

H. Homosexuality. 1. Basis. a. Homosexuality is incompatible with military service. The presence in the military environment of persons who engage in homosexual conduct or who, by their statements, demonstrate a propensity to engage in homosexual conduct, seriously impairs the accomplishment of the military mission. The presence of such members adversely affects the ability of the Military Services to maintain discipline, good order, and morale; to foster mutual trust and confidence among service members; to ensure the integrity of the system of rank and command; to facilitate assignment and worldwide deployment of service members who frequently must live and work under close conditions affording minimal privacy; to recruit and retain members of the Military Services; to maintain the public acceptability of military service; and to prevent breaches of security.

"Tips for Inquiry Officers of Cases Involving Members Who State They Are Homosexuals," Air Force Judge Advocate General's Memo, Attachment 1, Sections 1–3, November 3, 1993

1. You have been appointed to serve as an inquiry officer in a case involving a member stating he or she is homosexual or bisexual. Making such a statement is homosexual conduct that subjects the member to involuntary separation action because the statement creates a rebuttable presumption that the member engages in, attempts to engage in, has a propensity to engage in, or intends to engage in homosexual acts. Moreover, if the member has received educational assistance, special pay, or bonuses, the member may be subject to recoupment of an amount of government benefits proportional to the amount of the member's military service that has not been fulfilled.

2. The purpose of the inquiry is to determine if the commander possesses credible information upon which to initiate separation action or if other action should be taken because the member has made a false statement to avoid service. The intent of the member in making the statement also must be examined because it is highly probative to the issue of recoupment. The purpose of the inquiry is not to discover evidence of homosexual acts or to ferret out other homosexuals in the military. As an inquiry officer (IO), you must look at all relevant evidence to enable you to make a finding on the truth of the statement by the member that he or she is homosexual. You also should make a finding on the member's purpose for stating he or she is homosexual or bisexual.

3. You initially should interview the subject member. Ensure you notify counsel if the member already has retained counsel. You also should interview the following persons:
   a. Parents and siblings. If the member does not provide this information, DD Form 398 should have this data.
   b. Look at the DD Form 398 for any other possible leads for interview subjects.
   c. School counselor and advisor.
   d. Any other knowledgeable school officials.
   e. School career development office; did the member interview for civilian jobs? Did the student apply for fellowships, internships, etc., that would have been displaced by military service?
   f. Roommates and close friends, including people the subject dated.
   g. Mental health records.
   h. AFIT {Air Force Institute of Technology} program manager. Did the member apply for deferment of military service? If the member is in medical school, was the member assigned to intern in an area of medicine he or she did not want?
   i. Air Force career manager.

Guidelines for Fact-Finding Inquiries into Homosexual Conduct,
"Enlisted Administrative Separations," Department of Defense
Document 1332.14, Enclosure 4-1, Sections C, D, and E,
December 21, 1993

C. Bases for Conducting Inquiries

1. A commander will initiate an inquiry only if he or she has credible information that there is a basis for discharge. Credible information exists when the information, considering its source and the surrounding circumstances, supports a reasonable belief that there is a basis for discharge. It requires a determination based on articulable facts, not just a belief or suspicion.

2. A basis for discharge exists if:

   a. The member has engaged in a homosexual act.

   b. The member has said that he or she is a homosexual or bisexual, or made some other statement that indicates a propensity or intent to engage in homosexual acts; or

   c. The member has married or attempted to marry a person of the same sex.

3. Credible information does not exist, for example, when:

   a. The individual is suspected of engaging in homosexual conduct, but there is no credible information, as described, to support that suspicion; or

   b. The only information is the opinions of others that a member is homosexual; or

   c. The inquiry would be based on rumor, suspicion, or capricious claims concerning a member's sexual orientation; or

   d. The only information known is an associational activity such as going to a gay bar, possessing or reading homosexual publications, associating with known homosexuals, or marching in a gay rights rally in civilian clothes. Such activity, in and of itself, does not provide evidence of homosexual conduct.

4. Credible information exists, for example, when:

   a. A reliable person states that he or she observed or heard a Service member engaging in homosexual acts, or saying that he or she is a homosexual or bisexual or is married to a member of the same sex; or

b. A reliable person states that he or she heard, observed, or discovered a member make a spoken or written statement that a reasonable person would believe was intended to convey the fact that he or she engages in, attempts to engage in, or has a propensity or intent to engage in homosexual acts; or

c. A reliable person states that he or she observed behavior that amounts to a non-verbal statement by a member that he or she is a homosexual or bisexual; i.e., behavior that a reasonable person would believe was intended to convey the statement that the member engages in, attempts to engage in, or has a propensity or intent to engage in homosexual acts.

D. Procedures

1. Informal fact-finding inquiries and administrative separation procedures are the preferred method of addressing homosexual conduct. This does not prevent disciplinary action or trial by courts-martial when appropriate.

2. Commanders shall exercise sound discretion regarding when credible information exists. They shall examine the information and decide whether an inquiry is warranted or whether no action should be taken.

3. Commanders or appointed inquiry officials shall not ask, and members shall not be required to reveal, whether a member is a heterosexual, a homosexual, or a bisexual. However, upon receipt of credible information of homosexual conduct (as described in Section C, above) commanders or appointed inquiry officials may ask members if they engaged in such conduct. But the member should first be advised of the DoD policy on homosexual conduct (and rights under Article 31, UCMJ {Uniform Code of Military Justice}, if applicable). Should the member choose not to discuss the matter further, the commander should consider other available information. Nothing in this provision precludes questioning a member about any information provided by the member in the course of the fact-finding inquiry or any related proceeding, nor does it provide the member with any basis for challenging

the validity of any proceeding or the use of any evidence, including a statement by the member, in any proceeding.

4. At any given point of the inquiry, the commander or appointed inquiry official must be able clearly and specifically to explain which grounds for separation he or she is attempting to verify and how the information being collected relates to those specific separation grounds.

5. A statement by a Service member that he or she is a homosexual or bisexual creates a rebuttable presumption that the Service member engages in, attempts to engage in, has a propensity to engage in, or intends to engage in homosexual acts. The Service member shall be given the opportunity to present evidence demonstrating that he or she does not engage in, attempt to engage in, or have a propensity or intent to engage in homosexual acts.

6. The Service member bears the burden of proving, by a preponderance of the evidence, that he or she is not a person who engages in, attempts to engage in, has a propensity to engage in, or intends to engage in homosexual acts.

E. Legal Effect

The procedures in this enclosure create no substantive or procedural rights.

"Homosexual Administrative Discharge Board/Show Cause Hearings," in "Memorandum of the Department of the Navy," Code 34 Re: Administrative Discharge Board/Show Cause Hearings, June 1994

Introduction

With the recent implementation of the new homosexual conduct regulations throughout the Department of Defense, Code 34 continues to monitor individual cases to ensure full and fair application of the regulations. The following guidance is intended only for the recorders assigned to administrative separation boards or Boards of Inquiry, and should not be presented to the members, legal advisors, or the respondent's counsel. Our goal is not to dictate the final board results, but rather to ensure fair and consistent application of the DOD and DON regulations concerning homosexual conduct.

In order to ensure a fair result at any administrative proceeding, it is essential that the members appointed fully understand the applicable directives, regulations, and instructions. The recorder, as well as the legal advisor (if appointed), largely shoulders the burden of "educating" the members, when necessary, on the ins and outs of the applicable law or regulations. The regulations concerning homosexual conduct in the Navy, while lengthy and detailed, are actually quite straight forward. As these regulations are newly implemented, however, most military members will be considering and applying them for the first time at an administrative proceeding. Accordingly, it is important that the recorder take the necessary time to ensure that the members fully understand how the regulations work.

The objective is to ensure that the Navy's regulations are applied properly, and that the board results are fair, consistent, and appropriate, under the circumstances.

What follows are some generalized pointers—presented in bullet format—for conducting administrative discharge boards or show cause hearings convened pursuant to the new homosexual conduct discharge policy. Though specifically derived from our experiences in "statement" cases vice "acts" cases, these tips are applicable to both.

I. General

Call Code 34 to discuss cases.

Code 34 provided significant input to the drafters of the "new" policy and the implementing regulations. We are now deeply involved in defending both the "old" and "new" homosexual policies from judicial assault, and have been for several years. We have also provided assistant recorders for several high visibility cases in recent months. We are a valuable clearing house for information, insights and ideas, and a sounding board on how the policy should be applied at the administrative hearing stage of the process.

When necessary and appropriate, Code 34 will send an assistant recorder.

In select cases, we have sent Code 34 attorneys to the field as assistant recorders. We will continue to do so when necessary. The factors to consider when asking for (or being offered) a Code 34 assistant are the likelihood of litigation, the precedential value of the issues presented by the case, the active involvement of organized homosexual litigation support groups, and the press or congressional interest.

II. Pre-Hearing Preparation

Know the statute, DoD Directive and CNO message thoroughly.

This is probably the single most important tip to pass along. The facts in these cases tend to be relatively straight forward, and usually not disputed. The case turns on the application of the regulations to those facts. Take particular note of the definitions. Understand completely the difference between homosexual "status" {*sic*}. They are themselves conduct which permit the reasonable inference of specific past and/or future acts. Carefully consider the implications of the rebuttal presumption in light of the express words used by the respondent in a particular case.

Coordinate with Convening Authority before the hearing.

Ensure the CA knows all of the facts of the case and understands how the regulations apply to the case. Encourage the detailing of the legal advisor, preferably someone with prior judicial experience. Encourage the detailing of experienced, level-headed officers as members.

Obtain and review all prior administrative hearing records or court records in the case.

In some instances there may have been a prior administrative hearing or proceeding in federal district court. A careful review of these papers will reveal the nature of the case the respondent is likely to present.

Be creative.

The measure of success may well turn on thorough and innovative preparation for the hearing. As the advocate of the command, the recorder should use imagination to research the facts of the case. Where the case is premised on a statement alone, the recorder should attempt to find evidence to corroborate the statement and to sustain the presumption flowing logically from the statement. In terms of hearing preparation, the goal of the recorder is to build the strongest case possible. Although a statement alone may constitute a prima facie case, a recorder should present the board with additional evidence demonstrating that a discharge is warranted by the unequivocal desire of the respondent to commit criminal acts. . . .

III. Voir Dire

Focus members on the policy.

Ask the members about their attitude toward homosexuality. Then ask them if they can agree to apply the regulations regardless of their personal feelings about homosexuality. A member should not be disqualified simply because he or she has an opinion regarding homosexual conduct in the military. A member can properly sit if he or she can put aside their personal feelings and beliefs and apply the regulations, as written.

IV. Evidentiary Issues Generally

Evidence designed to attack the homosexual policy is not relevant.

There are many documents, studies, reports, etc., in existence concerning what the policy should be with regard to homosexuals in the military. If these documents are offered by the respondent, object. This is not an issue for Board consideration. The policy question was resolved by Congress and the President. The Board may not overrule the policy, nor choose to disregard the implementing regulations.

Occasionally, a respondent will offer the same documents to support the notion that the arguments underlying the rebuttable presumption are invalid. They will contend that just because a person admits a homosexual orientation doesn't mean they will commit homosexual acts, and these studies prove their point. Object. This is a thinly veiled attack on the policy. What evidence has the respondent offered to rebut the presumption raised by an admission of homosexuality? If the answer is none, then the real purpose for seeking admission of the documents is transparent. Even if some evidence is offered in rebuttal, the relevancy link between that evidence and the aforementioned studies is at best only tenuous.

V. Opening Statement

Keep members' focus strictly on the relevant issues.

Invite the members' attention to the requirements of their appointing letter. . . . Walk them through it so they can understand how it works. Be certain the members understand their job is to apply the regulations to the facts in the case before them. It is not their prerogative to pass judgment on the policy itself. . . .

VI. Witnesses

Challenge evidence portraying the respondent as a model sailor.

Respondents frequently use witnesses to demonstrate good military character. Point out on cross (if possible) that public denunciation of homosexual policies may be inconsistent with good military character. The wearing of one's uniform, or identifying oneself as a member of USN while visibly supporting homosexual interests may violate Uniform Regulations and the Standards of Conduct. Where applicable, point out that the respondent has been serving in a less than demanding/non-operational billet. Has there been any adverse impact on the command?

VII. Case in Rebuttal

If the respondent attempts to rebut the presumption, analyze critically the language used. We have seen respondents offer statements, written or oral, sounding as though they were attempts at rebutting the presumption, but were instead nothing more than broad, general acknowledgments of the policy, or half-hearted commitments to obey the law.

VIII. Closing Argument

Focus on the issues as you did in the opening argument.
Once again, review the policy with the members. Show them how it specifically applies to the case. Drive home the reasonableness of the homosexual acts to the extent the evidence permits. Do not easily accept the characterization of the respondent as a model sailor

"Memorandum for Secretaries of the Military Departments. Subject: Implementation of Recommendations Concerning Homosexual Conduct Policy," Undersecretary of Defense, August 12, 1999

The Department of Defense is committed to the fair and even-handed application and enforcement of its policy on homosexual conduct in the military. An April 1998 report responded to the Secretary of Defense tasking {*sic*} to review how well the Department's policy on homosexual conduct is being applied and enforced. That report provided an analysis of the data on separations for homosexual conduct in Fiscal Year 1997, as well as a discussion of various issues arising under the policy, and made several recommendations. Since that time, my office has continued to analyze the data and issues discussed in the April 1998 report, as well as the data concerning separations based on homosexual conduct in Fiscal Year 1998. It is now appropriate to take the actions outlined below to ensure that the Department's policy is being properly applied and enforced.

First, as the April 1998 report makes clear, the majority of homosexual conduct discharge cases involve minimal or no investigation; that is also confirmed by the data that were analyzed for Fiscal Year 1998. As a result, many installation-level attorneys have not had occasion to build practical expertise in the special rules applicable in this area. Accordingly, the April 1998 report found that, in more complex investigations, it has become common practice for installation judge advocates to consult for advice with more experienced judge advocates in higher headquarters legal offices. The review recommended that the Department issue guidance specifying that such consultation is recommended before initiating investigations into alleged homosexual conduct.

Second, the April 1998 report concluded that little or no investigation should be necessary in most cases where a service member has made a statement acknowledging his or her homosexuality and does not contest separation. The report recognized, however, that it is appropriate in some circumstances to undertake an investigation to determine whether recoupment of financial benefit is warranted, or whether a service member's statement may have been fabricated in an effort to avoid a service obligation. To ensure appropriate review of such cases, the report recommended that prior authorization at the Military Department secretarial level be obtained for any substantial investigation of this nature.

Third, the April 1998 report noted that each Service devotes substantial effort to training commanders and attorneys of the Department's homosexual conduct policy. Notwithstanding these efforts, some commanders, attorneys and investigators report that they have not received training. Accordingly, the report recommended that the Military Departments issue guidance directing that Service Inspectors General include as a specific item of interest for inspection the training of all those charged with implementing the homosexual conduct policy.

In order to implement the recommendations and findings of the April 1998 report, I request that you issue guidance as follows:

Recommend that, to promote consistent and fair application of the law and policy, installation-level staff judge advocates consult with senior legal officers at higher headquarters prior to the initiation of an investigation into alleged homosexual conduct. This guidance should make clear that the responsibility to determine when credible information exists—i.e., to determine whether the information reported supports a reasonable belief that a service member has engaged in homosexual conduct, such that an investigation is appropriate—remains with commanders. Commanders are best equipped to assess the credibility of the information provided, taking into account, for example, whether the stress of basic training may affect the reliability of a statement.

Ensure that initiation of any substantial investigation into whether a service member made a statement regarding his or her homosexuality for the purpose of seeking separation be approved at the Military Department secretarial level.

Ensure that Service Inspectors General include as an item of specific interest in their inspections the training of those charged with application and enforcement of the policy on homosexual conduct—i.e., commanders, attorneys, and investigators.

Please provide your draft implementing guidance on these matters to Mr. Frank Rush, Principal Deputy Assistant Secretary of Defense for Force Management Policy, within 30 days.

Department of Defense Press Release Concerning
Anti-Harassment Plan, July 21, 2000

Department of Defense Issues Anti-Harassment Guidelines

Secretary of Defense William S. Cohen received and approved the Department of Defense working group's action plan to eliminate all forms of harassment today. As recommended in the plan, the Department adopted an "overarching principle" that emphasizes that harassment for any reason undermines good order and discipline and has no place in the armed forces.

In addition, the Department intends to adopt the rest of the 13-point "action plan" that focuses needed attention on the problems of mistreatment generally and harassment of alleged or perceived homosexuals in particular. The plan ensures that commanders are ultimately responsible for training personnel on the Department's anti-harassment policies and holding accountable harassers and those who tolerate harassment. It also clearly states that information regarding sexual orientation is never necessary for a harassment complaint to be taken seriously. In that regard, it encourages the Services to teach all personnel, especially supervisors, that persons who receive such complaints must not ask about sexual orientation and persons who report harassment ought not disclose such information. Everyone must also be trained to understand the consequences of violating these principles.

A Department-wide directive will be issued outlining the key tenets of the overarching principle. It will emphasize that mistreatment, harassment and inappropriate comments or gestures, including those based on sexual orientation, are not acceptable.

Training and its effectiveness also featured prominently in the working group's deliberations and recommendations. One new initiative is the action plan's requirement that the Services must review their training programs annually to ensure they contain all information required by law and policy. It also requires them to tailor their programs to their audiences. To measure training effectiveness and compliance with DoD policy, the Services will be required to ensure feedback or reporting mechanisms are in place to measure knowledge, behavior, and climate.

Undersecretary of the Air Force Carol DiBattiste chaired the working group which was established by Cohen on March 24, 2000, to examine the findings of a Department of Defense Inspector General report on harassment of military personnel who are alleged or perceived to be homosexual. The group was comprised of senior civilian and military officials from each Service who met regularly for four months to consider such issues as eliminating mistreatment, harassment, and inappropriate comments or gestures; training; reporting of harassment; enforcement of policies prohibiting harassment; and measurement of anti-harassment program effectiveness.

In the course of its review, the working group requested and reviewed public comment, information on individual Service anti-harassment efforts, and briefings on the DoD survey from the DoD Inspector General and principles of behavior from the Behavioral Science Faculty at the U.S. Military Academy.

Sources

Chapter 1

Boswell, John. "Battle-Worn: Gays in the Military, 300 B.C." *New Republic* 208 (May 1993): 15–18.

Homer. *The Iliad.* Translated by Richard Lattimore. Chicago: University of Chicago Press, 1962.

Plutarch. *The Dialogue on Love.* Vol. 4 of *Moralia.* Cambridge, MA: Harvard University Press, 1961.

———. *Pelopidas.* In *Lives.* Revised by A. H. Clough. Boston: Little Brown, 1905.

Virgil. *The Aeneid of Virgil.* Book 9. Translated by Alan Mandelbaum. Berkeley: University of California Press, 1971.

Xenophon. *Anabasis.* Vol. 2 of *The Greek Historians.* Translated by Henry G. Dakyns. Edited by Francis R. B. Godolphin. New York: Random House, 1942.

———. *The Constitution of the Spartans.* Vol. 2 of *The Greek Historians.* Translated by Henry G. Dakyns. Edited by Francis R. B. Godolphin. New York: Random House, 1942.

———. *Symposium.* In *The* Apology *and* Crito *of Plato and the* Apology *and* Symposium *of Xenophon.* Introduction and translation by Raymond Larson. Lawrence, KS: Coronado Press, 1980.

Chapter 2

Aeschylus. *Prometheus Bound.* Translated by Herbert Weir Smyth. Cambridge, MA: Harvard University Press, 1956–57.

———. *The Suppliant Maidens.* Translated by Herbert Weir Smyth. Cambridge, MA: Harvard University Press, 1956–57.

Aristides. *Panathenic Oration.* Translated by C. A. Behr. Cambridge, MA: Harvard University Press, 1973.

Aristophanes. *Lysistrata.* Vol. 1 of *Aristophanes: The Eleven Comedies.* London: Athenian Society, 1912.

Arrian. *The Anabasis of Alexander.* Vol. 2 of *The Greek Historians.* Translated by Edward J. Chinnock. Edited by Francis R. B. Godolphin. New York: Random House, 1942.

Blundell, Sue. *Women in Ancient Greece.* London: British Museum Press, 1995.

Diodorus Siculus. *Diodorus of Sicily.* Books 2, 4, 17. Translated by C. H. Oldfather. Cambridge, MA: Harvard University Press, 1953.

Herodotus. *The Histories of Herodotus of Helicarnasus.* Book 4. Vol. 2 of *The Greek Historians.* Translated by George Rawlinson. Edited by Francis R. B. Godolphin. New York: Random House, 1942.

Isocrates. *Panegyricus.* Translated by George Norlin. Cambridge, MA: Harvard University Press, 1928.

Justin. *The History of Justin, Taken out of the Four and Forty Books of Trogus Pompeius.* Translated by Robert Codrington. London: William Gilbert, 1654.

Lysias. *Funeral Oration.* Translated by W. R. M. Lamb. Cambridge, MA: Harvard University Press, 1967.

Pausanius. *Description of Greece, Attica.* Book 14. Translated by W. S. Jones. Cambridge, MA: Harvard University Press, 1959.

Quintus Curtius. *The History of Alexander.* In *Works of Quintus Curtius.* Translated by John C. Rolfe. Cambridge, MA: Harvard University Press, 1956.

Quintus Smyrnaeus. *The Arrival, Deeds, and Death of Penthesileia, the Amazon Queen.* In *The War at Troy: What Homer Didn't Tell.* Translated with an introduction and notes by Frederick M. Combellack. Norman: University of Oklahoma Press, 1968.

Seneca. *Hyppolytus* or *Phaedra.* Translated by Edmund Prestwich. London: George Boddington, 1651.

Strabo. *The Geography of Strabo.* Book 11. Translated by W. Falconer. London: Henry G. Bohn. 1856.

Suetonius. *Julius Caesar.* In *The Twelve Caesars.* Translated by Robert Graves. London: Penguin, 1979.

Chapter 3

Dugdale, Sir William. "The Proceedings against the Knights Templars in the Kingdom of England." In *Monasticon Anglicanum.* 1718. Reprinted in Gershon Legman, *The Guilt of the Templars.* New York: Basic Books, 1966.

Gilmour-Bryson, Anne. "Sodomy and the Knights Templar." *Journal of the History of Sexuality* 7 (October 1996): 151–183.

Chapter 4

Court Martial of James Ball. ADM 1/5266. Public Record Office. Kew, United Kingdom.

Court Martial of John Coise. ADM 1/5267. Public Record Office. Kew, United Kingdom.

Court Martial of Henry Bicks. ADM 1/5296. Public Record Office. Kew, United Kingdom.

Court Martial of Robert Garbut. ADM 1/5301. Public Record Office. Kew, United Kingdom.

The Gentleman's Magazine 15 (February 1745): 106.

Washington, George. "General Orders." In vol. 11 of *The Writings of George Washington from the Original Manuscript Sources, 1745–1799*. Edited by John C. Fitzpatrick. Washington, DC: United States Government Printing Office, 1934.

Chapter 5

Court Martial of Bartlet Ambler. ADM 1/5369. Public Record Office. Kew, United Kingdom.

Court Martial of Hepburn Graham. ADM 1/5376. Public Record Office. Kew, United Kingdom.

Gilbert, Arthur N. "The *Africaine* Courts-Martial: A Study of Buggery in the Royal Navy." *Journal of Homosexuality* 1 (1974): 111–122.

Chapter 6

Burg, B. R. "Ganymede at Sea." In *An American Seafarer in the Age of Sail: The Erotic Diaries of Philip C. Van Buskirk, 1851–1870*. New Haven, CT: Yale University Press, 1994.

Calamus Lovers: Walt Whitman's Working-Class Camaradoes. Edited by Charley Shively. San Francisco: Gay Sunshine Press, 1987.

Drum Beats: Walt Whitman's Civil War Boy Lovers. Edited by Charley Shively. San Francisco: Gay Sunshine Press, 1989.

Melville, Herman. "A Peep through the Subterranean Parts of a Man-of-War." In *White Jacket*. New York: Harper Brothers, 1850.

———. "The Social State in a Man-of-War." In *White Jacket*. New York: Harper Brothers, 1850.

Sheridan, P. H. "Collecting Forage." In vol. 1 of *Personal Memoirs of P. H. Sheridan, General, United States Army*. New York: Charles L. Webster, 1888.

Whitman, Walt. *The Correspondence, 1842–1867*. Edited by Edwin Haviland Miller. New York: New York University Press, 1961.

Chapter 7

"Alleged Immoral Conditions and Practices at the Naval Training Station, Newport, R.I." From *Report of the Committee on Naval Affairs*, United States Senate, Sixty-seventh Congress, First Session, 1921. Washington, DC: United States Government Printing Office, 1921. Reprint, New York: Arno Press, 1975.

Morgan, Ted. "The Newport Scandal." In *FDR: A Biography*. New York: Simon and Schuster, 1985.

Chapter 8

Bérubé, Allan. "Why We Fight." In *Coming Out under Fire: The History of Gay Men and Women in World War II*. New York: Free Press, 1990.
Loeser, Lewis H. "The Sexual Psychopath in the Military Service." *American Journal of Psychiatry* 102 (July 1945): 92–101.

Chapter 9

Army Regulation 600-443. Department of the Army, Washington, D.C., April 10, 1953.
Army Regulation 635-98. Department of the Army, Washington, D.C., July 15, 1966.
Army Regulation 635-100. Department of the Army, Washington, D.C., January 21, 1970.
"Department of Defense Press Release concerning Anti-Gay Harassment Plan." July 21, 2000.
"Enlisted Administrative Separations." Department of Defense Directive 1332.14, January 28, 1982.
"Guidelines for Fact-Finding Inquiries into Homosexual Conduct, Enlisted Administrative Separations." Department of Defense Document 1332.14, Enclosure 4-1, Sections C, D, and E, December 21, 1993.
"Homosexual Administrative Discharge Board/Show Cause Hearings." In "Memorandum of the Department of the Navy, Code 34 Re: Administrative Discharge Board/Show Cause Hearings," June 1994.
"Lecture for the Indoctrination of WAVE Recruits on Subjects of Homosexuality." 1952. Reprinted in Allen Bérubé and John D'Emilio, "The Military and Lesbians during the McCarthy Years," *Signs* 9 (1984): 759–775.
"Memorandum for Secretaries of the Military Departments. Subject: Implementation of Recommendations Concerning Homosexual Conduct Policy." Undersecretary of Defense, August 12, 1999.
"Report to the Honorable John W. Warner, U.S. Senate: Homosexuals in the Military, Policies and Practices of Foreign Countries." United States General Accounting Office, June 1993.
"Standards and Procedures, Appendix A to Part 41." Office of the Secretary of Defense, 32 C.F.R. chapt. 1, July 1, 1993.
"Tips for Inquiry Officers of Cases Involving Members Who State They Are Homosexuals." Air Force Judge Advocate General's Memo, Attachment 1, Sections 1–3, November 3, 1993.

Permissions

Index

UCMJ. *See* Uniform Code of Military Justice
Uncleanness, 122, 128, 129–30, 131, 133
Uniform Code of Military Justice, 267, 276

Valentinian, Emperor, 71
Van Buskirk, Philip C., 162, 163–75, 191
Vatinius, 63
Vendôme, Maréchal de, 10
Venereal disease, 249, 256; frequency among homosexuals, 238–39
Vermandois, Compte de, 10
Veterans benefits denied for homosexuals, 252, 254
Vice Italien, 23
Vidal, Gore, 227
Virgil, 9, 19
Volcens, 21, 22, 23

Walsh, Senator David A., 192
Washington, George, 120
Watson, Lt. Henry B., 165
WAVES, 252
Wells, Sumner, 192
White Jacket (Melville), 162, 175, 178
White, Minor, 226
Whitman, Walt, 162; correspondence, 180–90
"Why We Fight" (Bérubé), 224–231
William of Tyre, 68
Women in Ancient Greece, 28

Xenophon, 5, 24, 25, 37

Young Men's Christian Association (Newport, R.I.), 192–98

Zeus, 11, 12, 13, 55, 59

About the Editor

B. R. Burg is a professor of history at Arizona State University and the author of numerous books and articles on naval history and the history of human sexuality, including *Sodomy and the Pirate Tradition,* also available from NYU Press.